NEW ZEALAND JESUS

NEW ZEALAND JESUS

SOCIAL AND RELIGIOUS TRANSFORMATIONS OF AN IMAGE, 1890–1940

GEOFFREY TROUGHTON

PETER LANG

Bern·Berlin · Bruxelles · Frankfurt am Main·New York · Oxford·Wien

Bibliographic information published by die Deutsche Nationalbibliothek
Die Deutsche Nationalbibliothek lists this publication in the Deutsche National-
bibliografie; detailed bibliographic data is available on the Internet
at ‹http://dnb.d-nb.de›.

British Library Cataloguing-in-Publication Data: A catalogue record for this book is available
from The British Library, Great Britain

Library of Congress Cataloging-in-Publication Data

Troughton, Geoffrey, 1972-
New Zealand Jesus : social and religious transformations of an image, 1890-1940 / Geoffrey Troughton.
p. cm.
Includes bibliographical references (p.   ) and index.
ISBN 978-3-03-431047-5
1. New Zealand--Church history--19th century. 2. Jesus Christ--History of doctrines--19th century.
3. Protestant churches--New Zealand--Doctrines--History--19th century. 4. New Zealand-
-Church history--20th century. 5. Jesus Christ--History of doctrines--20th century. 6. Protestant
churches--New Zealand--Doctrines--History--20th century. I. Title.
BR1480.T76 2011
232.0993'0904--dc23
                                2011029981

Cover illustration: detail of a World War One memorial window, Jesus with children,
from St John's Presbyterian Church, Wellington. Photo: Duncan Babbage.

Cover design: Rowan Heap

ISBN 978-3-0343-1047-5

© Peter Lang AG, International Academic Publishers, Bern 2011
Hochfeldstrasse 32, CH-3012 Bern, Switzerland
info@peterlang.com, www.peterlang.com

Printed in Switzerland

Table of Contents

Acknowledgements

One consequence of writing a book is the accrual of many debts. While these are too many to recount or repay here in full, I do wish to express gratitude to friends, family and colleagues whose inspiration, advice and forbearance have made this venture possible.

This book began life as a thesis that attempted two main things: first, to examine New Zealand perceptions of Jesus as a subject of interest in its own right and relevant to historians of modern Christianity generally; second, to address a more local concern of approaching the history of Christianity in New Zealand in a fresh manner. I wanted to write about New Zealand Christianity in a way that brought together religious, social and cultural history more closely than most existing local studies, and in a way that would be valuable for the broadest spectrum of New Zealand historians. To the extent that these ambitions have been realised, I am indebted to supervisors, colleagues and others who have offered critical feedback at different times. In particular, I express deep appreciation to Associate Professor Peter Lineham who offered such generous friendship and superb supervision of the original project, as did Professor Ivor Davidson. I also benefited from the support and advice of colleagues in the History programme at Massey University, including Professor Margaret Tennant and Drs Kerry Taylor and James Watson, and Professors Kerry Howe and David Thomson.

Since 2008, it has been my pleasure to be part of the Religious Studies programme at Victoria University of Wellington. Special thanks to my colleagues there for their wonderfully supportive spirit, and also especially to Professor Paul Morris and Associate Professor Chris Marshall for their particular encouragement and advice. I also acknowledge the assistance of the Faculty of Humanities and Social Sciences at the University in time and resources to complete this book.

Finally, I express deepest gratitude to my family: first, to my parents David and Rosemary for their unwavering generosity and support; finally and especially to Adrienne for constant patience, love and companionship, as well as to Harry, Jacob, Aria and Millie. I love you each, and dedicate this book to you.

List of Abbreviations

AJHR	*Appendices to the Journal of the House of Representatives*
ANZ	Archives New Zealand, Wellington
ATL	Alexander Turnbull Library, Wellington
CC	*Church Chronicle*
DNZB	*Dictionary of New Zealand Biography* (online edition)
ENZ	*Encyclopaedia of New Zealand*
EP	*Evening Post*
JRH	*Journal of Religious History*
MAC	*Minutes of Annual Conference, Methodist Church of New Zealand*
MW	*Maoriland Worker*
NZB	*New Zealand Baptist*
NZH	*New Zealand Herald*
NZJH	*New Zealand Journal of History*
NZMBC Link	*New Zealand Methodist Bible Class Link*
NZMT	*New Zealand Methodist Times*
NZOYB	*New Zealand Official Year Book*
NZPD	*New Zealand Parliamentary Debates*
NZ Tablet	*New Zealand Tablet*
ODT	*Otago Daily Times*
PCANZARC	Presbyterian Church of Aotearoa New Zealand Archives Research Centre, Dunedin
PCNZ	Presbyterian Church of New Zealand
PGA	*Proceedings of the General Assembly of the Presbyterian Church of New Zealand*
PGS	*Proceedings of the General Synod of the Church of the Province of New Zealand*
TS	*Truth Seeker*
YCU	*Yearbook of the Congregational Union of New Zealand*

1. Jesus, History and Religion in New Zealand

The central claim of Christian revelation is that God became incarnate in the person of Jesus of Nazareth. Orthodox Christian belief emphasises that Jesus was God, but also that he lived a fully human existence. Yet the ways in which his life have been understood and interpreted have varied substantially over time. This book addresses pervasive ways in which New Zealanders thought about Jesus, and what they made of him, during the years from approximately 1890 to 1940. It considers ways that Jesus was spoken of, contexts in which he was especially invoked and ends for which he was employed.

The analysis that follows interprets Jesus historically as an ideal and religious justification. It hinges on three key premises: that Jesus has a history; that religious transformations are invariably bound up in social and cultural change; and finally, that Jesus talk can be highly reflexive, especially when focused on the dimensions of his humanity. That principle of reflexivity was a basic insight propounded in Albert Schweitzer's devastating critique of the so-called 'Quest of the Historical Jesus', published in 1906. Having surveyed the efforts of the eighteenth- and nineteenth-century writers to interpret Jesus in historical rather than doctrinal terms, Schweitzer concluded that reconstructions of Jesus' life typically revealed as much about authors and their times as their subject.[1] People always view others out of the dimensions of their own personality and experience. Methodologically, Schweitzer's observation suggests that interpretations of Jesus can also be useful historically, shedding light on the wider social context in which discourse about him is located.

Jaroslav Pelikan's seminal work *Jesus through the Centuries* was perhaps the earliest attempt to utilise these insights in evaluating changing images of Jesus over the long span of Christian history.[2] More

---

1   Albert Schweitzer, *The Quest of the Historical Jesus: A Critical Study of its Progress from Reimarus to Wrede*, W. Montgomery (trans.), 2nd ed., London: A. & C. Black, 1911.

2   Jaroslav Pelikan, *Jesus through the Centuries: His Place in the History of Culture*, New Haven: Yale University Press, 1985.

recently, Pelikan's approach has been employed in further studies, especially relating to North America.[3] Like these earlier works, this book treats Jesus as a subject, but also as a lens into changing social and religious values. It differs from them, however, in two matters of scope.

First, and most obviously, this book concerns representations of Jesus in New Zealand. Indeed, it is the first historical analysis to do so, and one of few book-length treatments to address a nation outside of North America. New Zealand has never been claimed as a 'Jesus nation', as the United States has, but is nevertheless well suited for such a study. For one thing, the country's size makes the task comparatively manageable. At the beginning of the twentieth century, New Zealand was a small and far-flung outpost of the British Empire, religiously comprised of a range of denominations and sects and attuned to cultural and religious currents circulating around the Empire and English-speaking world. Though small, it was subject to many of the complex transformations that affected Western cultures and societies, and these played out locally in interesting and significant ways.

A national study of this kind provides a framework for considering the religious and social consequence of ideas, as well as the local character of religion, spirituality and society. These themes have not been well traversed in terms of the nation's historiography. In fact, New Zealand history writing has often been criticised and considered remarkable for the strength of its secularist tradition and its consequent neglect of the nation's religious past.[4] By contrast, analyses of images of

---

3   Stephen Prothero, *American Jesus: How the Son of God Became a National Icon*, New York: Farrar, Straus and Giroux, 2003; Richard Wightman Fox, *Jesus in America: Personal Savior, Cultural Hero, National Obsession*, San Francisco: HarperSanFrancisco, 2004; Stephen J. Nichols, *Jesus Made in America: A Cultural History from the Puritans to the Passion of the Christ*, Downers Grove: IVP Academic, 2008.

4   For example, John Stenhouse, 'God's Own Silence: Secular Nationalism, Christianity, and the Writing of New Zealand History', *NZJH*, 38:1, 2004, pp.52-71; Allan K. Davidson, 'New Zealand History and Religious Myopia', in Susan Emilsen and William W. Emilsen (eds), *Mapping the Landscape: Essays in Australian and New Zealand Christianity. Festschrift in Honour of Professor Ian Breward*, New York: Peter Lang, 2000, pp.205-21. Though see more recently, John Stenhouse, 'Religion and Society', in Giselle Byrnes (ed.), *The New Oxford History of New Zealand*, Melbourne: Oxford University Press, 2009, pp.323-56.

Jesus such as this necessarily place religious, social and cultural history in close relation.

The second feature distinguishing this book from earlier Jesus studies concerns periodisation. Whereas Pelikan emphasised epochal shifts over time, and the North American studies traversed their national story from origins to the present, this work focuses on the more tightly defined years from 1890 to 1940. This narrower focus enables a relatively thick description of religious and cultural dynamics in New Zealand society. The particular period is also a significant one in terms of social and cultural change, as can be attested in a number of ways. These years were a hinge, for example, between the popularity of images like William Holman Hunt's *The Light of the World* (1851-1853) and the smiling, laughing figure of the late-twentieth century Jesus Movement. That transition was not specific to New Zealand, but did have a distinctive local refraction. In terms of New Zealand history, these years are also widely acknowledged as pivotal ones in the transition from a settler society to the emergence of a 'modern' nation.[5] Finally, this book focuses on representations drawn from within the Pakeha (European) world, rather than those of the indigenous Maori population. A more comprehensive account would need to contend with both. The narrower focus makes particular sense in relation to this period, however, since the Maori population was never smaller, and Maori and Pakeha worlds were never more separate, than during these decades.

Jesus-centred religion

This period also witnessed the rise of a new kind of Jesus-centred religiosity. In one sense, Jesus had always been central to Christian doctrine and piety. Nevertheless, during the early decades of the twentieth century it became more attractive to frame religious commitment and teaching in relation to him than it had in earlier times. Appeals to Jesus changed and acquired new value. The strength of this

5   See, for a classic analysis, Erik Olssen, *Building the New World: Work, Politics and Society in Caversham 1880s-1920s*, Auckland: Auckland University Press, 1995.

pattern among Protestant Christians indicated a changing focus in which the balance of religious authority shifted from Scripture to Jesus.

Jesus-centred piety ascribed a preeminent position to Jesus devotionally, in justifications for ideas and behaviour, and in interpreting the nature of true Christianity. The widespread idea that an Age of the Incarnation had come suggested a focus on Jesus' human attributes, though a new fascination with his personality was perhaps more critical in distinguishing twentieth-century views from earlier Jesus-centred piety. Typically, religion in this mode emphasised four main characteristics: Jesus' life, rather than his death, and its importance as an example and repeatable pattern; Jesus' teaching, rather than doctrine concerning him, as a basic source of religious authority; Jesus' personality, alongside his character; and finally, his social interactions, rather than his divinity or the ontological nature of his relationship with God the Father.

Growing attention to Jesus in this manner occurred at a time when new interest in the individual and notions of society were emerging amidst complex social, intellectual and cultural change. Jesus the individual became a symbol and touchstone amid the contests and uncertainties of the age. He reflected cultural priorities, but was also a tool for reshaping religion in the light of transformations within society – thus enabling Christianity to be remoulded using a central resource from within Christian tradition.

Jesus-centred Christianity was partly a response to the churches' concerns about the place of religion in society and the continuing influence of religion. While 95% of census respondents were still formally Christian, the churches faced considerable challenges. Some of these concerned adaptation to the changing landscape of increasingly industrialised, urbanised and educated societies, and the increase of alternative associational options. Others involved seemingly resistant attitudes to religion that ranged from overt hostility to alleged apathy or indifference. Even where such attitudes prevailed, esteem for Jesus was generally high. By focusing on Jesus, the devout were appealing to the most attractive and uncontroversial core of Christianity. Arguably, this also entailed rejection of doctrinal or systematic theology, which was often perceived as befuddling and divisive.

Concerns about the continuing social influence of religion led to repeated calls for presentation of a clear, simple and unified Christian message during this period. In 1916, Anglicans called for an end to disputation, urging that all 'modern theories, quibbles and shibboleths' be dismissed in favour of 'a few easily grasped cardinal and irrefragable principles'.[6] Emphasis on Jesus accorded well with such an approach. In 1900, W.H. Griffith Thomas, a leading English evangelical Anglican and Principal of Wycliffe Hall in Oxford, published a text that expressed something of this general mood. His *Christianity is Christ* stressed the centrality of Jesus to the Christian message: 'Christ is essential, Christ is fundamental, Christ is all'.[7] It also claimed a vital connection between the 'Christ of Experience' and the 'Christ of History', highlighting orthodox belief in both the humanity and deity of Christ. It went further, however, in asserting the necessity of 'experiencing' the personality of Jesus through the mediating role of the Holy Spirit.

According to D.G.S. Rathgen, Thomas' book caused something of a sensation in New Zealand when it appeared.[8] This may exaggerate the case a little, but certainly the language was widely utilised. It was particularly beloved of evangelicals, who were at times quite anti-dogmatic and found in its simplicity and focus an ideal rallying cry. Thus, in 1922, the Rev. Walter McLean resolved the question 'What is Christianity?' in a single word:

> CHRIST! Christianity is Christ! He is the whole of Christianity! Christianity and Christ, Christ and Christianity are one. That is an answer that will mean much or little, everything or nothing, according as a man has or has not had personal experience of Christ.[9]

This language, and the concerns it addressed, were not narrowly or peculiarly evangelical. Writing later in the period, one correspondent in the *New Zealand Methodist Times* proposed that this simple focus on Christ was also the key to increasing church attendance. In an article on 'Empty Pews and How to Fill Them', the writer noted:

6   *PGS*, 1916, p.6.
7   W.H. Griffith Thomas, *Christianity is Christ*, 2nd ed., London: Longmans, Green and Co., 1909, p.118.
8   D.G.S. Rathgen, 'The Church in New Zealand 1890-1920, With Special Reference to W.A. Orange', LTh Hons thesis, New Zealand Board of Theological Studies, 1969, p.55.
9   *Outlook*, 13 February 1922, p.3.

The late Dr. Rutherford Waddell, asked to define Christianity in a thousand words commented that he could define it in three words: "Christianity is Christ." Similarly the writer, asked to give his views on how to fill empty Churches in a thousand words considers he can do better than Dr. Waddell and sum it all up in two words "Christ first".[10]

The Rev. J.K. Archer's sermon to the Baptist Union in 1910 illustrates the role that social concerns played in shaping this kind of discourse. An Englishman, Archer had been ordained into the Baptist ministry in 1891. He served in pastorates around the north of England before arriving in New Zealand in 1908, when he became the minister at the Baptist Church in Napier. A noted preacher, and an activist and controversialist by temperament, Archer was a keen supporter of the Christian socialist tradition.[11] His address to the Union gathered his concerns together in a sermon that focused squarely on Jesus. Archer claimed that, 'A thing is not true because a good man says it, or right because a good man does it.... It is true, if true at all, because it harmonises with the teaching of Jesus, and false if it does not'. He then applied this principle to issues ranging from war to evangelism and smoking, concluding that 'Jesus, and Jesus only. Jesus, rightly understood, interpreted, applied, is the solution of all social, national and international problems'. Archer's approach aimed to extend evangelical devotional commitment to Jesus into public life, to destroy 'the distinction between sacred and secular by making all life sacred'. His claims for Jesus in doing so were formidable. Jesus was the object of true faith, the source of spiritual energy and the exemplary man. He was central to Archer's vision of a Christianised society, and also to Christian strategy.

But why did Jesus seem to provide the answer to such concerns? Kerry Howe has noted the 'very powerful strands of cultural plasma' that linked New Zealand with centres of ideas and values in Europe.[12] The great movements that affected European culture and religion were therefore also evident locally. Even relatively contemporary changes were often only separated by a matter of months from New Zealanders,

10 NZMT, 9 May 1936, p.3.
11 NZB, January 1911, pp.11-13; M.P. Sutherland, 'Pulpit or Podium? J.K. Archer and the Dilemma of Christian Politics in New Zealand', *The New Zealand Journal of Baptist Research*, 1, 1996, pp.26-46.
12 K.R. Howe, *Singer in a Songless Land: A Life of Edward Tregear, 1846-1931*, Auckland: Auckland University Press, 1991, pp.44-45, quote p.44.

many of whom read avidly and were attuned to developments abroad. The focus on Jesus was partly attributable to the confluence of a number of these cultural and religious shifts. In particular, the priority placed on Jesus reflected impacts related to the Enlightenment, Romanticism, the rise of psychology and notions of personality.

Some particularly important factors derived from Enlightenment legacies. Enlightenment thinking emphasised the capabilities and authority of the reasoning subject and cultivated scepticism toward tradition. It often contrasted Reason with the purported irrationality and superstition of religion and the weakness of its traditional proofs. Out of this framework, interpretations of religion and history emerged that profoundly influenced perceptions of Jesus and helped to explain some of his appeal. Enlightenment emphases did not necessarily lead to secularisation or supplant religious outlooks. They did, however, contribute to changes in the way religion was understood and configured.

For example, Enlightenment priorities strengthened a correlation between religion and morality. Hence, Immanuel Kant dismissed 'supernatural' religion as being inimical to reason, but emphasised the ethical functions of religion instead. This closer association of religion with ethics paved the way for increased focus on the teaching of Jesus and his human existence. Esteem for Jesus remained, though he was often principally understood as a moral archetype and reformer, or as a teacher of common sense.[13] If Jesus possessed a special nature, it consisted in the excellence of his moral teaching and personal virtue.

Liberal Protestant theologies like those descended from Albrecht Ritschl and Adolf von Harnack built upon these assumptions in emphasising the ethical significance of Christianity.[14] For Ritschl, a truly religious view of Jesus emphasised what he actually did: namely, he lived in obedience to God the Father in ways appropriate to the Kingdom of God. Jesus was therefore primarily a moral example, and the Kingdom an ethical one. In Harnack, such notions were transposed into the idea that the 'essence of Christianity' was not so much about belief as a way of life that systematised dogma had made unintelligible. This

---

13   Arthur F. Holmes, *Fact, Value, and God*, Grand Rapids: Eerdmans, 1997, pp.128-31; James Yerkes, *The Christology of Hegel*, Missoula: Scholars Press, for the American Academy of Religion, 1978; Pelikan, pp.182-93.

14   John Macquarrie, *Jesus Christ in Modern Thought*, London: SCM Press, 1990, p.253.

essence was described in the primitive Christianity of Jesus' Kingdom teaching, rather than in teaching about him.[15] Kingdom language and notions of ethical Christianity were often taken up in social gospel theologies that sought to address the problems associated with social change, industrialisation and urbanisation. Crucially, these themes were evident in much of the Jesus language that circulated in New Zealand.

Another associated legacy related to notions of history. Enlightenment sensibilities encouraged the growth of historical consciousness, especially using methods that emphasised change, human agency and natural causation. Treated scientifically, history and historical criticism became means for accessing truth. As Peter Hinchliff has noted, British Christians reacted to new notions of history in a variety of ways.[16] One important response embraced historical criticism, making the historical Jesus authoritative and turning him into the fount of authentic Christianity. Liberal Protestants, in particular, stripped away the supernatural elements associated with Jesus' life hoping to find the kernel of true religion it contained. This approach was exemplified in the 'lives' written by John Seeley, Ernest Renan and David F. Strauss, which New Zealanders were clearly familiar with.[17] Strauss's *Life of Jesus* dismissed the supposedly primitive supernatural worldview of most of the New Testament, claiming that its stories expressed theological truths rather than historical facts. Though appropriated by many radical critics of Christianity, his treatment of Jesus retained a reverential tone.[18] Strauss supported the 'idea' of divinity joined with humanity, but disconnected this from the historical person of Jesus. His Jesus was the realisation of Hegel's Absolute in history.[19] Curiously, then, quests for the historical

---

15 Macquarrie, pp.261-63.
16 Peter Hinchliff, *God and History: Aspects of British Theology, 1875-1914*, Oxford: Oxford University Press, 1992.
17 John Seeley, *Ecce Homo*, 17th ed., London: Macmillan, 1883 (1865); Ernest Renan, *The Life of Jesus*, (trans.) London: Trubner, 1863; D.F. Strauss, *The Life of Jesus Critically Examined*, George Eliot (trans.), London: SCM Press, 1975 (1835). J.G.S. Grant, *Critical Examination of 'Ecce Homo'*, Dunedin: Mills, Dick & Co., 1867; William Williams, *Remarks Upon 'Ecce Homo'*, Auckland: Cathedral Press, 1867.
18 See Timothy Larsen, *Contested Christianity: The Political and Social Context of Victorian Theology*, Waco: Baylor University Press, 2004, pp.43-58.
19 Stanley J. Grenz and Roger E. Olson, *20th-Century Theology: God & the World in a Transitional Age*, Downers Grove: InterVarsity Press, 1992, p.38; Colin J.D.

Jesus could actually lead to quite abstract formulations of him as an ideal type.

Classically, Enlightenment interpretations of history were shaped by teleological assumptions, with human history presented as a narrative of progress. This mood was characteristic of modernity in general. It was also evident in Romantic and Darwinian ideas, and in the confidence generated by technological improvements. Notions of progress were imbibed into the social, political and material spheres, but also in morality. By the late nineteenth century, optimistic assessments of human moral potential were widespread. Jesus fitted in this milieu. Humanity was less in need of salvation than an example to live up to, and this is what he seemed to provide. On the other hand, twentieth century kergymatic theologies began to resist this buoyant temper. These questioned the usefulness of history for faith, and so distinguished between the 'Jesus of history' and the 'Christ of faith', according a privileged position to the latter.

Perhaps the most important cultural influences shaping interest in Jesus derived from the rise of Romanticism and notions of personality. For all its diverse threads, Romanticism essentially arose as a direct response to the rational impulses of the Enlightenment. In contrast to reason, Romanticism prioritised 'will, spirit and emotion', along with the glories of untamed nature.[20] It celebrated the 'living, breathing, whole human being'.[21] Idealisation of humanity led to an emphasis on simplicity, rusticity and primitivism. The allegedly dehumanising tendencies of mass production, industrialisation and the machine age were deplored. Humanism flourished, and the individual personality was idolised, especially in the Great Man tradition exemplified in Thomas Carlyle's study of heroes and hero worship.[22]

In New Zealand, religious interaction with Romanticism was shaped as much by this general mood as by any particular philosophical or

---

Greene, *Christology in Cultural Perspective: Marking Out the Horizons*, Grand Rapids: Eerdmans, 2003, p.143.

20 David Bebbington, *The Dominance of Evangelicalism: The Age of Spurgeon and Moody*, Downers Grove: InterVarsity Press, 2005, p.148.

21 James M. Byrne, *Religion and the Enlightenment: From Descartes to Kant*, Louisville: Westminster John Knox Press, 1996, p.75.

22 Thomas Carlyle, *On Heroes, Hero-Worship and the Heroic in History*, Lincoln: University of Nebraska Press, 1966 (1841).

theological formulations. But religious Romanticism was a significant phenomenon. Friedrich Schleiermacher's challenge to the narrowest forms of Enlightenment rationalism was an important progenitor of subsequent approaches. His critique distinguished religion from metaphysics and morality, and located it in the heart and dispositions.[23] Schleiermacher's theology cohered with Romantic priorities and was oriented to notions of religious 'feeling' and experience of redemption. Jesus figured prominently, not as a moral hero or ideal of the Enlightenment type but as a real historical person.[24] In general, Romantic sensibilities were diffused in the religious sphere somewhat later than in literature, art and history. David Bebbington has argued that the Romantic influence in religion built as the nineteenth century progressed. Among evangelicals, Romantic tastes were only being eclipsed by the middle of the twentieth century.[25]

The cult of personality that emerged in the twentieth century was effectively a form of modernist Romanticism. According to Warren Susman, the rise of a 'culture of personality' marked a pervasive cultural shift away from a nineteenth-century 'culture of character' based on ideas of self-improvement and self-help.[26] Shaped around notions of individual prowess and psychological interpretations of the self, the culture of personality responded to urban distress and other modern problems by celebrating the power of the individual, especially in its ability to effect change and bend the world to its will. In a sense, it reformulated the heroic tradition for a psychological age. The disciplines of history, psychology and sociology all cohered with the new mood, as did modern biography and child-centred education. Jesus-centred religion was also arguably a manifestation. It seemed kinder and gentler, affirmed the individual and supported simple practical religiosity in relation to a universally admired model.

In this mélange of influences, religion centred on Jesus seemed particularly appealing. It affirmed human experience, as well as notions of brotherhood and solidarity that were proving attractive in the

---

23 Macquarrie, p.193; Claude Welch, *Protestant Thought in the Nineteenth Century: Volume 1, 1799-1870*, New Haven: Yale University Press, 1972, p.65.
24 Greene, pp.104-8.
25 Bebbington, *Dominance*, pp.148-83.
26 Warren I. Susman, *Culture as History: The Transformation of American Society in the Twentieth Century*, New York: Pantheon Books, 1984, pp.271-85.

community at large. Advocates for more inclusive theologies therefore tended to regard Jesus as an ally. In the late nineteenth century, New Zealand Presbyterians became embroiled in a number of theological controversies. In 1888, William Salmond was tried for heresy on account of his attack on the doctrine of Double-Predestination.[27] Salmond felt that his advocacy of the 'larger hope' was expressive of the direction in which the 'whole Church' was heading – away from the 'hard and stern logic' of earlier Calvinism.[28] Salmond's tract was not primarily Christological, though the issue did concern the scope of the Atonement. Nonetheless, his discussion was punctuated with references to 'the love of God and the mercy of Christ'. The instinct toward more inclusive theology was supported by 'the boundless love of Christ'.[29] Notably, when the Rev. James Gibb was later tried for heresy he also called for greater emphasis on Jesus. Attacking the purportedly narrow and punitive aspects of Calvinism, Gibb asserted that Christ provided the model for Christian living, not the Ten Commandments.[30]

Questioning of the nature of the Atonement during the early twentieth century was also shaped by a desire to affirm both the love of God and human moral capacities. Hence, the Rev. John Gibson Smith's attack on penal-substitution made it clear that the Atonement indicated God's 'holy mercy' rather than his 'retributive justice'.[31] W.H. Fitchett's account of the 'ideals and methods' of Methodism for the Centenary of Australasian Methodism in 1915 included a chapter outlining Methodist approaches to the Atonement. Significantly, Fitchett emphasised that Methodist teaching 'refuses to think of God the Father as an angry Judge, with Christ as our Substitute, bearing the actual penalty of our sins'. He conceded that the Substitutionary, Governmental and Moral Influence theories were all necessary to an 'adequate explanation'.

27 Simon Wood, 'Liberalism and Heresy: An Examination of the Controversy Surrounding William Salmond's The Reign of Grace', BA Hons research essay, University of Otago, 1991.

28 William Salmond, *The Reign of Grace: A Discussion of the Question of the Possibility of Salvation for All Men in This Life, or in the Life to Come*, Dunedin: James Horsburgh, 1888, p.34.

29 Salmond, *Reign of Grace*, pp.36, 57.

30 See *ODT*, 5 July 1888. On Gibb, and his trial for heresy in 1890, see Laurie H. Barber, 'James Gibb's Heresy Trial, 1890', *NZJH*, 12:2, 1987, pp.146-57.

31 John Gibson Smith, *The Christ of the Cross, or, The Death of Jesus Christ in its Relation to Forgiveness and Judgment*, Wellington: Gordon & Gotch, 1908, p.299.

However, Fitchett also stressed the universal character of salvation, and argued that 'identification' rather than 'substitution' was the best characterisation of Christ's relation to humanity in his atoning work.[32]

In other contexts, some commentators promoted reflection on Jesus as a way to improve personal and social morality. In 1922, the Anglican *Church Chronicle* carried comments by the British Christian socialist James Adderley. These repudiated notions of God as an angry king or indifferent sovereign in favour of God's nature as Father. According to Adderley, Christians needed to focus more on Jesus, for the divine qualities of mercy and forgiveness were most clearly expressed in him:

> We rattle off the creeds about His perfect humanity, but how great a responsibility we take upon ourselves when we thus declare our faith! We get angry with the liberals who write books about the human life of Jesus and His ethics, because, perhaps they do not seem quite orthodox about His divinity. Yet is [sic] often in these very books that we find a much greater faith in the importance of love and mercy and forgiveness than in more catholic manuals.[33]

In fact, Adderley's critique went further in describing frustrations with the official Church. 'Why is it', he questioned, 'that so often outside Church circles we find a greater faith in the sacred humanity of Christ than we do within?' Thus, Jesus could appeal as a symbol for the necessity of reform, even of the Church itself.

Themes and trajectories

The preceding discussion of the sources of Jesus-centred religion has highlighted a number of prominent motifs. These are taken up in subsequent chapters, which address predominant images thematically and in relation to contexts that shaped the way Jesus was viewed. Images have also been considered in the light of significant debates in New Zealand historiography.

---

32   See W.H. Fitchett, *What Methodism Stands For*, Melbourne: Printed by T. Shaw Fitchett, 1915, pp.44-55.
33   *CC*, April 1922, p.59.

Chapter 2 assesses a range of approaches to Jesus in Christian doctrine and devotion, highlighting the pattern of growing Jesus-centredness focused on notions of Jesus' humanity and personality. Jesus was invoked in a range of ways, however, and not all emphasised these features. The chapter therefore addresses some of the terminology and vocabulary associated with Jesus and its usage, and limits to the pattern of Jesus-centredness. It establishes that interest in the humanity of Jesus was clearly increasing and acquiring new value, even if this never entirely supplanted other ways of thinking.

Not all references to Jesus were couched in conventional devotional terms. Chapter 3 addresses a counter-image of him, in which a prophetic 'anti-Church' Jesus functioned as the churches' leading critic. This was widely appropriated, though for strikingly different ends. It was sometimes applied as a voice of external critique, but was also used as an argument for reforming, reviving, or reinvigorating the churches from within. For some the anti-Church Jesus heralded the overthrow of the Church, for others its renewal. While purposes for applying the image differed, the critique relied on a shared premise that ecclesiastical legacies had distorted and even corrupted Jesus' message.

In many ways, the twentieth-century pattern of Jesus-centred Christianity emerged out of social change, and especially from concern about the social problems that change created. Consequently, Jesus featured prominently in the language of social reform. Chapter 4 addresses ways that Jesus appeared in discourses related to social campaigning, much of which built on language and ideas that had been established in previous decades. Precise issues varied, ranging from debates about alcohol to contests within the labour movement and in relation to conceptions of socialism. In whichever context, invoking Jesus provided a moral underlay to social debates. He was particularly cited in the interests of the poor, of workers, and those with an agenda for social reform. Appeals to him provided a common language, though the tangible influence of this language was less clear.

Ideas presented to children are an excellent medium for analysing cultural values. Chapter 5 addresses images of Jesus that arose out of the enormous investment in religion for children. Religious activity was concentrated in the childhood years during the early decades of the twentieth century. Sunday schools, campaigns for religious education in schools and family religion were all emphasised primarily with a view to securing children's religious identities. The chapter examines a range of contexts in which children encountered religious ideas, and evaluates the messages communicated there. It finds that Jesus occupied a central space in the religious discourse of childhood, and that the person described to children was also particular to childhood in certain ways. Significantly, childhood was also a prime context in which growing Jesus-centredness within Protestantism was expressed.

Finally, the religiosity of men was a topic of debate and concern during this period, especially in relation to the age of transition to adulthood when more males than females ceased active participation in organised religion. Chapter 6 considers images of Jesus that were used to address anxieties about these issues. In particular, it highlights attempts to use a manly Jesus to bolster religion among youth, working men and soldiers in the wake of World War One. Some categories of religion for boys were explicitly invoked – particularly the heroic. After the war, this heroism was typically defined in military terms. However, the manly Jesus was essentially an instrumentalist attempt to reach men who were expected to be resistant to organised religion. Consequently, it was more of a presentation technique than a wholesale reinterpretation.

As they did at other times, New Zealanders interpreted Jesus' life in diverse ways between 1890 and 1940. Notwithstanding this diversity, reference to Jesus acquired new value and he became a more important focus. Part of the change was a new emphasis on humanity conceptualised as personality. Attention to the personality of Jesus influenced a range of areas, from devotional patterns and methods of evangelism to justifications for social priorities. The appeal of Jesus-centred Christianity reflected a broader cultural flow in which religious discourses were embedded. The images of Jesus assessed here open a window into that milieu, and deepen our understanding of the changing shape of religion in New Zealand society.

2. The Turn to Personality

Jesus' humanity became an increasingly central reference point within Christian devotion and spirituality during the early decades of the twentieth century. The increasingly personalised connotations of Jesus-centred language and spirituality, however, were not entirely un-contested. In 1919, one Anglican correspondent in the Diocese of Wellington noted the trend, but complained that over-familiarity with Jesus was one of the 'most questionable tendencies of modern thought and expression':

> Men are being taught to fraternise with the Nazarene instead of to approach the Cross of Jesus Christ with reverent and humble adoration. It seems that any phraseology is permitted to-day when men speak of Christ.... The name of Christ has been sufficiently bandied about, and, in the opinion of many, lowered during the last few years. It is high time that we began to regard Christ not so much as just one of ourselves, but rather to endeavour to make ourselves one with Him. This will never be achieved by the encouragement of 'familiarity' with His Sacred Name. He must be lifted up, not dragged down.[1]

In short, Jesus-centred devotion seemed vulgar and irreligious, capturing all too well 'the purblind overweening individualism of the day'.

Reactions of this kind highlighted that ways of speaking about Jesus varied. Moreover, while much Jesus language emphasised his humanity and personality, not all of it implied Jesus-centredness. Conservatives, for example, invoked him often, but also repudiated characteristically Jesus-centred emphases as evidence of liberal trends in theology. Nevertheless, a turn to Jesus-centredness did take place, and ultimately influenced even more conservative traditions. This chapter examines streams of sentimental piety, Catholic spirituality and doctrinal debate, where Jesus language abounded but with limited emphasis on personality. It then considers contexts in which the turn to personality was more evident, notably in representations in literature, art and the language of mission.

---

1   *CC*, September 1919, p.132.

Sentimental piety

In 1916, the Anglican Primate's address to General Synod claimed that the general attitude of the community to religion was one of indefinite and sentimental acceptance.[2] Churchill Julius' observations suggested that sentimental piety lacked doctrinal clarity, but also implied that it was widely held. Strikingly, Jesus was a major focus in the kinds of popular affective devotion to which he referred. Where affective piety engaged him directly, however, it typically emphasised experience and emotion rather than Jesus as an historical person. These were deployed to encourage genuine religious commitment, since this mattered more than the details of Jesus' personality or historical existence.

Sentimental expositions of Jesus' ministry often emphasised his compassion, contrasting that with mere religiosity. Preaching on Mark 1.41, for example, the Rev. J. Anderson Reilly from the small provincial town of Seddon noted that 'the yearning of the human heart is not so much for the religion of the Priest and the Levite as that of the Samaritan'. Like the Samaritan, Jesus responded to lepers with compassion: 'the tears started to His eyes; His heart ached, and the blood flowed quicker through His veins as He thought of the terrible tragedy behind that leprous look'.[3] Similar ideas could also be found in Catholic devotional literature. One contribution in the *New Zealand Tablet* noted that compassion was the hallmark of Jesus' life:

> Compassion ruled in the heart of the Divine Lover of souls, compassion for the weakness of His creature whom He came to save, and hence the thought of man's sin was with Him – in childhood, in boyhood, in all the lonely years of suffering, overwhelming Him in Gethsemane, darkening His last hours on Calvary.[4]

Indeed, reflection on Jesus' suffering and 'yearning for souls' were arguably mainstays of Catholic piety.

'Sweetness' was one of the great adjectives and praise words of the age. It was used in the Protestant vernacular to describe singing and fellowship, but also individuals – primarily, though not exclusively,

2   *PGS*, 1916, p.6.
3   *Outlook*, 3 January 1927, p.17.
4   *NZ Tablet*, 10 February 1921, p.45.

women and children. Thus, Michael Faraday, a leading nineteenth-century English scientist, was also lauded as 'one of the most sweet and simple of Christians'.[5] In relation to Christians, sweetness described warmth, sincerity and an absence of pretence. As a descriptor of Jesus, it further implied beauty, excellence and a heart-warming presence in the believer's soul. The term was used widely in the language of adoration. One Anglican Christmas sermon used the text of Psalm 72.18-19 to reflect on the theme of Jesus' sweetness, invoking the chorus of a well-known nineteenth-century hymn:

Sweetest note of seraph song;
Sweetest Name on mortal tongue;
Sweetest carol ever sung,
JESUS, precious JESUS.

Predictably, the reflection concluded with another classic hymn by John Newton, 'How sweet the name of JESUS sounds'.[6]

Music played an important role in forming and expressing religious convictions. The local hymnic tradition was largely derived from abroad, with little contextualised production appearing before the second half of the twentieth century. Trans-denominational hymns tended to be especially popular. Notably, many of the best-loved hymns in the popular musical corpus invoked the Saviour's tenderness and comfort, reflecting Oliver Duff's contention that New Zealanders' sought solace by turning 'back to religion in sorrow and trouble'.[7] Hymns like 'Rock of ages', 'Abide with me', 'Jesus lover of my soul' and 'Lead kindly light' all fitted within this framework. Others like 'Nearer my God to Thee' addressed God, but spoke of heaven as being in the 'Saviour's love'. Use of many of these as accompaniments during screenings of *The King of Kings* in 1928 indicated their popularity. In Wellington, one reviewer suggested potentially suitable music, but doubted there was room for 'Lead kindly light' or 'Nearer, my God to Thee'. That advice was ignored. Both featured alongside other favourites like 'Abide with

---

5   *NZB*, June 1931, p.166.
6   *CC*, December 1927, p.203 (original emphasis).
7   Oliver Duff, *New Zealand Now*, Wellington: Department of Internal Affairs, 1941, p.40.

me' and 'Rock of ages' in Wellington, while 'Lead kindly light' was also used in Auckland.[8]

Gospel songs, especially in the Ira Sankey tradition, were also popular. His music poured into New Zealand from the mid-1870s in connection with a revivalist movement modelled on Dwight L. Moody's methods. Sankey's songbook was imported in that context, but circulated more widely. Missions led by R.A. Torrey and Charles Alexander in 1902, and J. Wilbur Chapman with Alexander in 1912-13, extended this influence. Sankey shaped Alexander's style, and a third of Alexander's mission hymnbook drew directly from *Sacred Songs and Solos*.[9] This music caught the ear and lodged in the memory, and was still popular in the 1930s when the Sunday night choir on the 'Friendly Road' radio station run by Colin Scrimgeour (also known as Uncle Scrim) styled itself as the 'Sankey Singers'. Though widely known, it became particularly established in the evangelical churches, in evangelistic meetings, the home and with youth. Even the Modernist theologian H.D.A. Major reflected that singing 'Moody and Sankey hymns' had constituted one of the pleasurable aspects of Sunday school attendance.[10]

Analyses of this gospel hymn tradition have noted an increasing concentration on Jesus and changing approaches to him during the nineteenth century. According to Sandra Sizer, Isaac Watts' hymns were ten times more likely than Sankey's to focus on Jesus' role as mediator, but the latter referred to Jesus more often. Sankey's approach to Jesus favoured themes of grace and salvation, refuge, help and guidance, and referred to him frequently as loving and beloved.[11] A loving, yearning saviour reflected patterns of softening theology; emphasis on heaven fitted questioning of eternal damnation. These characteristics have also been described as leading Sankey close to a 'cloying sentimentality'

8   *CC*, March 1928, p.40; *EP*, 16 June 1928, p.7; *NZH*, 15 March 1928, p.12; *NZH*, 23 March 1928, p.15.

9   Joan Mansfield, 'The Music of Australian Revivalism', in Mark Hutchinson and Stuart Piggin (eds), *Reviving Australia: Essays on the History and Experience of Revival and Revivalism in Australian Christianity*, Sydney: Centre for the Study of Australian Christianity, 1994, p.137.

10   Clive Pearson, Allan Davidson and Peter Lineham, *Scholarship and Fierce Sincerity: Henry D.A. Major, The Face of Anglican Modernism*, Auckland: Polygraphia, 2005, p.81.

11   Sandra S. Sizer, *Gospel Hymns and Social Religion: The Rhetoric of Nineteenth-Century Revivalism*, Philadelphia: Temple University Press, 1978, esp. pp.171-73.

which Alexander, if anything, pushed further.[12] Such sentimentality has also been connected with a purported 'feminisation' of piety during the nineteenth century. According to Mary De Jong, feminine social stereotypes predominated in this popular evangelical hymnody, with Jesus cast variously as a lover, friend and victim.[13] On the other hand, gospel hymns also presented Jesus as a leader, upon whom believers depended for strength, consolation and companionship. Surrender, emotion and intimacy were made central to the salvation process.

Jesus therefore featured prominently in the discourse of sentimental piety, and in revivalist forms which made constant appeals to the 'power of Jesus Christ' and the need to make a 'decision for Jesus'.[14] In some senses, this approach made personality central, with salvation constructed relationally in terms of Jesus' friendship. Crucially, however, these leading attributes were spiritualised rather than historicised, since emphasis on companionship seldom translated into reflection on Jesus' lived humanity. The motif contrasted with earlier emphases on a more distant creator, but the focus on Jesus' personality related to his ability to convince, lead and save. Personalism was closely allied with the salvation of the divine Christ, the Son of God.[15]

Sentimental approaches to Jesus were shaped by the 'Romantic gale' that David Bebbington argues swept over evangelicals in the 1920s, influencing conservative and liberal alike.[16] Notions of Jesus' humility, simplicity and sympathy fitted comfortably with Romantic priorities. While humanity and personality were important, Romanticism worked more with ideals than specifics. The accent was on religious feeling and affective response. Sentimental piety in the Romantic mode imagined Jesus through these lenses. Intimacy and emotion were

12 Mansfield, pp.129, 137.
13 Mary G. De Jong, '"I Want to Be Like Jesus": The Self-Defining Power of Evangelical Hymnody', *Journal of the American Academy of Religion*, 54:3, 1986, pp.461-93.
14 *Outlook: Illustrated Memento of the Torrey-Alexander Mission, August-September 1902*, pp.15-16.
15 For example, R.A. Torrey's address in *Outlook: Illustrated Memento*, pp.41-43.
16 David W. Bebbington, *Evangelicalism in Modern Britain: A History from the 1730s to the 1980s*, Grand Rapids: Baker, 1989, pp.80-81, 181-84; Bebbington, *Dominance*, pp.148-83.

regarded as channels to religious devotion. Cultivation of this spiritual relationship was central to development in the religious life.

The interaction between embodiment and sentiment also owed something to modernist cultural preoccupations. Caroline Daley notes that overt physicality and display of the body became more common in the early twentieth century, when 'the emphasis was on the body rather than the mind, when activity and rationality were celebrated and passivity and irrationality decried'.[17] Modernist reconstitution of Jesus as a robust, manly activist consciously departed from the 'pail, limp Jesus' of conventional devotional piety.[18] Yet, physicality also served a function in sentimental piety. Materiality and the body were conduits to the intimacy and emotion that fired religious commitment. Protestants tended to make the connection textually. Hymns like 'When I survey the wondrous cross' invoked the physical marks of the crucifixion as a vehicle to consecration. The pattern was particularly pronounced, however, in the material culture of Catholic devotion where Jesus' wounded body was supposed to inspire love, adoration and commitment.

Catholic spirituality

The Jesus of New Zealand Catholicism was shaped by a refashioning of Irish Catholic religiosity during the 'devotional revolution' led by Cardinal Cullen in the mid-nineteenth century. This had a flow-on effect to New Zealand, where the Catholic community was largely comprised of Irish Catholic migrants. Post-famine Irish Catholicism was rich in devotional associations and artefacts, and these shaped local forms. Sodalities and lay associations encouraging institutional participation proliferated, while Catholic homes were identified by devotional markers such as religious images including those of Jesus, Mary and the Saints.[19]

17 Caroline Daley, *Leisure and Pleasure: Reshaping and Revealing the New Zealand Body, 1900-1960*, Auckland: Auckland University Press, 2003, p.5.

18 Harold Segel, *Body Ascendant: Modernism and the Physical Imperative*, Baltimore: Johns Hopkins University Press, 1998, p.220.

19 S.C. MacPherson, 'A "Ready Made Nucleus of Degradation and Disorder"? A Religious and Social History of the Catholic Church and Community in Auckland

Catholic approaches to Jesus emphasised the Passion. Indeed, the devotional system provided countless ways to contemplate the grace expressed through his sacrifice and broken body. The emphasis was evident in periodicals and occasional literature, and central to the drama and ritual of the Mass – attendance at which was becoming increasingly common.[20] In 1921, an article in the *New Zealand Tablet* claimed that the Blessed Sacrament held the key to Jesus' character, and therefore to Christian character in general:

> It is a new day in a man's life when he realises that here in the Blessed Sacrament is the summing up of all the works of Jesus – His mercy, His pity, His infinite loving kindness. It makes life worth living. The first desire of the Catholic heart will be to return love for love; to atone in some way for the negligence and indifference of the world... to respond in some way to that Divine yearning that brought Him from heaven to Nazareth and Calvary, and now makes Him as it were the Prisoner and Bondsman of His own love.[21]

Catholics also distinguished between the Sacrament of the Eucharist and the Sacrifice of the Mass. Jesus' death was a present sacrifice and permanent institution of the Church. Therefore, the Mass invited reflection not only on the Passion, but also union with the Church.

Catholic spirituality gave visual emphasis to the death of Jesus in other ways. Although also acceptable to some Anglicans and Lutherans, the crucifix, rather than an empty cross, was a distinctively Catholic form. Within churches, the crucifix was the principal ornament of the altar where it recalled 'that the Victim offered on the altar is the same as was offered on the Cross'.[22] In homes, crucifixes were displayed as markers of identity and devotion. The Stations of the Cross were found around the interior of many churches. These provided a narrative account of Jesus' suffering and death, and a focus for reflection during the season of Lent. Because they were displayed throughout the year, the Stations witnessed to Christ's suffering outside the Holy Season.[23]

1870-1910', MA thesis, University of Auckland, 1987, p.91; *NZ Tablet*, 5 January 1922, p.45.

20 Hugh Jackson, 'Churchgoing in Nineteenth-Century New Zealand', *NZJH*, 17:1, 1983, pp.43-59.

21 *NZ Tablet*, 10 February 1921, p.45.

22 'Altar Crucifix', *Catholic Encyclopedia*, New York: Robert Appleton, 1907-1912.

23 *NZ Tablet*, 20 March 1919, p.23; *NZ Tablet*, 13 May 1938, pp.3-4.

Devotion to the Sacred Heart of Jesus was perhaps the most distinctive practice of this period. Modern impetus for the devotion dated to Margaret Mary Alacoque (1647-1690), but strengthened during the nineteenth century, culminating in Pope Leo XIII's consecration of humanity to the Sacred Heart on 11 June 1899. Though established in Australasia during the nineteenth century, the devotion flourished between World War One and Vatican II.[24] Reinvigoration followed circulation of a pastoral letter of the Archbishops and Bishops of Australasia. This called for re-consecration to the Sacred Heart on 29 June 1919, through reading an Act of Consecration.[25] In subsequent years, the month of June became a focal point for reflection.

Display of Sacred Heart images was a central element. These adorned churches in a range of forms including paintings, statuary and glass. They were also prominent in Catholic homes where some devout families placed pictures in every room.[26] The displayed heart stood for the moral and spiritual qualities of the man, and was emblematic of Christ's love. The bishops' letter emphasised that Jesus' heart was the most loving, generous, tender and compassionate of all. Devotion to it would renew spiritual vigour and reciprocal love. As the bishops explained, 'Love is the guiding principle of all our Saviour's conduct towards us. He asks only love in return for His countless benefactions.... He is ready to obliterate the greatest crimes, if there is but love'.[27]

By accentuating his wounds, the Sacred Heart icon also expressed Christ's sorrow at the world's rejection, incorporating motifs related to the Passion and Eucharist. Sacred Heart spirituality made devotees feel loved, but also 'reminded the Faithful that Jesus was close to them through the bond of common suffering. Catholics often found consolation in moments of sorrow by comparing their sufferings to those of Christ'.[28]

---

24 Katherine Massam, *Sacred Threads: Catholic Spirituality in Australia, 1922-1962*, Sydney: New South Wales University Press, 1996, pp.62-63; MacPherson, p.91.

25 *NZ Tablet*, 26 June 1919, pp.17-19.

26 Patrick O'Farrell, *Vanished Kingdoms: Irish in Australia and New Zealand*, Kensington: New South Wales University Press, 1990, p.87.

27 *NZ Tablet*, 26 June 1919, p.19.

28 Bernard F. Cadogan, 'Lace Curtain Catholics: The Catholic Bourgeoisie of the Diocese of Dunedin, 1900-1920', BA Hons dissertation, University of Otago, 1984, p.88.

Sacred Heart devotion has been interpreted as an effort to keep Catholic spirituality 'in touch with the emotional side of life, validating the compassion which drives people to action'.[29] According to Patrick O'Farrell, it also indicated a lack of balance within the spirituality of Irish Catholicism which exalted sentiment and activity at the expense of thought or contemplation.[30] Sacred Heart iconography in New Zealand reflected the *l'art saint sulpice* style that had become the international fashion of Catholic art by the end of the nineteenth century, but which contrasted markedly with a highly politicised version that circulated simultaneously elsewhere.[31] Intriguingly, though critical of its extension to Marian devotion, the prominent Baptist minister J.J. North's attack on Catholicism unwittingly affirmed its affective emphasis. In so doing, North highlighted the broader appeal of this form of devotion:

> The humanity of Christ bridges the gulf between God and man. No woman's heart is as tender as the heart of Jesus.... No prayer should be diverted from His ear. No worship, which belongs to Him alone should be bestowed on His creatures. Pity and power have their home in the heart of Jesus, for Jesus is one with the Father.[32]

On the other hand, more assertive forms of lay Catholic spirituality were also evident during the interwar years, some of which centred on Jesus. Notably, Christopher van der Krogt highlights the feast of Christ the King, arguing that, 'the proclamation of Christ's kingship represented a renewed determination to wrest the initiative in the struggle with a hostile society'.[33] This tone was evident elsewhere, for example, in the New Zealand National Eucharistic Congress during celebrations for the local centennial of Catholicism in 1938.[34]

---

29   Cited in Massam, p.63.
30   Patrick O'Farrell, *The Catholic Church and Community: An Australian History*, rev. ed., Kensington: New South Wales University Press, 1985, p.213.
31   Raymond Jonas, *France and the Cult of the Sacred Heart: An Epic Tale for Modern Times*, Berkeley: University of California Press, 2000.
32   J.J. North, *The Plain Points of Protestantism*, Auckland: H.H. Driver, 1938, pp.44, 48.
33   Christopher J. van der Krogt, 'More a Part than Apart: The Catholic Community in New Zealand Society 1918-1940', PhD thesis, Massey University, 1994, p.81.
34   See *N.Z. National Eucharistic Congress, Wellington, February 1-4 1940: Souvenir Programme*, Christchurch: Printed by Whitcombe & Tombs, 1940.

Overall, Catholic approaches tended to correlate Christ and Church closely. In 1910, Archbishop Francis Redwood proclaimed Jesus as the 'noblest scion of humanity, the consummate model of perfection'. This verdict, he contended, was universally accepted among all true Christians, and even those 'writers who have shorn Him of the splendour of His miracles and prophecies, and brought him down to the lowest level which the cold fancy of unbelief could conceive'. The reference was to Strauss, Renan, Harnack and John Stuart Mill, whom Redwood characterised as 'unrelenting assailants' of Jesus' Godhead.[35] Redwood claimed that no life could better have manifested God's love and nature than did 'Jesus the prophet of Galilee'. He hailed Jesus' 'fortitude' and 'celestial sweetness', and the 'sublime inspiration' of his teaching. He also credited Christ as the moral force that gave shape to 'the Christian religion'. The marvels of 'true religion', however, were clearly those of the Catholic faith. Christ had been the Saviour and King of mankind for nineteen centuries, swaying 'the destinies of the Catholic world' and framing its civilisation. His achievements symbolised the promise of Catholicism.

This willingness to use Jesus as a symbol of denominational identity was marked within Catholicism. It reflected Catholic ecclesiology as much as Christology, though it may also have been reinforced by a minority position within New Zealand society. The result was a rather emblematic Jesus. Catholic approaches characteristically focused on the Passion, and made Jesus' wounded body the primary evidence of his humanity and a focal point of spiritual reflection. Like many Protestants, Catholics believed that emotion could facilitate religious commitment, and cultivated this through Passion imagery. There was, however, much less interest in Jesus' personality. Partly as a consequence of their approach to the Bible, Catholics also appeared less concerned to use Jesus' life as a direct religious model.

---

35   Francis Redwood, *Jesus Christ Yesterday, To-Day, and For Ever*, Dunedin: NZ Tablet, 1910, pp.1-2.

The humanity of Jesus and doctrinal conflict

Questions concerning the person and work of Christ, and the humanity of Jesus, have always been crucial in Christian theological reflection. They remained a central element in doctrinal debates of the early twentieth century. Questioning of the Virgin Birth, for example, was a staple of Modernist interpretation, but a point of concern for those anxious about the contemporary tendency to treat Jesus as 'a merely natural man'.[36] Interpretations of the Atonement were another important site of contest. For some, attitudes to the humanity of Jesus became an important indicator of doctrinal error. For example, the Brethren evangelist C.H. Hinman claimed that it was a tendency of heterodox religious groups to enthuse over the humanity of Jesus:

> In a patronising kind of way the Theosophist, Unitarian, and Spiritist can speak of the Lord as a wonderful teacher and moralist: they can extol His virtues as man, and admire His self-sacrifice and self-effacement, but they combine with others in denying his proper deity.[37]

Conservative Christians feared that over-emphasis on Jesus suggested that his humanity was all that mattered, or perhaps the only reality.

While responses varied, one typical conservative reaction was to increase the devotional emphasis on Jesus, even as emphasis on his personality and humanity was resisted. In theological debates, Jesus language often became a focal point for other contests, especially those concerning the role and nature of Scripture. Significantly, Hinman's tract highlighted that the question of Christ's divinity was crucial because of its central place in the 'present-day attack upon the Word of God'. Similarly, Isaac Jolly's review of John Gibson Smith's controversial work *The Christ of the Cross* noted that the author's repudiation of the expiatory view of the Atonement avoided any detailed examination of the relevant Scriptures. In Jolly's estimation, expiation was so woven into the fabric of the New Testament that criticisms like Smith's could

---

36   *Reaper*, July 1924, p.138.
37   C.H. Hinman, *The Deity of Christ. As Seen Before Incarnation. In Incarnation. Among Men. In His Works. In His Death and Resurrection. In His Coming Reign and Glory*, Palmerston North: E. Whitehead Print, 1907, p.2.

'in no way affect the doctrine of the Atonement with those to whom Holy Scripture speaks with authority'.[38]

These theological differences were most evident in the growing conflict between conservative and Modernist positions during the interwar years. Significantly, the 'Fundamentalist' reaction against Modernism at this time was defined primarily in terms of biblical fidelity and doctrinal purity. Approaches to the Bible were deemed central, and the higher biblical criticism isolated as a chief cause of deviations from orthodox Christian faith. Jesus also provided an important rallying point for the conservative position. Nowhere was this more evident than in the rhetoric surrounding the Great Bible Demonstration of 1929. The event was organised in Auckland as a counter to the publicity surrounding a visit from England of the New Zealand-raised Modernist theologian H.D.A. Major.[39] On 14 March, about 3,000 people attended a gathering at the Town Hall that the *Reaper* described as a reply to Modernist 'attacks upon our holy and historic Faith'.[40] The occasion included addresses by 'several ministers of the Gospel and prominent Christian men of the city', as well as prayers, Bible reading and singing.

Most presentations criticised Modernism directly, and in some way addressed the nature and reliability of the Bible. Echoing the basic argument of the American theologian Gresham Machen, the leading Baptist minister the Rev. Joseph Kemp argued that Fundamentalism and Modernism were different religions, since Modernism denied basic Christian claims such as the deity of Christ.[41] Kemp judged such teaching to be subversive of faith, morals and the minds of the young. C.J. Rolls provided a more explicit focus on biblical issues in his address on 'The Trustworthiness of the Bible'. So did the Rev. Evan R. Harries, whose talk on the 'The Antidote to Modernism' urged listeners to 'Take the Bible as It Is', 'Read the Bible as God's Self-Revealing Message' and 'Read the Bible as God's Word to You'.

Crucially, resistance to Modernism and concern for doctrinal purity were also construed in terms of loyalty and faithfulness to Jesus Christ.

38   *Outlook*, 1 August 1908, p.7; cf. John Gibson Smith, *The Christ of the Cross*.
39   Clive R. Pearson, 'H.D.A. Major and English Modernism, 1911-1948', PhD thesis, University of Cambridge, 1989; cf. Pearson, Davidson and Lineham.
40   The citations here and following draw from, 'Special Report on the Great Bible Demonstration', *Reaper*, April 1929, pp.26-40.
41   J. Gresham Machen, *Christianity and Liberalism*, London: Victory Press, 1923.

The Rev. A.A. Murray of the independent United Evangelical Church spoke on the 'Infallibility of Jesus Christ'. Chastising Modernists for their refusal to accept Jesus' own scriptural and doctrinal interpretations Murray asserted that Jesus' teaching was 'entirely free from error and positively authoritative and final. We believe that the authority of the Scriptures rests upon the authority of Jesus Christ'. Significantly, Murray pinpointed acceptance of the 'kenotic theory' as a contributor to Modernism's failings. Modern kenotic Christology had been recently popularised in the English-speaking world by the English Anglican theologian and bishop Charles Gore. It posited an emptying of Jesus' divine attributes in becoming human, which conservatives took as a denial of his full divinity. By contrast, Murray made great play of pointing his audience to Christ, exhorting the gathered to 'build lives on Jesus Christ' with quotations from the hymn 'On Christ the solid rock I stand'. Indeed, the use of hymns throughout the event illustrated the power of appeal to Jesus. The Demonstration opened with the national anthem followed by a rousing rendition of 'All hail the power of Jesus' name'. Others included 'Jesus shall reign where'er the sun' and 'The Church's one foundation is Jesus Christ her Lord'.

Another prominent individual at the meeting was Dr W.H. Pettit, a General Practitioner and former medical missionary in India. In the interwar years, Pettit became a leading public critic of Rationalism and theological Modernism. He was instrumental in the formation of the Crusader movement and the Inter-Varsity Fellowship of Evangelical Unions (IVF) in the early 1930s. Reflecting later on the IVF's secession from the Student Christian Movement (SCM), Pettit highlighted the early evangelicalism of the latter organisation as demonstrated in its attitudes to Scripture and Christology.[42] He noted John R. Mott's formative role, praising his 'fearless and uncompromising... witness to the deity of Christ, His Virgin birth, His atoning death, His bodily resurrection, and His second advent'. Moreover, he cited Mott's belief that 'a Movement confessing and proclaiming the deity of Christ would attract Christians from every denomination and keep them true to the faith'. By contrast, Pettit complained that the SCM bore 'no clear witness to the infallibility of the Holy Scriptures, which is the ground of

---

42   W.H. Pettit, *Experiences in Christian Work Among New Zealand Students*, IVF Papers no. 2, New Zealand: IVF, n.d.

all our belief. The result was that the influence of the Higher Criticism and Modernism was early felt in that Movement'.

A reverential language of Christ's lordship was allied to resistance to Modernism and higher biblical criticism throughout the period. The Presbyterian controversialist P.B. Fraser's *Biblical Recorder*, one of the most outspoken organs of conservative theology, characterised Modernism as 'the religion of corrupt Christian idealism plus "science" and good advice.... Jesus of Nazareth, with them is either a hero to be applauded, or a God who only operates from Rome'.[43] References to 'the Lord Jesus Christ' in this context became markers of fidelity to historic Christian belief, especially in relation to the divinity of Jesus and the penal-substitution model of the Atonement. Thus, after World War One the *Biblical Recorder* railed against German theology, claiming:

> The new theology belittles our Lord Jesus Christ. It takes away His Supernatural birth, His Deity, His Resurrection, and His Atonement for sins. These great truths and the power of Christ to regenerate and miraculously change men have Christianised the barbarous and brought the wonderful changes wrought among the heathen. Reverse the order, take away the Bible as the Word of God, tell men they do not need the blood of Christ and the regeneration of the Holy Spirit, and you lead the civilised back to barbarism.[44]

Similarly, the Rev. Thomas Miller also employed reverential address in questioning the orthodoxy of the Principal of the Presbyterian Theological Hall John Dickie's *The Organism of Christian Truth*, especially in its treatment of the Atonement. Miller argued that his opposition was warranted, 'In view of the clear and consistent teaching of the Word of God on the death of our Lord Jesus Christ, and in view of our Church's subordinate standards'.[45]

A distinctive set of discourses therefore existed in which Jesus was invoked often, but primarily with reference to his divinity, or as a marker of other concerns. In contexts of formal theological contestation, a desire among conservatives to preserve 'biblical authority' discouraged

43 *Biblical Recorder*, August 1931, p.227.
44 *Biblical Recorder*, January 1919, p.7.
45 *PGA*, 1932, p.26. See John Dickie, *The Organism of Christian Truth: A Modern Positive Dogmatic*, London: James Clarke, 1931; Geoffrey S. King, '"Organising Christian Truth": An Investigation of the Life and Work of John Dickie', PhD thesis, University of Otago, 1998.

thorough exploration of Jesus' humanity. To some extent, these aimed to reclaim the divine Jesus as the true Jesus and thus rescue him from experimentalists. Nevertheless, the pressure that generated such strong responses indicated the growing influence of the more liberal position. This rising tide of interest in the humanity of Jesus ultimately shaped more conservative forms. It was also strikingly evident in religious literature and Protestant material culture.

The life of Jesus in literature

Whatever impact Schweitzer's work had on the 'Quest of the Historical Jesus', it did not staunch the flow of semi-biographical studies from scholarly popularisers, preachers and literary figures in the English-speaking world. By 1935, one writer in the Presbyterian denominational newspaper the *Outlook* observed that 'Every man of note has to write his book on Jesus'.[46] While many nineteenth-century examples of the genre had been produced by liberal Protestants using the tools of critical scholarship, a more devotional tone was evident in later works. Daniel Pals has noted that many Victorian 'lives' stressed the importance of Jesus' humanity, but adopted a moderate stance on biblical criticism. Like F.W. Farrar's exceptionally popular *Life of Christ*, they romanticised their subject and his life in ancient Palestine in order to appeal to a mass market. Late Victorian volumes of this kind aimed to settle believers' anxieties, especially those aroused by questioning of the Jesus' historicity and challenges to supernatural belief.[47] The twentieth-century lives read by English-speaking audiences characteristically picked up on this devotional tone, whilst also determining to communicate Jesus' humanity and personality more effectively.

Readers evidently recognised the new emphasis and appreciated it. Writing in 1939, J.J. North opined that:

---

46 *Outlook*, 29 July 1935, p.13.
47 Daniel L. Pals, *The Victorian 'Lives' of Jesus*, San Antonio: Trinity University Press, 1982. See F.W. Farrar, *The Life of Christ*, New York: A.L. Burt, 1907 (1874), which went through over 30 editions.

No man could read a "Life of Christ" dated a century back and then read a modern life… without feeling that what was obscure and remote has been transfigured and become contemporary, and this not because of additions introduced, but because of the neglected and misunderstood humanity of Jesus.[48]

For North, this new approach revealed a compelling personality: 'We see Him more completely man than any man, and from Whom the men of to-day are never able to divert their gaze. He haunts us, at once human and divine. He is both the hero and the Lord of the world'.

The genre proved popular. One volume by Giovanni Papini created a sensation when published, and remained perhaps the most loved of the interwar lives.[49] According to North, it epitomised the 'modern' approach. Papini's fictionalised biography was exceptionally well-received abroad, becoming a top-five fiction seller in North America. Such acclaim undoubtedly contributed to its local appeal. In 1923, the Bible Class magazine *Four Square* highlighted the book, paying particular attention to its international success.[50]

Part of Papini's appeal was literary. The author had been a journalist and poet, and brought these skills to bear in 96 impressionistic episodes. Reviewers noted the 'arresting originality' of the style and language of his work, and its vivid depiction of Jesus' life.[51] Reviews also signalled that the author's own story was important.[52] Papini had repudiated religion early in life, and his early literary career had been iconoclastic and controversial. At one point, he courted scandal by speculating that Jesus and John had shared a homosexual relationship. He began research on Jesus' life with sceptical intent, but converted to Roman Catholicism in 1921 while completing the book. Christians embraced Papini as a latter-day Saul of Tarsus and heralded his work as one of consummate devotion.[53] The author was a trophy of grace.

Papini's portrait of Jesus was fresh, but affirmed key orthodox doctrines. For instance, though not everyone was convinced, Papini seemed certain that he had unearthed proof of Jesus' divinity. He also

48   J.J. North, *'Me a Christian!' 'Why Not?'*, Auckland: H.H. Driver, 1939, p.12.
49   Giovanni Papini, *The Story of Christ*, Mary Prichard Agnetti (trans.), London: Hodder and Stoughton, 1923.
50   Prothero, p.108; *Four Square*, June 1923, p.325; *Four Square*, July 1923, p.344.
51   *NZMBC Link*, 24 July 1924, p.1.
52   *Outlook*, 24 September 1923, p.7.
53   *Four Square*, June 1923, p.325; Papini, xxii-xxiv.

believed that the Resurrection was incontrovertible. Papini claimed that he respected the Bible but saw an apologetic need for works like his. No life of Jesus could be more beautiful and perfect than the Gospels, 'But who reads the Evangelists to-day?' Every generation needed to translate the 'old Gospel' anew: 'In order that Christ may always be alive and eternally present in the lives of men, it is absolutely necessary to resuscitate Him from time to time'.[54] Earlier portrayals of Jesus were dismissed as 'ice-cold abstractions', while he launched a thinly-veiled attack on Friedrich Nietzsche. All of this pointed to an appealingly radical tone. Papini chided traditional devotion, claiming that he wanted his book to be edifying, 'Not at all in the sense of mechanical religiosity, but in the human and virile sense of remaking souls'. Lives created for the devout invariably exhaled a musty staleness, 'an obnoxious odour of extinguished candle, a stench of evaporated incense and bad oil, which takes away one's breath'.[55] Youth magazines revelled in this language, and cited extracts that emphasised Jesus' forceful personality and his practical attention to social need:

> Of all subvertors, Jesus is the greatest. He is the Mendicant, who distributes alms; One who, Himself naked, clothes the naked; One who, Himself famishing, yet feeds others. He is the miraculous and superhuman Pauper, who changes the falsely rich into paupers and makes the poor truly rich.[56]

Other lives of Jesus circulated widely, particularly during the interwar years. Written in the same year as Papini's volume, J. Paterson Smyth's *A Peoples' Life of Christ* often featured among recommended books for Bible Class and older Sunday school scholars.[57] Basil Mathews wrote books for children and adults. In 1935, the *Outlook* rated his *A Life of Jesus* the best of the lives of Christ then currently available. According to the reviewer, it avoided the usual pitfalls of the genre, which included producing a mere diatessaron, a purely imaginative biography, or a series

---

54 Papini, viii-ix.
55 Papini, xvii, vix-x.
56 *NZMBC Link*, 24 July 1924, p.1.
57 J. Paterson Smyth, *A Peoples' Life of Christ*, London: Hodder and Stoughton, 1921; cf. *Sunday School and Bible Class at Work: Text-Book for Teacher-Training Classes, Study Groups, and General Use*, 2nd ed., Melbourne: Joint Board of the Graded Lessons of Australia and New Zealand, 1936, p.119.

of incidents turned into sermonettes.[58] Theologically liberal Americans like Bruce Barton and Harry Emerson Fosdick were also fascinated by Jesus' personality, and their interpretations of his life in contemporary terms were widely cited.[59] Some of Shailer Mathews' social gospel interpretations of Jesus were also considered 'notable'.[60]

Though not a 'life of Jesus' as such, T.R. Glover's *The Jesus of History* was also influential during this period. Glover was a notable English Baptist and classical scholar at Cambridge University. His book on Jesus was republished frequently and distributed widely following its appearance in 1917. Originally delivered as a lecture series on the historical Jesus in India during 1915-16, the work was unmistakably apologetic. Glover aimed to provide a scholarly argument for Christian faith in the light of questions raised by historical criticism. Though recognising that the Gospel accounts were not biographical, he did explore Jesus' personality to some extent. The need to experience Jesus, and the centrality of Jesus to Christianity, were greater emphases.[61] Glover observed:

> the fact must weigh enormously that wherever the Christian Church, or a section of it, or a single Christian, has put upon Jesus Christ a higher emphasis – above all where everything has been centred in Jesus Christ – there has been an increase of power for Church, or community, or man.[62]

New Zealanders also read popular religious novels like the American Congregationalist minister Charles M. Sheldon's *In His Steps*. In this, members of the fictional First Church of Raymond vowed, after cajoling by their minister, to consider 'what would Jesus do?' before undertaking any action.[63] The book was a social gospel novel. It aimed to inspire

58   Basil Mathews, *A Life of Jesus*, New York: R.R. Smith, 1931; cf. *Outlook*, 29 July 1935, pp.13-14.
59   Bruce Barton, *A Young Man's Jesus*, Boston: Pilgrim Press, 1914; Bruce Barton, *The Man Nobody Knows*, Indianapolis: Bobb's-Merrill, 1925; Harry Eemerson Fosdick, *The Manhood of the Master*, rev. ed., London: Wyvern, 1958 (1913).
60   *NZMT*, 19 July 1921, p.9.
61   T.R. Glover, *The Jesus of History*, London: Hodder and Stoughton, 1965 (1917), p.154.
62   Glover, p.16.
63   Charles M. Sheldon, *In His Steps: What Would Jesus Do?*, London: Frederick Warne, 1928 (1896).

Christians to self-sacrificing action by emulating Jesus' example. By 1933, Sheldon estimated that 23 million copies had sold in 21 languages, though some scholars believe this to be overly generous.[64] In any case, the book was well received in New Zealand. One early commentator in the *Outlook* claimed that Sheldon's books were among the 'most potent factors in the life to-day, working for the elevation of public morals and the achievement of righteousness in our midst'.[65] The concept of following 'in his steps' became established thereafter in the vernacular. Sheldon eschewed scholarship, preferring an 'untheological Christianity' focused on simple love for God and humanity. Apparently, this practical and somewhat moralistic tone appealed to New Zealand readers.

None of Sheldon's many later works rivalled the popularity of *In His Steps*, though some proved more controversial. A sequel, *Jesus is Here!*, took reflection on Jesus a step further when, instead of merely considering what Jesus might do, the Rev. Henry Maxwell and his congregation found that Jesus actually became present in their midst.[66] The book was not well received. Amongst other grievances, contemporary observers complained that it transgressed a boundary by imagining Jesus' humanity in contemporary terms. One reviewer in the *Outlook* believed that 'adverse criticism was due to the feeling that no one should attempt to picture in a novel what might happen if Jesus were actually to appear in the world a second time in human form'.[67]

Contrasting reaction to the two works was significant. While Jesus could serve as a moral inspiration, attempts to update him were evidently problematic. Negativity partly reflected residual reticence about imaging the divine. It also indicated the difficulty of portraying a specific Jesus in generally acceptable terms. *In His Steps* had issued a universally applicable call to reflective ethical conduct, in which common associations of Jesus with moral excellence fitted well. Notwithstanding Sheldon's confidence about what Jesus might have done, the essential premise of that novel left the implications open. The sequel was perhaps too definite, and hence its suggestions were more easily resisted.

64   Ronald C. White and C. Howard Hopkins, *The Social Gospel: Religion and Reform in Changing America*, Philadelphia: Temple University Press, 1976, p.143.
65   *Outlook*, 24 February 1900, p.43; cf. *Outlook*, 25 August 1906, p.21.
66   Charles M. Sheldon, *Jesus is Here! Continuing the Narrative of In His Steps*, New York: George H. Doran, 1914.
67   *Outlook*, 28 March 1927, p.15.

Art

Perceptions of Jesus were reflected in, and shaped by, the way he appeared in material culture. The Reformation of the sixteenth century did not so much expunge images as redefine suitable places and uses for them. Consequently, these patterns remained important for Protestant and Catholic alike. Within the material culture of Protestant religiosity, emphasis on Jesus' human attributes and representation of his personality became increasingly important characteristics.

In New Zealand as elsewhere, 'word-centred' Protestants continued to cultivate iconographic vocabularies, notably in illustrated Bibles, Bible-story books for children and other decorated literature. In addition to the pious and quasi-religious verse that appeared in many homes, there were also favoured images of Jesus. These included illustrations by Gustave Doré, and depictions by Heinrich Hofmann and Harold Copping. New Zealand missionaries in the Punjab used some of the latter as evangelistic tools. As one report to the Presbyterian missionary magazine the *Harvest Field* noted, 'Harold Copping's pictures have made some excellent coloured slides, and these show more vividly than much talk ever could the reality and beauty of a Life once lived on earth for all men'.[68]

William Holman Hunt's *The Light of the World* was perhaps the most widely disseminated and influential image of Jesus for Protestants during the twentieth century. The painting had become prominent in the mid-nineteenth century following favourable reviews by John Ruskin. A few windows based on the image were installed in Anglican churches in the 1890s, which indicated something of its popularity. Its local reputation grew considerably, however, when the third of three versions of the painting visited in 1906 as part of a tour of the British Empire.[69]

The painting was exhibited in New Zealand between 15 April and 28 May 1906, before returning again for display at the International Exhibition in Christchurch between November 1906 and April 1907.

---

68   *Harvest Field*, May 1938, p.10.
69   Geoffrey Troughton, '*The Light of the World* at the End of the World, 1906', *Journal of New Zealand Art History*, 28, 2007, pp.1-15; Jeremy Maas, *Holman Hunt & The Light of the World*, London: Scolar Press, 1984.

During the initial sojourn, it aroused great excitement as large crowds turned out to see it, filling substantial public venues. In Auckland, over 50,000 people came to the Mackelvie Gallery in one week. The *Auckland Weekly News* reported that the crush on the final Sunday was barely containable, with members of the 'fair sex' emerging 'breathless and by no means so neat in appearance as when they entered'.[70] In Christchurch, queues of up to one thousand waited outside the Canterbury Society of Arts Gallery.[71] A letter to the painting's owner, Charles Booth, asserted that 'No person or event has moved Dunedin with a tithe of the intensity of interest that the picture has done'. The writer estimated that no less than 120,000 people viewed the painting there, despite a city population of less than 60,000.[72] In smaller centres, such as Timaru, crowds were similarly overwhelming. By late July 1907, when the painting finally departed the region, the tour's organiser estimated a total Australasian attendance of at least four million out of a population of just over five million people – though this included a highly optimistic calculation of viewings at the International Exhibition.

The enthusiastic overall response reflected the convergence of art with entertainment, imperialism and religion. Nevertheless, the work was widely hailed as religious art, and for many people viewing it was a kind of a religious experience. Significantly, despite its allegorical nature, responses to the work frequently emphasised its depiction of Jesus' humanity. As one commentary noted, 'This Christ, for all His symbolised divinity, is magnificently human'. One preacher spoke of the sense of the nearness of God the painting engendered. Another observer commented on the fellow-feeling that flowed from the subject's face, asserting that it was the face of 'the Son of Man rather than the traditional countenance of the Son of God'.[73]

To the extent that viewers perceived a human Jesus, he was distinctly mawkish and pious. He was the Man of Sorrows. His bearing was grave and noble, and marked by a countenance of 'deep solemnity...

70 *Auckland Weekly News*, 26 April 1906, p.29.
71 *Press*, 19 May 1906, p.8; *Lyttelton Times*, 19 May 1906, p.8.
72 J.H. Roy to Charles Booth, 4 June 1906, Charles Booth Papers, Ms797/II/91/3, Special Collections, University of London Library, London; *Auckland Weekly News*, 31 May 1906, p.25.
73 *ODT*, 23 May 1906, p.2; *Press*, 21 May 1906, p.9; *EP*, 4 May 1906, p.6.

blended with dignity'.[74] An apparent lugubriousness reflected the great yearning in the subject's soul: 'The face of Christ standing lonely with His lantern is wistful, with a wistfulness which seeks human fellowship'.[75] There is evidence that some viewers expected to see more humanity and personality depicted. As the *Taranaki Herald* reported:

> Many good and devout people take exception to the expression of the face. Some think "The Light of the World" should depict an expression of hope and cheerfulness, instead of which is readily conveyed to the mind by the words of Isaac Watts, "See from His head, His hands, His feet, sorrow and love flow mingled down."[76]

Another correspondent from Napier acknowledged the artistry of the work, but noted that they expected to see 'a gentler face outlined of Him who came and suffered for mankind'.

Observers' interpretations actually isolated morals, 'lessons', and principles more than anything especially personal. Thus, James Craigie hoped that the painting would excite 'a more lively appreciation of that great Christian love and charity of which it is emblematical'.[77] Viewers may have been conscious of the humanity of Jesus in the painting, but read its message according to their understanding of his divine mission. Jesus was a gentle, pleading saviour seeking reconciliation. This vision appealed particularly to Protestants shaped by conversionistic and pietistic models. Support for the painting was most evident among low church Anglicans, Presbyterians and Methodists, who appreciated its allegory. Ironically, the painting was also heralded as a 'sermon in oils', signalling a Protestant instinct for 'the word' as well as conversionism. Numerous sermons drew moral and spiritual 'lessons from the great picture'.[78] Its central meaning was already reasonably transparent, and had been widely published. Few could have missed the imagery drawn from Revelation 3.20, which was by then a favoured evangelistic text.[79]

74   *Press*, 16 May 1906, p.7.
75   *EP*, 4 May 1906, p.6.
76   *Taranaki Herald*, 17 April 1906, p.7.
77   *Timaru Herald*, 22 May 1906, p.6.
78   *Outlook*, 19 May 1906, pp.22-23.
79   Revelation 3.20: 'Behold I stand at the door and knock; if any man hear my voice and open the door, I will come in to him and sup with him, and he with me' (Authorised Version).

46

Consequently, there were hopes that many would 'open their hearts to Jesus and let Him come in' on account of viewing it.[80] Given New Zealanders' reputed ambivalence about revivalism, the painting may have been instrumental in making that language respectable.

The fact that Protestants were so taken with the humanity of Jesus in the painting was significant, not least because it indicated that they were consciously looking for it. Responses also highlighted growing appreciation of the power of embodiment as a mediator for religious feeling. As a 'sermon in oils', *The Light of the World* was thought to transcend mere artistry, appealing to the 'reverence for the divine' resident 'Deep in the hearts of even the most careless and frivolous'.[81] Contemplation of the 'nobility of the sacred figure' of Jesus would lead to devotion and commitment. As one correspondent suggested, 'To gaze on the symbolical painting is to inspire holy sentiments'.[82]

The Light of the World arguably became one of the most recognisable works of religious art in the country. The exhibition was a major cause, since it aided dispersal of reproductions. A lucrative trade in postcards of the work accompanied the tour.[83] Major newspapers also published full-page reproductions. In Christchurch, the *Lyttelton Times* reported that the *Canterbury Times* would print a supplement to its regular weekly edition to include a 'most artistically reproduced' copy of the painting, 'well suited for framing, as an adornment for a room'. In expectation of increased demand the *Times* planned to print 'several thousand extra copies'.[84] *The Light of the World* lived on in other ways in more overtly religious contexts. In 1906, numerous sermons utilised stories, texts and symbolism drawn from the painting. This continued for many years; the painting remained a favoured preaching illustration, and was used widely for evangelistic and religious education purposes. Framed copies of the work were displayed in many churches. From 1912, a version of *The Light of the World* comprised one panel of the altar reredos at Woodend near Christchurch.[85] The picture also became a favourite subject for stained glass windows.

80   *Outlook*, 19 May 1906, p.3.
81   *Press*, 19 May 1906, p.8.
82   *Lyttelton Times*, 15 May 1906, p.2.
83   Maas, pp.167-68; *Manawatu Evening Standard*, 30 April 1906, p.8.
84   *Lyttelton Times*, 15 May 1906, p.2.
85   *Church News*, March 1912, p.3.

Stained glass

In many ways stained glass windows epitomised a style that attempts to personalise Jesus were moving away from. As J.J. North described, the stained glass Jesus was often 'The stiff Christ of the church windows'.[86] Nevertheless, there were hints of a changing emphasis even in this conservative medium. Fiona Ciaran's detailed catalogue of Canterbury sources indicates that Jesus was the predominant subject of ecclesiastical windows. Two-thirds of 711 examples identified in the province included some depiction of the life of Christ.[87] Of these, the most common themes related to Jesus' death, resurrection and ascension, as well as his childhood and Johannine themes of Jesus as the Good Shepherd and Light of the World. Images of Jesus were often found in the sanctuary where the symbolism of Jesus' death and resurrection related obviously to celebration of the Eucharist.

The Canterbury evidence makes clear the appeal of stained glass to particular forms of religiosity. It appeared in churches of all the main denominations, but overwhelmingly among Anglicans and Catholics. Presbyterians and Methodists had some, but at rates significantly lower than their share of the population.[88] Imagery relating to the life or teaching of Jesus was proportionally more common within the Protestant churches, while Anglicans particularly favoured the Johannine symbols. Catholics had a higher proportion of windows devoted to the saints, though Anglicans also depicted the apostles. Eucharistic and Passion imagery featured in Anglican and Catholic churches.

The timing of installation reflected changes in Protestant religiosity. Most early installations in the province were in Anglican and to a lesser

---

86 North, 'Me a Christian!', p.12.
87 Fiona Ciaran, Stained Glass Windows of Canterbury, New Zealand: A Catalogue Raisonné, Dunedin: University of Otago Press, 1998, p.75. Following discussion derives from analysis of Ciaran's catalogue.
88 Of the 711 windows, the proportions by denomination are: Anglican (49.8%), Catholic (17.1%), Presbyterian (9.3%), and Methodist (3.3%). The denominational proportions for Canterbury in 1906 were: Anglican (45.6%), Catholic (12.4%), Presbyterian (19.8%), and Methodist (12.8%); cf. Census, 1906, p.97. The comparison assumes that the proportion of population was to some extent reflected in the number of churches for each denomination.

extent Catholic churches. This reflected devotional priorities, and the relative wealth of Anglicanism in Canterbury. Of 493 windows in place in the province by 1940, 335 had been installed after 1900.[89] Significantly, only 22 of the 66 Presbyterian windows in the catalogue had been fitted by 1940 (including 14 in a single church at Cave). All 22 were fitted after World War One. Aside from those at Cave and an insignia of the burning bush at Knox Church in Waimate, all dealt with facets of Jesus' life and teaching, or his evangelistic appeal. Similarly, only 6 of the 28 Methodist windows in the sample were installed prior to World War Two, and all of these concerned Christ.

Ciaran notes that ecclesiastical windows drew from a range of sources including medieval and renaissance styles. New images and themes emerged in the nineteenth century, but there was often a lag time between British trends and New Zealand installations, especially during the Victorian era.[90] Glass was often used for memorial purposes, which explains why so many windows appeared in the years following each of the two World Wars. Prior to the Second World War, however, there was little local context evident in designs for church windows.[91] Consequently, the Jesus who appeared in New Zealand stained glass art was firmly contextualised within European traditions.

Introduction of glass into Canterbury's Methodist and Presbyterian churches was a significant departure. The increasingly respectable and settled position of Protestant churches in the province probably encouraged the change. Another factor was arguably the influence of the *Light of the World* tour. Ciaran's catalogue lists 17 windows modelled on the painting, mostly in rural churches. The earliest nineteenth century examples were Anglican. Two more were installed in 1917, and another three in the interwar years. Presbyterian windows based on the work were installed from 1935, especially after World War Two.[92] Fraser's Art Glass Company in Dunedin also supplied windows to a number of Methodist churches in the 1930s.[93] *The Light of the World,* and its evangelistic message, may have provided an acceptable iconography that

---

89 Ciaran, p.219.
90 Jock Phillips and Chris Maclean, *In the Light of the Past: Stained Glass Windows in New Zealand Houses*, Auckland: Oxford University Press, 1983, p.26.
91 Ciaran, pp.84-85.
92 Ciaran, p.215.
93 *NZMT*, 28 October 1933, p.6.

helped to establish the medium from the interwar years. The fact that preferred Protestant images concerned Jesus' life and teaching seems particularly striking. Factoring in delays in stained glass production, increasing use of the medium from the interwar years evidently reflected the increasingly Jesus-centred nature of Protestantism during the period. In effect, windows became justifiable within this changing context.

Film

Film became a significant cultural force during the first half of the twentieth century, and provided further opportunities for encountering depictions of Jesus. In particular, its warmth and immediacy offered fresh perspectives on Jesus' humanity. Writing in 1945, Gordon Mirams claimed that New Zealanders adopted the motion picture earlier and more enthusiastically than most other countries; on a per capita basis, they spent more time and money on picture-going than any country bar the United States. Only tea-drinking, he surmised, was a more popular diversion.[94] Some statistical evidence supports his assessment. Nerida Elliott cites estimates that 320,000 people per week attended picture theatres by 1916.[95] In 1926, the figure was closer to 600,000.[96] By the end of World War Two, film-going was still among the most popular leisure pursuits. New Zealand had one movie theatre for every 3,000 persons in 1943, compared with one in 8,700 in the United States.

The rise of film had profound effects. Mirams noted the cultural impact on habits, customs and attitudes, claiming that 'If there is any such thing as a "New Zealand culture", it is to a large extent the creation of Hollywood'.[97] Patterns of leisure changed. Some churches worried that movie-going was effectively an alternative to religious association, and threatened religious education and morality. The coarser aspects of

---

94   Gordon Mirams, *Speaking Candidly: Films and People in New Zealand*, Hamilton: Paul's Book Arcade, 1945, p.5.
95   Nerida J. Elliott, 'Anzac, Hollywood and Home: Cinemas and Film-Going in Auckland 1909-1939', MA thesis, University of Auckland, 1989, p.119.
96   *EP*, 25 November 1926, p.8.
97   Mirams, p.5.

film content also raised concern. Religious groups were among those that feared what on-screen crudity and violence would do to children and the tone of society. Agitation spearheaded by the New Zealand Catholic Federation, with support from churches, the Woman's Christian Temperance Union (WCTU) and the Young Men's (YMCA) and Women's Christian Associations (YWCA), became instrumental in the development of film censorship apparatus in the form of the Cinematograph-films Censorship Act, 1916.[98]

Religious people also saw the potential benefits of film. In 1916, A.H. Norrie, a Presbyterian home missionary, was organising screenings around Whangamomona on his Pathé Free Home Cinematograph machine. Shows included films on biblical subjects such as *The Finding of Moses* and *The Prodigal Son*, though most of his material was not religious at all.[99] In Australia, Herbert Booth helped produce an evangelistic multimedia show, *Soldiers of the Cross*, which combined short films with slides, hymns, sermons and prayers.[100]

Many early films, including epics like *Ben Hur* and *Quo Vadis*, addressed religious themes in a generally reverential manner. A smaller number concerned Jesus directly, though it is not clear how many of these reached New Zealand. Certainly, by 1917, New Zealanders were viewing depictions of Jesus on film, for in March that year the newly established Film Censor's office passed both *The Life of Christ* and *Intolerance* for screening.[101] The latter decision proved controversial. Made in 1916, *Intolerance* was directed by the American D.W. Griffiths and featured four separate stories from four distinct eras, each reflecting the theme indicated in the title. One portrayed Jesus. While this accounted for just 12 minutes of the three-hour film, the idea of Jesus as a victim of intolerance was fundamental to the project as a whole.[102]

98 Paul Christoffel, *Censored: A Short History of Censorship in New Zealand*, Wellington: Department of Internal Affairs, 1989, p.12; *NZPD*, vol. 177, 1916, p.572.

99 A.H. Norrie to W. Jolliffe, 6 November 1916, Mr Jolliffe Correspondence, 1916-17, IA 83, Envelope 10, ANZ.

100 Robert K. Johnston, *Reel Spirituality: Theology and Film in Dialogue*, Grand Rapids: Baker Academic, 2000, p.32.

101 Registers of Films, 12 Sept 1916 to 31 May 1917, IA 60, 6/1, ANZ.

102 W. Barnes Tatum, *Jesus at the Movies: A Guide to the First Hundred Years*, Santa Rosa: Poleridge Press, 1997, pp.33-34.

There had been opposition to the film before it came to New Zealand. In America, complaints by the WCTU focused on its critical portrayal of social purity reformers, who seemed to be caricatures of WCTU members.[103] Griffiths had used Jesus' miracle at Cana to make explicit anti-prohibition messages, but he also found other ways of associating social up-lifters with hypocrisy. In Britain, the film ran foul of censorship laws prohibiting depictions of Jesus on film and on stage.

In New Zealand, controversy over *Intolerance* was sparked primarily by debates in Dunedin. Audiences were initially alerted to the film through international reviews, notably in the Australian stage magazine *The Green Room*.[104] When the censor William Jolliffe passed the film without amendment, criticism followed. Armed with negative opinion from Australia, a review in the *Dunedin Evening Star* promptly condemned the film, while Presbyterian, Methodist and Baptist preachers in the city denounced it shortly thereafter.[105] A meeting in early June addressed the issue, and led to a delegation petitioning G.W. Russell, the Minister of Internal Affairs.[106] In his representations to Russell, R.S. Gray, the Baptist minister at Hanover Street, conveyed concerns that the film was sacrilegious – especially in its depictions of Jesus and his Passion, and a sequence that portrayed Christ stumbling under his cross.[107] This complaint reflected long-standing discomfort with the theatre in general as well as resistance to rendering Jesus' life on stage. Many Christians simply regarded the Passion an unsuitable subject for dramatic treatment. Indeed, in light of the furore, Russell criticised Jolliffe for failing to act and urged him to follow overseas precedents in establishing a list of prohibited subjects. Russell felt that

103 Alison M. Parker, 'Mothering the Movies: Women Reformers and Popular Culture', in Francis G. Couvares (ed.), *Movie Censorship and American Culture*, Washington: Smithsonian Institution Press, 1996, p.77.
104 The Rev. Winslade to W. Jolliffe, 22 May 1917, Jolliffe Correspondence, 1916-17.
105 *Eltham Argus*, 12 June 1917, in Mr Jolliffe's Papers – General, 1916-1923, IA 83, Envelope 9, ANZ.
106 Lisa Cutfield, 'Silent Film and Censorship in New Zealand, 1908-1928', BA Hons long essay, University of Otago, 1994, p.34. Similar meetings occurred in Christchurch, Wellington and Auckland; cf. *EP*, 10 July 1917, p.3.
107 Report of the deputation, IA 1, 13/11/25, ANZ.

the British Board of Film Censors' ban on representations of Christ and nudity provided a suitable model, but Jolliffe resisted this advice.[108]

Further issues related specifically to *Intolerance*. While the portrayal of Jesus was orthodox in many respects, the movie cast him in more iconoclastic terms than earlier reverential depictions had. Drawing comparisons between Christ's suffering and other stories undermined the sense that Jesus' suffering and death was unique, and removed his Passion from its more familiar ritual context. More importantly, the redemptive interpretation of his death was also diminished. Jesus' humanity was effectively highlighted at the expense of his divinity.

In fact, the issue of representing Christ was only one area of concern. Most of the debate concerned morality rather than sacrilege, with correspondence complaining about violence and sexual immorality, including depictions of rape and sexual assault. Thus, Kingsley Wigglesworth, writing as Honorary Secretary of the Methodist Lay Preachers Meeting in Christchurch, directed Jolliffe to reports referring to its sensuality, nudity and immorality.[109] Gray had argued against showing 'the living figure of Christ', but also raised objections with the Minister concerning vampire women, indecorous dress, and pictures that brought marriage into contempt or lowered 'the sacredness of family ties'.[110] Cultural factors also seem to have been important. American dominance in the film industry led some commentators to interpret the film's objectionable features as part of a wider problem. Commenting on *Intolerance*, the minister at Knox Presbyterian Church in Dunedin complained that 'These malignant exhibitions of sensuality and vice, these prurient plays that came to us from America present the worst phases of American life, and should be banished out of our midst'.[111]

After World War One, the movie industry became progressively more commercialised, leading to increased rates of film-going during the 1920s and 1930s. The commercial drive came largely from America, which was the source of most of the films entering New Zealand. The influence of Hollywood generated considerable discussion, including attempts to promote British film instead. In 1920, the *New Zealand*

---

108 Cutfield, p.35; Chris Watson and Roy Shuker, *In the Public Good: Censorship in New Zealand*, Palmerston North: Dunmore Press, 1998, p.31.
109 K. Wigglesworth to W. Jolliffe, 15 June 1917, Jolliffe Correspondence, 1916-17.
110 *EP*, 10 July 1917, p.3.
111 *Eltham Argus*, 12 June 1917.

Times reported on a resolution adopted by the Council of Education, 'That encouragement be given to British picture films, as the present preponderance of American films does not encourage morality or the growth of a knowledge of the British Empire'. In 1926, however, the same newspaper reported that 95% of the 450 films coming to New Zealand in 1927 were expected to be American.[112]

In an increasingly commercial environment, American filmmakers like Cecil B. DeMille began to recognise the potential profitability of religion. According to R.K. Johnston, DeMille responded to a growing market for the illicit within an increasingly secular culture. Though personally religious, he also understood the morality of the flapper era and gave the public what it wanted with 'a religious gloss over salacious scenes'.[113] His *Ten Commandments* (1923) was indicative of the new approach, and portrayed sensuous orgies within the moral context of the giving of Torah. When DeMille embarked on filming a life of Christ there was further controversy, partly because of lingering reservations about depicting Jesus on film. In New Zealand, W. Bower Black noted retrospectively that another of DeMille's projects, *The King of Kings*, had aroused much discussion, with some critics thinking it should never have been shown.[114]

The King of Kings followed a tradition handed down from Renan in giving a sexually alluring Mary Magdalene a central role, and by surrounding Jesus with adoring females. Aware of the financial risk involved, however, DeMille also worked hard to ensure religious support for his film by engaging religious consultants. The religious community was potentially lucrative, and distributors similarly worked to allay their potential concerns.[115] In New Zealand, there was extensive advertising in the denominational press, including brief character descriptions and endorsements from religious leaders. Preview screenings were arranged for church leaders. The Anglican *Church Chronicle* reviewed one for

---

112 See *NZ Times*, 18 June 1920; *Press*, 3 September 1926; *EP*, 25 November 1926; *NZ Times*, 26 November 1926, in Film Censor: Loose Papers, News Clippings, 1918-27, IA 83, ANZ.

113 Johnston, p.33.

114 W. Bower Black, *Shepherd of Souls*, Christchurch: Presbyterian Bookroom, 1952, p.14.

115 Robert S. Birchard, *Cecil B. DeMille's Hollywood*, Lexington: University of Kentucky Press, 2004, p.216.

ministers and clergy in Wellington at the De Luxe Theatre in Courtenay Place on 7 February 1928. Its report noted misgivings about biblical films and referred to unfavourable reviews in the *Church Guardian* and *London Spectator*. However, it judged that the motivation inspiring the film was sincere, which was 'the wish to spread the knowledge of our Lord to "the uttermost parts of the earth."' [116]

When the film opened, newspaper reports emphasised its accessibility to ordinary viewers' tastes. According to the *New Zealand Herald*, critics claimed it was not merely a biblical film, but one that 'every man, whatever his thought, can understand and appreciate. Throughout it surges with infinite humanity, with tenderness, with beauty, and never does it overstep the bounds of good taste'. [117] Reviews paid tribute to the spirit of reverence in the movie, and its faithfulness to the 'spirit of the original story in the Bible'. [118] There were oblique references to controversy. Some people apparently objected to the idea that, as a carpenter, Jesus profiteered from making crosses. The *Evening Post* also noted that the film contained many apocryphal interpolations which were 'quite inessential to a dignified representation of the ministry of Jesus when on earth, but, seemingly, they are indispensable elements in commercial cinematography'. [119] Most focused on the film's orthodoxy and conservatism. One supplement to the *New Zealand Herald* noted that *The King of Kings* had 'probably caused more bitter argument and diverse opinion than any other picture yet made', but concluded that it was not revolutionary in theme or treatment: 'It did not upset, as so many church authorities apparently like to think, the common conception of Christ. DeMille simply followed the Bible as closely as possible'. [120]

Sensing an opportunity, the churches rallied behind the film and appropriated it for devotional purposes. Reports of its success in evangelistic terms helped to bolster support. The *New Zealand Herald* carried testimony from one patron who claimed to have attended Sunday school and church all their life, and 'earnestly studied the Bible', but believed that 'the three hours I have spent viewing this picture have given me a deeper and more real understanding of the life and teachings

116 *CC*, March 1928, pp.39-40.
117 *NZH*, 15 March 1928, p.12.
118 *NZH*, 5 April 1928, p.15; *NZH*, 12 April 1928, p.13.
119 *CC*, March 1928, p.40; *EP*, 16 June 1928, p.7.
120 *Supplement to the NZH*, 7 April 1928, p.9.

of Christ than all else'.[121] Others reported witnessing the transformation of crowds who entered as amusement seekers, only to exit three hours later 'silent and thoughtful, awed and subdued, with a look of wonder and wistful inquiry in their tear-stained eyes'.[122] Crucially, responses were credited to the film's evocation of Jesus' humanity. The film was:

> a magnificent sermon, which needs no translation, set forth as it is in the universal language of the eye which renders the message of the Gospel in eloquent testimony.... With bold, but sympathetic, strokes he does away with any merely symbolic representation, and depicts Christ as a flesh and blood figure.[123]

According to Ian Faulkner, Colin Scrimgeour had been interested in 'moving pictures' as an evangelistic medium from about the middle of 1927. Through the 1920s, Scrimgeour had served in a series of rural home missions for the Methodist Church before his appointment as the inaugural missioner at the Auckland Central Mission in 1927. Whilst there, Scrimgeour developed a reputation for innovative practical and evangelistic work. The success of *The King of Kings* helped convince him of film's value in this endeavour. On 29 October 1928, he received authorisation to hire the Strand Theatre for Sunday evening services. For the first few weeks he used clips from the movie as part of these special services. The theatre had a capacity of 1,500 seats, but was frequently full. At times, up to 400 were reputedly unable to receive entry.[124] For a populist like Scrimgeour, film represented a boon. His experimental services partly succeeded because of their novelty and on account of his personal charm. There was also the fact that film was inherently well suited to conveying the warmth, emotion and personality that reflected his approach to religion.

The epic scale and grand spectacle of *The King of Kings* contributed to its success. Moreover, its heroic style and scale were felt to do justice to the film's subject. Despite the commercial imperatives driving it and DeMille's sensual embellishments, the movie helped to make film

---

121 *NZH*, 7 April 1928, p.17.
122 Black, *Shepherd of Souls*, p.14.
123 *NZH*, 18 April 1928, p.14.
124 Ian F. Faulkner, *The Decisive Decade: Some Aspects of the Development and Character of the Methodist Central Mission, Auckland, 1927-1937*, Christchurch: Wesley Historical Society, 1982, pp.7-8.

depictions of Jesus more acceptable. The supposed sincerity and evangelistic intent of the film helped. In turn, acceptance was justified by the feeling that Jesus' essential character had been revealed. The advent of film technology facilitated different kinds of experience, which shaped perceptions of Jesus. Above all, film conveyed immediacy and provided vivid and memorable images. These features aided engagement with personality and were precisely the aspects that religious use of the film drew upon. Writers and preachers who continued to refer to *The King of Kings* did so because its scenes conveyed emotional impact. Thus, Bower Black could claim that 'in the spell of Jesus cast on a great audience the picture found its justification and its purpose'.[125]

The language of outreach and missions

Churches' attempts to extend their community influence often invoked Jesus. These efforts were exerted in diverse ways and contexts, some of which will be considered in following chapters. One important area related to missions. Foreign missionary activity was a distinctive feature of Protestant religious life during this period, though it was most closely associated with conservative theology. Justifications for mission were intimately tied to Jesus. Earlier Protestants emphasised the motivating factors of human sinfulness and the glory of God. By the later interwar years, however, it had become more common to find the missionary task framed with reference to Jesus' example.

In keeping with evangelical priorities, missionary work was closely related to Jesus as well as to scriptural injunctions. In particular, supporters of foreign mission pointed to the 'Great Commission' of Matthew 28.18-20 as a foundational justification. In his history of the New Zealand Baptist Missionary Society, the Rev. H.H. Driver declared that it existed 'First and chiefly, because Jesus Christ bade his followers to go into all the world, and preach the gospel to every creature'. The Great Commission applied to individuals, which made mission a matter of simple obedience:

125 Black, *Shepherd of Souls*, p.14.

We knew that His royal command had never been revoked, and applied to us as it did to those who first heard it.... Our Society rests, therefore... upon the solid foundation of the Will of Christ the Lord. It is not based upon human opinions. It was not formed to gratify any unworthy ambition. It was established with the one grand aim of carrying out the command of the Lord Jesus Christ.[126]

As David Bosch has noted, the Great Commission lent moral authority. The text became a defensive bastion, 'as if the protagonists of mission were saying, "How can you oppose mission to the heathen if Christ himself has commanded it?"'[127]

The conviction that missionary activity was Jesus' work provided confidence and reassurance, and a focal point for calls to commitment. It also heightened a sense of obligation. When financial giving to missionary work fell behind targets in the 1920s, Methodists were reminded that they had a direct duty to Christ:

We may and should deny ourselves. We cannot deny Christ. We cannot deny our Lord of that which He needs. He is taking up this collection. When we give to Missions, we give to Him. Were He to come round to us individually and press the claims of His Kingdom in fields afar, we should each give a little more.[128]

During the depression of the 1930s, Presbyterian children were encouraged to give financially to a building for the Maori mission in the central North Island because Jesus wanted them to. J.G. Laughton expressed appreciation for the children's efforts to 'present Jesus with a house of worship at Reporoa for His birthday in 1932', and assured them that Jesus was very thankful.[129]

Hugh Morrison's study of the Protestant missionary movement in New Zealand reinforces the view that motivations were complex, and varied to some extent over time.[130] In whatever form, however, love for Jesus remained a central motif. Experience of Jesus' love was the route

126 H.H. Driver, *Our Work for God in India: A Brief History of the N.Z.B.M.S.*, Dunedin: H.H. Driver, 1914, p.10.
127 David Bosch, *Transforming Mission: Paradigm Shifts in Theology of Mission*, New York: Orbis, 1991, pp.340-41.
128 *NZMT*, 3 February 1923, p.2.
129 *Break of Day*, 24:10, 1932, pp.1, 5.
130 Hugh D. Morrison, '"It is our Bounden Duty": The Emergence of the New Zealand Protestant Missionary Movement, 1868-1926', PhD thesis, Massey University, 2004.

to commitment. As A.H. Collins expressed, 'our wayward hearts must be captured by Jesus, and His love must breathe its aroma of peace and heavenly joy before we can have an abiding sense of the greatness of the missionary cause'.[131] Experience created reciprocal love for Jesus, expressed in grateful service – a sense of duty and obligation that Collins called 'love to Jesus Christ and pity to the heathen'. As one commentator explained in 1926, 'If the love of Christ is a constraining power in any man's life it will compel him to give of what he possesses to satisfy his brothers' need.... A stay-at-home Christianity is not real Christianity'.[132]

This language often coincided with sharp juxtapositions between light and dark, Christian and heathen, civilisation and depravity, though that tone existed alongside an emphasis on Jesus' compassion. Bosch contends that late nineteenth-century foreign missionary work was increasingly conceptualised in terms of response to the love of God and the pitiful state of non-Christian people, rather than a response to the glory of God.[133] The need of the non-Christian world featured more prominently, and Christians were called to reach out to this world 'constrained by the love of Jesus'. Thus, one missionary prayer calendar from 1905 depicted a map of India, in which images of famine-stricken Indians contrasted starkly with a Christian congregation at worship. To the side, Christ's shadow fell on the starving while an outstretched arm reached to the map. The caption read: 'The touch of Christ upon India is one of compassionate longing and beseeching appeal'.[134]

The growth of missionary medical work fitted consistently with these ideas. The Baptist medical missionary Charles North regarded hospitals as facilities to care for 'the suffering poor in the name of the Lord Jesus Christ'.[135] Medical work and evangelisation were part of the same project, following the example of Jesus. Driver claimed that the first medical missionaries were 'led by common humanity as well as by the example and spirit of the Master to combine the ministry of healing with the preaching of the Gospel'.[136] Commenting on the opening of a

131 A.H. Collins, *The Interest of the Home Churches in Foreign Missions*, Auckland: Wright & Jaques Printers, 1899, p.9.
132 *NZB*, December 1926, pp.342-43.
133 Bosch, pp.285-91.
134 See Morrison, 'Bounden Duty'.
135 *Baptist Handbook*, 1911, p.78.
136 Driver, *Our Work*, p.59.

new dispensary at Chandpur, North assured Baptists that work carried out in the new building would prove an 'effective means of introducing men and women to the wonderful love of God in Christ'. Increased numbers would 'under these favourable conditions be more effectively treated, and told more clearly of the Great Physician'.[137]

In 1926, one report in the *New Zealand Baptist* highlighted that missionary motivations were becoming more complex.[138] Missionaries increasingly hoped to promote world peace, inter-racial brotherhood, social and industrial betterment and intellectual advancement. These were good, but the supreme missionary motivations were still conversion and duty – loyalty to 'Jesus Christ as Divine Lord and Saviour, a sense of the need of men for a way out of failure and sin, and a conviction that He alone shows the Way of Life, here and hereafter'. Most outgoing missionaries were felt to be 'actuated by such loyalty to Christ'. However, the writer noted that they needed also to be 'thoroughly grounded in faith and knowledge, and able to give the reasons for their conviction that the Gospel of Christ is the power of God unto salvation to everyone who believes on Him'. Similarly, Driver reiterated his earlier statements on missionary motivation:

> our Scriptures, with their pure and lofty morality, have refined and ennobled all who have yielded to their influence. And because we have the truth which makes men free, it is our bounden duty to declare it to all who are fettered by error and who grope in the darkness.... We were debtors to India, and in duty bound to do our best to impart to it the truth that makes men free.[139]

References to Jesus in the public discourse of mission combined certitude and sentiment, reflecting the traditions of revivalism and conversionist evangelical culture that nurtured missionary activity. A single Baptist missionary report in 1910 referred variously to 'the honey-sweet name of Jesus', his peace and his power, declaring that 'When once the fire of religion is kindled in a man's heart... sooner or later he will take refuge at the feet of Jesus Christ'.[140] In 1931, an article in the

---

137 *Baptist Handbook*, 1911, p.78.
138 *NZB*, October 1926, pp.276-77.
139 Driver, *Our Work*, pp.15, 21; cf. H.H. Driver, *These Forty Years: A Brief History of the N.Z.B.M.S.*, Dunedin: H.H. Driver, 1927, pp.11, 17.
140 *Baptist Handbook*, 1910, pp.72-73.

New Zealand Baptist contrived an image of Indian school children 'holding out their hands to us, whose lives are so full of sweet things'. Christians could respond by offering nothing else but Jesus: 'it is only as we bring Jesus within reach of their outstretched hands that we shall bring peace and happiness to their lives, and heal the hurt of India'.[141]

Missionary propaganda aimed to inform, inspire, and mobilise. By nature, it tended toward the triumphal. Alexander Don's history of the Presbyterian mission in the New Hebrides was conceived as a propaganda piece. It noted that 'The history of missions in the Pacific abounds with examples of dauntless heroism and sublime patience, and in such history the New Hebrides group has no mean share'.[142] An associated set of descriptors cast Christ in laudatory terms. H.H. Driver described the difficulties Baptist missionaries in India faced, but noted that, 'as followers of the Victorious Christ, we saw no reason for dismay, and resolved to go on in His name'.[143]

Missionary hymns reinforced ideals, and bore witness to a range of motivations. Some, like 'Hark the voice of Jesus is calling', emphasised that mission was Jesus' initiative and involved spreading the news of his saving love, whilst urging support for the cause. Appeals for participation and consecration were repeated in 'Ye servants of God' and 'Take my life and let it be', while 'Jesus shall reign' and 'Rescue the perishing' illustrated the confidence and emotion of missionary discourse. One of the most popular missionary hymns of the period was 'From Greenland's icy mountains'. This supplied romanticised images of foreign lands held in 'error's chains', but freed by the Christian message:

> Shall we, whose souls are lighted with wisdom from on high,
> Shall we to men benighted the lamp of life deny?
> Salvation! O Salvation! The joyful sound proclaim,
> Till earth's remotest nation has learned Messiah's name.

Such ideas could become allied to a jingoistic sense of cultural and religious superiority. Driver's sense of 'bounden duty' was awakened in

---

141 *NZB*, September 1931, p.280.
142 Alexander Don, *Light in Dark Isles. A Jubilee Record and Study of the New Hebrides Mission of the Presbyterian Church of New Zealand*, Dunedin: Foreign Missions Committee, PCNZ, 1918, p.12.
143 Driver, *Our Work*, p.17.

part by dismay at the 'puerilities, obscenities and absurdities' contained in Hindu sacred texts.[144] He was equally dismissive of the immorality and impurity of Indian Muslims, and clear that the decision to enter India owed much to the British presence there: 'Patriotism as well as piety called us to this glorious crusade'. Missionary commentators understood that the British Empire was flawed, and ultimately subservient to the Kingdom of God. However, they also perceived the hand of Providence providing opportunities for missionary expansion.[145]

Nevertheless, the missionary movement also helped to awaken awareness of cultural biases. Missions, interwar internationalism and increasing appreciation of Christ's humanity all encouraged self-conscious reflection on cultural assumptions. One consequence was an increased willingness to consider non-European representations of Jesus. At the end of the Second World War, Methodist young people were reminded that 'all races, colours and nationalities' claimed Jesus, and had their particular ways of portraying him:

> So wrapped up are we in our own conceits that we tend to think of Him as a white child, a European, and English babe. But the folk amongst whom Jesus lived were swarthy, and their high cheek-bones and long noses marked them as very different from Western European types.[146]

This yuletide reflection concluded that 'The gift of Christmas is the gift of Christ to the whole world. It is a gift of brotherhood, a gift of peace… it is not in the nature of small children to be unfriendly or to wage war'.

One of the most influential missionary books of the 1920s, E. Stanley Jones' *The Christ of the Indian Road*, discussed how Christ was 'becoming naturalised' in India. A leading American Methodist missionary and theologian, Jones argued that there was enormous interest in Jesus in contemporary India, due largely to Mahatma Gandhi. This interest portended a potential mass movement toward Christianity. Christianity was 'defined as Christ, not the Old Testament, not Western civilisation, not even the system built around him in the West, but Christ himself'. To be Christian was to follow Jesus, which meant that Christ had to be interpreted in terms of Christian experience rather than

---

144 Driver, *Our Work*, p.15.
145 *NZB*, November 1916, pp.210-11.
146 *Methodist Youth News*, December 1945, p.154.

argument.[147] One reviewer in the *Outlook* hailed Jones' work, delighting especially in its focus on 'Christ as a Person' and news that 'the principles and spirit and personality of Jesus are increasingly impressing themselves on the minds and hearts of men of goodwill in these great lands'. Significantly, one of the few complaints about the book derived from an Anglican critic who deplored Jones' depreciation of the role of the Church at the expense of the person of Christ.[148]

Numerous writers appropriated Jones' theme and terminology. In missionary contexts, the idea was often used to assert the humanity of Christ and humanitarian values. The Rev. A.W. Stuart's missionary sermon in 1927, 'The Christ of the World's Highways', was clearly inspired by Jones and utilised these ideas to make two key points.[149] First, that Jesus defied national limitation, and secondly, that no age could 'outgrow the Christ of the World's Highways'. Stuart argued that there was discontent in the world, but also a new mood of 'internationalism, of co-operation, of earnest desire to foster genuine brotherhood'. Only Jesus provided solutions to the problems and hopes of this present situation. Jesus wanted 'all men' to realise 'the dignity of manhood'. In response, men sought him as 'Liberator, as Friend, as Brother, as Lord'. In this context, non-European interpretations of Jesus circulated with some influence. Thus, J.J. North's list of contemporary witnesses to the 'wonderful humanity' of Jesus included Chiang Kai Shek, Sadhu Sundar Singh, Toyohiko Kagawa and T.Z. Koo.[150]

Jesus therefore occupied a central position in missionary discourse, though he appeared in a variety of ways. Notions of personality and humanity did not eclipse all other modes of address. However, it was significant that they became more evident even in an area of Protestant religiosity that was profoundly shaped by conservative assumptions.

In 1932, the death of the Rev. Rutherford Waddell sparked a remarkable outpouring of grief, reflecting his active presence within the Presbyterian Church and in national life over many years. Writing in a memorial

147 E. Stanley Jones, *The Christ of the Indian Road*, London: Hodder and Stoughton, 1926, pp.11, 33.
148 *Outlook*, 25 April 1927, p.11; *CC*, February 1927, p.30.
149 *NZB*, November 1927, pp.341-42.
150 North, *'Me a Christian!'*, p.13.

volume, another prominent Presbyterian minister, the Rev. James Gibb, commented on Waddell's religious faith. According to Gibb:

> He lived under the spell of Christ. To apply such a term to a man's feeling for Christ may not be quite orthodox; and our friend's theology, especially in his later years, was strongly conservative. The too common disparagement of Paulinism found no favour in his sight. He would with Dr. Glover have said that the Sermon on the Mount, apart from the salvation accomplished for us by Christ on the Cross, might well drive a man to despair. The Man of Nazareth was the Christ for him. Yet few men have ever surrendered themselves more whole-heartedly to the fascination of the life lived in the days of the Galilean spring. Its story held him all through and inspired him with a passion to serve.[151]

Waddell has often been viewed as a liberalising influence within New Zealand Presbyterianism on account of his progressive social attitudes. As Gibb's description indicates, he was also quite evangelical in his Atonement theology, support of missions and rejection of much higher biblical criticism. In many ways, he exemplified a form of moderate, liberal evangelicalism that was becoming increasingly important in New Zealand. This makes Gibb's description particularly interesting, for it describes an approach to Jesus in which his teaching and personality had great appeal, even if that appeal was balanced by other commitments.

However accurate Gibb's assessment of Waddell actually was, its appearance in such a laudatory volume was revealing. It highlighted some of the quite different connotations that references to Jesus implied, confirming that Jesus appeared in Christian discourse in complex ways. The assessment also demonstrated that Jesus' personality had become an important category. Various social, theological and even technological factors encouraged greater emphasis on Jesus' personality and human attributes during the period. Gibb's judgement suggested that the trend was not a marginal one, but was fairly close to the mainstream of New Zealand Protestantism.

---

151 J. Collie (ed.), *Rutherford Waddell: Memoir and Addresses*, Dunedin: A.H. Reed, 1932, p.10.

3. Anti-Church Prophet

One of the most striking and widespread representations during this period was of Jesus as a prophetic opponent of organised religion. Indeed, Jesus arguably became the iconic anti-Church figure of the age. The divine personality was also a man who challenged, confronted and confounded the churches. These misunderstood his identity so that the 'real Jesus' remained unknown to them. Jesus was a stranger, and often more confrontationally a critic of organised religion. Portrayals of this kind aimed to dissociate Jesus from organised religion, building on anticlerical and Romantic traditions that accentuated the gulf between Christ and institutions that were supposed to represent him.

Reasoning of this kind utilised favoured language and images. For critics of various stripes, the 'Christianity of Christ' and 'the religion of Jesus' became particularly important motifs for contrasting the dogma and tradition of the churches with the teaching and behaviour of Jesus. The themes were supported by an assumption that the religion of Jesus was pristine and undefiled. Bernard Lightman has noted that nineteenth-century agnostics' criticisms assumed that 'Victorian Christianity was a perversion of the original, pure religion as founded by Christ'. Thus, T.H. Huxley, who invented the term, saw Christ as an attractive symbol of true religious ideals, which contrasted the 'degenerate state of present day Christianity'.[1] Another factor was the widespread affection that existed for Jesus, partly on account of the positive images people encountered during childhood. Hence, the maverick New Zealand labour politician John A. Lee contrasted his warm attraction to Jesus with early fear of God and distaste for hypocrisy – appreciation, he claimed, that 'fluctuated between the admiration I might have felt for a conjuror and the sentiment I might have towards a warm-bosomed aunt'.[2]

A powerful set of images therefore distinguished Jesus from the religion of the churches, casting him as a stranger and prophet. In one

---

1   Bernard Lightman, *The Origins of Agnosticism: Victorian Unbelief and the Limits of Knowledge*, Baltimore: Johns Hopkins University Press, 1987, p.121.
2   John A. Lee, *Children of the Poor*, London: T. Werner Laurie, 1934, pp.67-69.

sense, these were determinedly unconventional. They were often promulgated independently of the institutional and devotional life of the Church, and interpreted Jesus in ways that consciously departed from orthodox Christian views. To this end, they highlighted that Jesus had symbolic significance outside of ecclesiastical contexts. On the other hand, interpretations of Jesus as a stranger and prophet had extra-ordinarily widespread appeal within Christian communities where they became a devotional type. The images were primarily a mode of argumentation in which the anti-Church Jesus provided a critique of power that supported diverse agendas for reform.

Jesus as a stranger to the churches

Foreign visitors to New Zealand sometimes noted that local interest in religion could be intense but idiosyncratic. André Siegfried commented that while religious activity retained an English form it had 'split up into a number of sects, in which the slightest shades of thought are represented'.[3] This proliferation extended to ideas about Jesus.

Amongst the various options there was some interest in 'sensational' lives of Jesus that often used scholarly rhetoric to advance unorthodox interpretations. One popular type of this literature has been termed the 'modern apocrypha' form of fictionalising biography.[4] Such works were typically preoccupied with the years between Jesus' childhood and ministry, and claimed to have uncovered knowledge of him that the churches had either ignored or deliberately suppressed. From the late nineteenth century, European fascination with the Orient fuelled interest in spiritualism and esoteric religion at precisely the time that comparative religion was emerging as a serious intellectual discipline. Consequently, many of these sensational lives were based in encounter

3   André Siegfried, *Democracy in New Zealand*, E.V. Burns (trans.), Wellington: Victoria University Press, 1982, p.311.
4   Mike Higton, 'English Popular Culture, Modern', in Leslie Houlden (ed.), *Jesus in History, Culture and Thought: An Encyclopedia*, vol. 1, Santa Barbara: ABC-CLIO, 2003, p.241; Theodore Ziolkowski, *Fictional Transfigurations of Jesus*, Princeton: Princeton University Press, 1972, p.13.

with Eastern religions. They upheld the enduring significance of Jesus' life, but transported him into novel religious settings. The implication was that existing Christian interpretations needed substantial modification.

Most of this literature was produced abroad, but attracted a small following in New Zealand. In 1894, Nicolas Notovitch wrote a life based on translations of 'The Life of Saint Issa', a manuscript allegedly uncovered in a Himalayan monastery. It purportedly accounted for the 'lost years' of Jesus' life, which Notovitch claimed were spent in India studying the teachings of the Buddha. Levi H. Dowling's *The Aquarian Gospel of Jesus the Christ* also placed Jesus in India and Tibet, but provided no documentary evidence of the kind offered by Notovitch. Instead, Dowling claimed to have drawn from the esoteric Akashic Records. Rosicrucianism reiterated similar interest in the 'known and unknown periods of the Great Master's life' through works like the *Mystical Life of Jesus*. Though Rosicrucianism never gained much support in New Zealand, writings like these did find their way into the country and perpetuated the tradition.[5]

Fictional biographies appealed to quasi-scientific independent religiosity, disappointment with religious institutions and interest in progressive politics. In 1931, one New Zealander reproduced selections of a text known as *Philochristus: Memoirs of a Disciple of the Lord*. Believing it to be 'the only true Gospel of the life and teaching of the Man of Nazareth', the anonymous author claimed that *Philochristus* had been written on Jesus' authority by a biographer of his choosing. The text supposedly portended a day when 'Jesus' socialism' would rule the world, and made plain the mystery of 'Joshua of Nazareth'. This Jesus' superiority spelled the end of religion on earth, and also marriage, which was merely a 'licence of adultery by priestcraft'.[6] In fact, the original biography was only as ancient as 1878, and had been penned by the English schoolmaster and mathematician Edwin A. Abbott.

5 Nicolas Notovitch, *The Unknown Life of Jesus Christ*, New York: Macmillan, 1894; Levi H. Dowling, *The Aquarian Gospel of Jesus the Christ*, London: L.N. Fowler, 1908; H. Spencer Lewis, *Mystical Life of Jesus*, San Jose: Supreme Grand Lodge of AMORC, 1929.

6 *Found at Last! The Lost Gospel: The Book That Nobody Knows*, Wellington: Evening Post Print, 1931, pp.3, 33-35; cf. *Philochristus: Memoirs of a Disciple of the Lord*, Boston: Roberts Brothers, 1878.

Some esoteric approaches presented Jesus as an example of enlightened mystical spirituality and the power of human potential. The credibility attached to Jesus provided a basis for advancing new religious ideas. Eileen Soper, for example, recounted her 'shocked delight' at a youthful clandestine encounter with a spiritual teacher facilitated by her father. This teacher instructed the children that 'though we were young in body we were old in soul and much wiser and more capable of goodness than we might have realised'. She urged them to conceptualise God as sunlight rather than a person, and to strive with intelligence and discipline for physical, mental and moral perfection, as a means to God's self-expression on earth. Through prayer they could make a conscious effort to ally themselves with 'our Best – God – and if we wished to know what a true child of God was like, we could find such a child in the person of our familiar Jesus'. According to Soper, this seemed 'more probable, more feasible, more practicable to one too egotistical to be capable of thinking of others before self, and moreover it bore out the command of the Parable of the Talents'.[7]

The literary outsider

Jesus figured in a small but significant way in the non-devotionally-inspired literary production of the early twentieth century. As Karl-Josef Kuschel has suggested, twentieth-century artists' imaginations were not captured by the Christ of 'churches and dogmas, not the Christ of theologians and priests, Christ the Redeemer and miracle-worker, the eternal Son of God, a second person of the Trinity, but the concrete Jesus of history'. In particular, the idea of Jesus as a revolutionary teacher, a heretic and outsider, provided fuel for the imagination.[8] Literary interest in Jesus sometimes incorporated quite strong anti-Church implications. Often, however, Jesus was employed more as a model of social exclusion. As a victim, outcast or outsider he provided a potent symbol

7   Eileen Soper, *The Green Years*, Dunedin: John McIndoe, 1969, pp.39-40.
8   Karl-Josef Kuschel, *The Poet as Mirror: Human Nature, God and Jesus in Twentieth-Century Literature*, London: SCM Press, 1999, pp.232, 234.

for prophetic critiques of society, and a model of simple, authentic and independent religious experience.

Arthur H. Adams was widely regarded as one of New Zealand's more promising poets in the late nineteenth century. Born at Lawrence in 1872, his first volume of poems, *Maoriland, and Other Verses*, was published to critical acclaim in 1899. In 1902, having recently departed for England, he published *The Nazarene: A Study of a Man*. The book was a meditation in verse on the life of Jesus as seen through the eyes of his contemporaries – Gospel characters such as Mary, Judas, John the Baptist and Pilate. As the subtitle suggested, it focused explicitly on Christ's humanity, asserting that Jesus was 'a man' like other men. According to the Prelude: 'He was of us, all human, brother, friend; / He strove, was vanquished, strove and won – a Man.' *The Nazarene* intimated that the story of Jesus was too often 'shadowed over by his divinity'. His humanity was shrouded by the 'waving of fine priestly hands', incense-smoke, and the throb of sonorous organs. Extracted from all this, a quite different Jesus would emerge.[9]

Despite his desire to liberate Jesus from tradition, certain aspects of Adams' portrait were thoroughly conventional. Images of the 'sweet Nazarene' as a dreamer and lover of children were common Romantic tropes, as was the vision of his heroic and kingly death. Yet, Adams' doctrinal approach was certainly not orthodox. He denied Jesus' divinity, claiming that the man himself had confounded the idea by refusing at all times to prove it. Furthermore, though gripped by the drama of Jesus' death, Adams resolutely repudiated the idea of a bodily resurrection:

> His body was not rapt in splendour up,
> But somewhere with us lies, his ashes sealed
> In some long-fallen tomb.[10]

Jesus existed in his continuing power to inspire, and through his participation in the cycles of death and rebirth common to all creation. The Jesus story was inspirational, but this did not require his divinity. MacDonald Jackson has suggested that the strength of *The Nazarene* lay in its 'psychological insight'. The work explored the force of Jesus'

9   A.H. Adams, *The Nazarene: A Study of a Man*, London: Philip Welby, 1902, pp.9-10.
10   Adams, *Nazarene*, p.11.

personality and its impact on those who encountered him.[11] It also examined the complex responses and inner conflicts that encounter with Jesus initiated. For Adams, focus on Jesus' humanity made investigation of psychological interplay and personality possible. Crucially, he suggested that the observations were only conceivable once the churches' interpretative frameworks had been discarded.

Consideration of the suffering and martyrdom of Jesus was a prominent feature of literary interest in him. That emphasis has sometimes been taken autobiographically to reflect the vocation of the suffering outcast artist.[12] In New Zealand, R.A.K. Mason's career is often held to epitomise the bleak condition writers faced in the literary 'wasteland' of the early twentieth century. Perhaps unsurprisingly, Mason's work also contained some of the most sustained reflection on Jesus of any local literature in this period. Mason's Jesus was not purely an autobiographical cipher, but it is clearly possible to interpret him as an image of the author as a victim of New Zealand society.[13]

Mason was concerned with the human Jesus, whom he distinguished from the divine Christ, or even God whom he rejected as hostile. While his Jesus was not divine in any traditional sense, Mason believed he should still be remembered and honoured. His poetry emphasised the intrinsic alienation and irrationality of human experience. In this, Christ recurred chiefly as 'the man persecuted by men and betrayed by God'.[14] He exemplified the human condition. Yet, awareness of his life could also deepen the solidarity and empathy necessary for improving human existence. Mason's motif of Christ the Beggar highlighted human suffering, but also compassion and hospitality. In 'On the Swag', Jesus

11 MacD. P. Jackson, 'Poetry: Beginnings to 1945', in Terry Sturm (ed.), *The Oxford History of New Zealand Literature*, Auckland: Oxford University Press, 1991, p.361.

12 John Albert, 'The Christ of Oscar Wilde', *American Benedictine Review*, 39:4, 1988, pp.372-403.

13 Joost Daalder, 'R.A.K. Mason: The Poet as a Pacific Christ', in Guy Amirthanayagam and S.C. Harrex (eds), *Only Connect: Literary Perspectives East and West*, Adelaide: Centre for Research in the New Literatures in English & East-West Centre, 1981, pp.311-20; Joost Daalder, 'The Religious Experience in R.A.K. Mason's Poetry', in Jamie S. Scott (ed.), *'And the Birds Began to Sing': Religion and Literature in Post-Colonial Cultures*, Amsterdam: Rodopi, 1996, pp.91-101.

14 Rachel Barrowman, *Mason: The Life of R.A.K. Mason*, Wellington: Victoria University Press, 2004, p.63.

figured as an archetypal outsider, ostracised largely because his true identity was veiled. By contrast, Judas also featured prominently in Mason's poetry as Jesus' antithesis, a figure of cruel human selfishness.

Mason was no friend of organised religion, or its leadership. Indeed, his poetic vision has been described as belligerently anticlerical.[15] His Jesus was linked with practical and experiential spirituality. Jesus exemplified the lonely, the misunderstood and victimised in society. He also provided a model of authentic spirituality that existed independently of religious organisation, notably through unmediated experience of God in Nature. This kind of spirituality was identifiable in Jane Mander's celebrated novel, *The Story of a New Zealand River*, in relation to the protagonist Alice:

> She had nothing of the gypsy in her, but she loved beauty, more especially the beauty that was created – as she would have put it – by the hand of God. And it was the hand of God that she saw in that night, in that mountain, that bush and that river.... She looked up at the stars, and she felt that God was there, and that His protecting arm was about her.[16]

Sentiments like these were expressed often among people unused or resistant to church attendance. E.M. Blaiklock, a leading New Zealand Baptist and a prominent classical scholar, described his non-church-attending father as a 'thoughtful theist' whose constant consciousness of the 'wonder of created things' confirmed his belief in God's existence. Blaiklock claimed that awareness of natural beauty ultimately led him to seek the perfection that lay behind it.[17] On the other hand, Elsie Locke became progressively disenchanted with organised religion, preferring instead her own kind of pantheism that saw God everywhere in nature.[18]

Some writers with strong religious commitments referred to Jesus in ways that linked readily with these forms of spirituality. Eileen Duggan's verse, for example, is often noted for its strong Celtic themes, attention

---

15   R.A.K. Mason, *Collected Poems*, Allen Curnow (ed.), Christchurch: Pegasus, 1962, p.76; Barrowman, *Mason*, p.63; Jackson, 'Poetry', p.366.
16   Jane Mander, *The Story of a New Zealand River*, Christchurch: Whitcombe & Tombs, 1920, pp.18-19.
17   E.M. Blaiklock, *Between the Valley and the Sea: A West Auckland Boyhood*, Palmerston North: Dunmore Press, 1979, pp.41-42.
18   Elsie Locke, *Student at the Gates*, Christchurch: Whitcoulls, 1981, pp.36-39, 54.

to the New Zealand landscape and religion.[19] Jesus featured in some of her work, though, perhaps as a consequence of her Catholicism, not particularly strongly. The Royal Christ was a prominent motif, but in the folksy and sentimental 'Legend of the Cuckoo' she also set forth an image of the young Jesus drawing spiritual lessons from creation.

Ursula Bethell's poetry was less popular in its own time, but also described religious sentiments evoked from the natural world. A committed Anglican, and possessed of a strong sense of social responsibility, Bethell observed that 'The *consciousness* of God came to me, as to many, chiefly in the solitudes of Nature'.[20] M.H. Holcroft praised her capacity to relate 'the anatomy of the land and the value of human experience', which was evident in rich natural and devotional imagery.[21] At times, Bethell imagined Jesus in this natural world, where he exemplified the idea that spiritual encounter and sustenance might be drawn from the created order:

So, long ago, I think, the Syrian Shepherd
Inhaled the sweet airs of his hills and valleys,
Drew in his breath and sang: Yahweh sustains me:
Lifted his head, and went his way rejoicing.[22]

The point here is that Jesus himself experienced God independently in harmonious relation with nature. This confirmed the authenticity of that form of spirituality, and demonstrated the possibility of true religious experience apart from the institutional life of the churches. Bethell's work suggested that contemplation of nature could lead directly to Jesus, and evoke reflection on his life. For her, the specificity of the Christian story lent substance to the existential encounter. The emphasis, however, was still on unmediated experience.

19   Eileen Duggan, *Selected Poems*, Peter Whiteford (ed.), Wellington: Victoria University Press, 1994, pp.18-20; F.M. Mackay, *Eileen Duggan*, Wellington: Oxford University Press, 1971, pp.10-22.

20   Bethell to M.H. Holcroft, 17 December 1939, cited in Ursula Bethell, *Collected Poems*, Vincent O'Sullivan (ed.), Wellington: Victoria University Press, 1997, xvii.

21   Stuart Murray, *Never a Soul at Home: New Zealand Literary Nationalism and the 1930s*, Wellington: Victoria University Press, 1998, p.83; see M.H. Holcroft, *Mary Ursula Bethell*, Wellington: Oxford University Press, 1975.

22   'Appel', in Bethell, pp.22-23.

The confrontational Christ

In some contexts, images constructed outside ecclesiastical contexts became more explicitly anti-Church. A fundamental anti-Church tenet suggested that Jesus was a stranger to the churches, in the sense that they had totally misunderstood him. Typical expressions of this idea claimed that the churches had buried Jesus beneath dogma and tradition. On the one hand, the beliefs of organised Christianity, especially regarding Jesus' divinity, were erroneous. On the other, church practices bore no resemblance to Jesus' life and teaching.

The notion of Jesus being a stranger to organised religion melded easily with claims of actual hostility between Jesus and the Church. Jesus was enlisted in complaints against 'institutional religion', and became the standard by which Christianity was judged. By this measure, the churches were criticised for their ignorance or active disregard, while their leaders were accused of misrepresenting Jesus and cultivating religious systems that conflicted with his actual teaching. Contemporary religious leaders were the modern counterparts of Jesus' original persecutors. As a logical counterpoint, Jesus supposedly resisted the contemporary Church as he had the religion of his own time. Organised religion opposed Jesus, and he was its chief adversary. The real Jesus was not only a stranger to the churches but also their leading critic.

There were clearly religious aspects to these claims, but also social and political ones. The ideas were particularly prominent in the arguments of radical socialists, and among Freethinkers and Rationalists. The combination of reverence for Jesus, anticlericalism and criticism of the churches had a long tradition in radical and socialist rhetoric. For instance, anticlericalism featured prominently in early French socialism and Marxism. While this eased, and positions became more fragmented over time, the tradition remained influential. But anticlericalism tended to thrive with Established religion, where perceptions of excess could gain a footing. In England, its appeal was limited by a weakening of Anglican power. More common, perhaps, were criticisms by British labour leaders of the hypocritical conditions imposed by professing

Christian employers.[23] Despite the lack of an official Established Church in New Zealand, surrogate forms did exist and made it easier for similar language and attitudes to flourish. Thus, James Watson has argued that anticlericalism seemed especially attractive to the independent working class who esteemed both intellectual and economic independence.[24]

J.H.G. Chapple exemplifies a number of these observations. On the one hand, he combined fierce intellectual independence with criticism of the churches, and enthusiasm for Freethought and socialism. He also demonstrates the movement from claims that churches misunderstood Christ into alleged opposition between the parties. Chapple had been active in the Salvation Army before ordination as a Presbyterian minister in 1903.[25] However, his attraction to Rationalism and socialist politics ultimately led to a breach with the Presbyterians and adoption of Unitarianism around 1910. In Maurice Gee's fictionalised account, this transition was marked by something of an epiphany wherein Chapple's understanding of Jesus was profoundly reconfigured:

And more and more it grew plain that what we must do was put aside Christ, sweep Him into the past, those dark and superstitious times in which He had his genesis, and turn to the real person, Jesus the man. And go on through him, as an example of goodness, to God, to the One, of whom we were a part.[26]

Chapple accused the churches of falsification by smothering biblical truths with creeds 'which would make Jesus a Deity'. They distorted Jesus' true nature and removed religion from the truth for which the world hungered, of 'Jesus the Carpenter and Divine Brother Man'.[27]

23 For example, Callum Brown, *The Social History of Religion in Scotland Since 1730*, London: Methuen, 1987, pp.175-76.

24 James Watson, 'An Independent Working Class?', in John E. Martin and Kerry Taylor (eds), *Culture and the Labour Movement: Essays in New Zealand Labour History*, Palmerston North: Dunmore Press, 1991, p.188.

25 See Frank W. Castle, *Annals of the Auckland Unitarian Church*, Auckland: Auckland Unitarian Church, 1981, pp.25-26; Geoff Chapple, 'Chapple, James Henry George, 1865-1947', *DNZB;* John Maindonald, *A Radical Religious Heritage: Auckland Unitarian Church and its Wider Connections*, rev. ed., Auckland: Auckland Unitarian Church, 1993, pp.11-13.

26 Maurice Gee, *The Plumb Trilogy*, Auckland: Penguin, 1995, p.88.

27 J.H.G. Chapple, *The Divine Need of the Rebel: Addresses from Texts from the Wider Bible of Literature*, London: C.W. Daniel, 1924, p.104.

Chapple's antipathy toward 'the churches' amplified in later years following his incarceration for sedition during World War One. Addressing the issue of war, Chapple railed against the seeming imperialism of Christian clergy, even though 'the founder of their religion was a rebel against the Empire of Rome'.[28] The churches were not only ignorant of Jesus, they revolted against him. In full rhetorical flourish, he proclaimed that 'The Churches are Anti-Christ'. In their connection with the war, he argued, 'they are really Anti-Christ – they who profess to follow the One of peace and goodwill, yet ever ready to fall over each other to serve the State when war is declared in the interests of imperialism, big commerce and capitalism generally'. By contrast, pacifists and conscientious objectors were objects of derision, but were 'nearer to the Nazarene than the Anti-Christ Churches'.[29] Chapple's language may have been more extreme than even that of his fellow radicals, but the general contours of his argument were familiar.

In some ways this Jesus was a rhetorical trope rather than a person. His historicity and humanity were less important than the uses for which he was deployed. Yet, Chapple still placed great emphasis on him. As the reference to pacifists and conscientious objectors indicated, it was not that Jesus was unknowable, but that he was most truly known outside the churches where his identity would not be obscured by emphasis on his divinity. One important function of this language was to support the legitimacy of non-institutional spirituality, or, conversely, to downplay the value of organised religion in general or church attendance in particular. The discourse also functioned as a form of ethical boosterism by suggesting the superior morality of agendas for reform.

Socialism and the labour movement

Debates about social reform constituted one important site in which the anti-Church Jesus appeared. Growing unionisation, the long depression

---

28   J.H.G. Chapple, 'The Growing Point of Truth' (unpublished manuscript), MS-Papers-4678-027, Maurice Gough Gee Papers, MS-Group-0193, ATL.
29   Chapple, *Divine Need*, p.73.

and the maritime strike of 1890 pushed labour issues closer to the centre of the social and political agenda. Socialism acquired cachet in New Zealand from the 1890s, and by 1900 was the leading ideological framework through which labour's aspirations were expressed. Socialism, however, was a house of many rooms.[30] In late nineteenth-century New Zealand the term was used broadly to describe emphasis on the social basis of human existence and commitment to improving social conditions. Margaret McArthur's analysis suggests that the socialism of that period largely prioritised altruism, community and cooperation over class, conflict and competition.[31] William Pember Reeves' Fabian articulation of the social laboratory had a particularly profound influence on the New Zealand socialist agenda.

These ideals were not uncontested. Radical and revolutionary socialism gained a following at times, particularly in association with the Red Feds between about 1908 and 1913.[32] The *Maoriland Worker*, which began in 1910 and became the official organ of the New Zealand Federation of Labour from 1911, was one place in which such views were expressed. Styled as a journal of 'industrial unionism, socialism and politics', it was the mouthpiece for labour's radical left, especially up until the great industrial confrontations of 1912 and 1913. Some editors retained this stance, but from 1916 when the New Zealand Labour Party (NZLP) was formed, and even more so from the end of World War One, contests between industrial and political methods were often evident. In its most radical phases, the editorial position of the *Maoriland Worker* echoed the industrial confrontation espoused by the International Workers of the World (IWW). While this approach gained traction for a time, the milder tradition on which New Zealand socialism was established attracted greater support over the longer term.

The relationship between Christianity, socialism and labour was conceived in a variety of ways, not least within the labour movement

---

30 See Anthony Wright, *Socialisms: Theories and Practices*, Oxford: Oxford University Press, 1986.

31 Margaret J. McArthur, 'Collectivist Tracts and Altruistic Sermons: A Study of "Socialism" in Late Nineteenth Century New Zealand', MA thesis, University of Canterbury, 1981, pp.21-22.

32 Erik Olssen, *The Red Feds: Revolutionary Industrial Unionism and the New Zealand Federation of Labour 1908-1913*, Auckland: Oxford University Press, 1988.

itself. For present purposes, it is sufficient to recognise that the idea of conflict between Jesus and the churches ran through much of the debate. It was evident within the Marxist labour tradition, which emphasised the destruction of capitalist institutions including the Church, but also among Fabian and state socialist groupings that had more support from within the churches. Indeed, the anti-Church Jesus represented a point of agreement between these streams. He was particularly evident prior to the mid-1920s in the period when organised labour was emerging as a significant force.

In 1890, Arthur Desmond produced one of the earliest New Zealand studies of Jesus as a social reformer. Desmond had been a rural worker in Hawke's Bay before a semi-itinerant career in political agitation on behalf of small settlers and workers. In Auckland, he became involved in journalism, briefly publishing his own paper before continuing his jibes against capitalism in other forums. Desmond's pamphlet claimed to be primarily concerned with the human Jesus, especially the 'heroic nobility of His thought and the grandeur of His deeds'. It also quite deliberately noted that the account did not deny the divinity of 'the Divine Democrat'. Desmond argued that Jesus' original opponents were driven by vested interests. These he described, somewhat anachronistically, as the 'heads of the Church, the owners of land, the owners of slaves, and the owners of capital'. More recently, theologians had suppressed the social element of Jesus' teaching, while clergy had betrayed him through their 'theology, gold-greed, and personal aggrandisement'.

Desmond preached the Christianity of Christ, consisting of social equality and duty towards one's fellow man. The churches had degraded this message through 'Dogma and denominationalism – bigotry and creed – belief and ceremony'. His solution was almost apocalyptic:

> What the world wants to-day is a MAN – a Leader – a heroic Champion of the Right – a ruthless demolisher of age-worn shams... whose clarion call shall ring round the world, inspiring millions to enlist beneath the standard of a new crusade, and go forth to battle unto death for the rights of man – for the cause of the poor.[33]

33   Arthur Desmond, *Christ as a Social Reformer*, Auckland: Arthur Cleave, 1890, pp.7-14. On Desmond, see Rachel Barrowman, 'Desmond, Arthur, fl. 1884-1894', *DNZB*; *Australian Dictionary of Biography*, vol. 8, Melbourne: Melbourne University Press, 1981, pp.291-92.

Whether that person was supposed to be Jesus or Desmond was not entirely clear, for Desmond was partly thinking about his own political prospects and positioning himself as a champion of the underdog.

As it transpired, much of his argument was plagiarised. Writing in the local press, Adam Kelly accused Desmond of pirating A. Van Deusen's 'Ecclesiastical Christianity versus Jesus' from New York's *Twentieth Century* magazine of 27 April 1889 – a claim he corroborated by publishing both articles. In one sense, this merely indicated the extent to which so much religious and political argumentation in New Zealand was derivative. Nevertheless, the work signalled important motifs that were reiterated in later meditations on the theme. Most notably, these included the idea of a fundamental gulf between the Christianity of Christ and the religion practised by the churches. Under its present leadership, contemporary Christianity had become enslaved to wealth, despising Jesus' ethical teaching as an 'unattainable chimera'. For Desmond, the best solution was to reform the Church by recapturing the true spirit of Jesus. For others, the breach merely indicated that organised religion must be swept aside. In either case, the fundamental arguments concerned ethics and ecclesiology, rather than Jesus directly. The focus of the anti-Church Jesus was primarily the Church.

Assertions that the Jesus of the churches was not the 'real Jesus' were repeated frequently in the labour press. Within international socialism, Jesus was contrasted with anti-socialists, or those deemed unsympathetic to working-class aspirations. The churches featured prominently among the groups classed this way. They were accused of hypocrisy, self-interest and protecting their own privileged position.[34] Claims that the churches perpetrated vice in Jesus' name appeared more commonly during periods of sharp conflict, such as industrial unrest and war. The charges were seldom linked directly to particular events within these disputes, though these may have contributed. More often, they highlighted the heightened state of conflict that existed, and the feeling that religious groups were at best only limited supporters of labour.

These kinds of objections had originally been formulated with Roman Catholicism or the Church of England in mind, since these were the wealthiest, most powerful and hierarchical forms of Christianity in

---

34   Donald M. Winters, *The Soul of the Wobblies: The I.W.W., Religion, and American Culture in the Progressive Era, 1905-1917*, Westport: Greenwood, 1985, pp.61-81.

the contexts in which the ideas arose. In New Zealand, however, the rhetoric was applied generally, with few concessions made for a substantially altered situation or in recognition of denominational differences. In fact, complaints were often directed at religious leaders as much as to the churches in general. Leaders were characterised as deceivers, and accused of being out of touch with ordinary workers' lives. Their greed for wealth and power allegedly led to conservatism. Complaints therefore highlighted that religious leaders' failings were at once spiritual and political. Support for the capitalist system was chided, even when it was tacit rather than explicit. One writer lamented, 'O Lord, shake up the parsons. They are so very slow in establishing Thy Kingdom on earth'.[35] Ministers were also derided for their hypocrisy. Critics enjoyed using biblical texts to shame their opponents, but appeared to take particular delight in using Jesus to expose double-standards among religious leaders. Thus, Margaret Thorn gleefully described the labour leader Robert Semple's attack on the Rev. Howard Elliott and the Protestant Political Association (PPA) as an unforgettable analysis of intolerance, and an 'ear-splitting post-mortem dissection of a parson professing faith in the gentle saviour of mankind'.[36]

One longstanding method of attacking institutional forms of Christianity focused on a distinction between real Christianity and 'priestcraft' or 'Churchianity'. There was a post-Reformation anti-Catholic aspect to the discourse, but also a radical one. As early as 1832, the controversial British radical and publisher Henry Hetherington was arguing that priestcraft, or 'priestianity', had become the great obstacle to the mental, moral, social and political improvement of the people. By contrast, the religion of Jesus was 'a plain, practical religion, unpolluted with mysteries, unencumbered with priests, and eminently calculated to generate... a love of truth, of justice, of liberty'.[37] The religion of Jesus would embarrass the churches and provide a moral flavour to reform.

Strategically, assailing the power of religious leaders was sometimes viewed as a way to strengthen support for the labour movement. One

35 *MW*, 21 July 1911, p.3.
36 Margaret Thorn, *Stick Out, Keep Left*, Elsie Locke and Jacquie Matthews (eds), Auckland: Auckland University Press, 1997, p.54.
37 Henry Hetherington, *Cheap Salvation; or, an Antidote to Priestcraft*, cited in Edward Royle, *Radical Politics, 1790-1900: Religion and Unbelief*, London: Longman, 1971, p.109.

letter to the *Maoriland Worker* claimed that priestcraft was one of labour's deadliest foes because of the influence priests had over women.[38] Others considered anticlerical rhetoric a potentially useful recruitment tool. J. Smith of Waimate contended that socialism was 'purely a Christian ideal and doctrine', but that it needed to stand against the 'colossal ignorance' of the modern churches. Smith argued that 'denunciation of the false teaching of the clergy' could be a 'powerful lever for agitation, and an incomparable means for recruiting our ranks for propaganda purposes'. One might thus remain faithful to 'our Christian watchword', yet 'disarm the enemy and arm Socialism'.[39]

There were confrontational overtones to the supposed distinction between the religion of Jesus and Churchianity. Pejorative terms like these referred to perversions. They suggested that pure religion had no rituals, but further that pure forms of Christianity could still perhaps be found. Blaming religious leaders also meant that criticism was directed at one particular class. Clerical influence blighted society in the same way that 'King-craft', 'diplomatist-craft' and 'merchant-craft' did.[40] Religious ills were therefore similar to other social evils imposed by the powerful. By returning to the religion of Jesus, organised Christianity could become a true religion of the people expressing socialist ideals. As one labour critic carefully clarified, 'lest we be misunderstood, we have not one word to say against true Christianity'.[41] This was a discourse of power favoured especially by those who felt, however subjectively, on the margins. Churches and religious leaders were conflated with the wider forces of 'society' that opposed Jesus and socialism equally. Thus, 'Religion provided him with a cross, Society with a tomb'. In its complicity with society's powerbrokers, religion had lost ethical power and capacity to nourish and reproduce itself.[42]

This kind of language reached its zenith during the years of heightened conflict around World War One. At points, socialist disputes with supporters of the war became almost hysterical. Pacifist sects like the Quakers were applauded, but the churches as a whole were heavily criticised. Despite 2,000 years of Christianity, a supposedly Christian

38   *MW*, 21 July 1911, p.15.
39   *MW*, 1 July 1914, p.6.
40   *MW*, 5 May 1915, p.1.
41   *Otago Liberal*, 9 September 1905, p.8.
42   *MW*, 11 July 1913, p.3.

civilisation had turned its back on Jesus and unleashed hell with their endorsement:

> The collective Church – that has for twice a thousand years rendered a lip service of Peace on Earth – spits in the face of its Christ of Peace, and in all lands shrieks in demoniacal frenzy for the crucifixion of the Christ idea and the Christ idealist.[43]

Claims that organised religion opposed Christ were part of a wider argument concerning the failure of social institutions, in which the vices and degradations of Christian civilisation were catalogued as evidence. Churches invoked the name of Jesus, but were accused of being essentially 'irreligious'. In 1920, the editorial in the Easter issue of the *Maoriland Worker* argued that interest in Jesus was running high, despite the churches' obstruction. Churches claimed to respect Jesus, but actually opposed him: 'Religions have been founded in his name; grand cathedrals in his honor; beautiful pictures, heavenly music, all these mock him and his gospel'. Nevertheless, the journal claimed that the time was ripe for the 'resurrection of the spirit of Christ, which has lain too long in the sepulchre of the Churches'.[44]

Labour anti-Church rhetoric commonly cast contemporary religious leaders as the Judases and Pharisees of Jesus' day. Like Judas, they had betrayed Jesus. In 1913, the *Maoriland Worker* also complained about ministers who undermined industrial action by volunteering to act as 'scabs'. In doing so, they sided with the oppressor against the oppressed in defiance of the plain example of 'the Divine Teacher'. The ministers were accused of prostituting their Master's teaching; 'soulless tools of capitalism', they had descended to a level even Judas could not reach:

> Those preachers, who, in consideration of pelf and place, range themselves upon the side of the oppressor, are surely greater betrayers than that despicable person of history who, for thirty pieces of silver, handed over the Carpenter of Nazareth, the Friend of the poor and the outcast, to a brutal authority.[45]

During World War One, ministers were also accused of becoming traitors for staying home and preaching the glories of war.[46]

43   *MW*, 22 December 1915, p.4.
44   *MW*, 7 April 1920, p.4.
45   *MW*, 26 September 1913, p.7.
46   *MW*, 20 January 1915, p.4.

Literature on religion and social reform frequently highlighted Jesus' conflicts with religious leaders. In one well-known English publication from later in the interwar period, John Lewis claimed that Jesus had embarked on a 'deliberate and devastating anti-religious campaign' because the religion of his day was an 'insuperable barrier to the coming of the Kingdom'. Lewis doubted that there could be any recovery of the Jesus of history within the churches; they were simply too reconciled to the existing social order.[47] By this time, the charge that modern religion was akin to that of Jesus' opponents was scarcely considered remarkable. False, hypocritical and self-serving Pharisaic religion denied people conditions that would make it possible to actually implement the Golden Rule. In this context, the whip of cords and Jesus' action in the Temple became favoured symbols of opposition to established authority. Thus, contemporary churches were challenged to account for their behaviour in the light of 'the action of the Divine Teacher, who whip in hand, scourged the money-changers from the temple'.[48]

The anti-Church Jesus image held fast to the idea that he stood aloof from organised religion. Spurning conventional religious practices, Jesus taught and practised a simple brand of religion. One writer claimed that:

he confounded the self-righteous, and made light of formal religion, and mocked the orthodox of his day, whose religion consisted in observing set times, and laws, and commandments.... To him creeds, churches, systems, sacraments and ceremonies were nothing.[49]

Modern Christianity was charged with inventing a superstructure of faith and doctrine out of its own vain imaginings. These were not only alien to the religion of Jesus, they were ideas he would actually repudiate: 'Hardly a claim made in the name of Christ to-day by the churches that take his name in vain but can be refuted out of his own mouth'.

47   John Lewis, 'The Jesus of History', in John Lewis, Karl Polanyi and Donald K. Kitchen (eds), *Christianity and the Social Revolution*, London: Victor Gollancz, 1935, pp.92, 102.

48   *MW*, 26 September 1913, p.7; cf. *MW*, 19 January 1912, p.16; *MW*, 14 March 1913, p.1; Tony Simpson, *The Sugarbag Years*, Auckland: Penguin, 1984, p.201.

49   *MW*, 7 April 1920, p.4.

One aspect of this argument related to church attendance. In response to an article by the Catholic Archbishop Francis Redwood on socialism and social order in the *Tablet*, one correspondent noted that 'Nothing in the sayings of Christ, as I read them, makes it obligatory on any follower of Christ to belong to a Church'.[50] The imperfections of the Church demonstrated that it was purely a human institution. Jesus' teaching represented genuine Christianity, divinely ordained, and defined in ethical terms. Practical but non-institutional Christianity might appear suspect to the conventionally religious, but was the expression Jesus approved. Thus, R.S. Mackay could claim:

> Many Socialists deny Christ with their lips, but accept Him by their lives, ideals, and the sacrifice they are prepared to make for the sake of their ideals. Many church-goers accept Him with their lips, but deny Him by their lives, and the objects they devote their energies to, principally their own material welfare. I think that if Christ himself were here to-day he would undoubtedly cast in his lot with the former, as being those who are carrying on His work.[51]

Freethought and Rationalism

Criticisms generated by Freethinkers and Rationalists were often similar to those from the political left, partly because the constituencies overlapped. As Bill Cooke has suggested, Rationalists were often socialists with an enduring interest in religion.[52] This connection was certainly one that Christian apologists made, especially in the turbulent years of labour unrest prior to World War One. By the 1920s and 1930s, the anti-Church Jesus was being most forcefully articulated in the rhetoric of Rationalism.

The extent of actual adherence to these groups is hard to trace, as is their influence. Freethinkers may have been less disposed to association than some other religious groupings. Moreover, a frequently confron-

50   *MW*, 30 July 1919, p.2; cf. *MW*, 16 July 1919, p.4.
51   *MW*, 27 January 1915, p.1.
52   Bill Cooke, *Heathen in Godzone: Seventy Years of Rationalism in New Zealand*, Auckland: NZ Association of Rationalists and Humanists, 1998, p.22.

tational and combative approach may have militated against broad appeal, but also ensured a greater profile and significance than numerical strength suggested. Census self-identification was always low, but fluctuated. According to the 1936 census, Rationalist numbers were was numerically very small by 1900, and only rose significantly in the later 1920s and 1930s.[53] From a mere 22 in 1901, there were 791 in 1911, before a decline to 430 in 1921, and sharp rise to 2,066 (0.14%) in 1936. Affiliation with Freethought grew from a stronger base of 2,856 in 1901 to 4,238 (0.42%) in 1911, but fell steadily to 925 (0.06%) in 1936. Freethinkers' organisation had collapsed in the late nineteenth century, but renewed growth around 1911 corresponded with the 'mission' of Joseph McCabe. Rationalism increasingly became the more fashionable term, and also benefited from the McCabe tour of 1910, as well as others by J.S. Langley in the late 1920s and again in the 1930s.[54]

After World War One, some Christians pointed to declining identification with Rationalism as evidence of the movement's sterility. Rationalists responded that it simply reflected the inadequacies of the census.[55] Active local organisations existed in Auckland, Christchurch and Wanganui in the 1920s, but these did not show up clearly in census figures. A substantial rise in the Object to State category was evident in Auckland province, however, and this was the centre of Rationalist organisation.[56] Professions of Agnosticism also rose steadily through these years, though the total remained small. The category of No Religion was larger in absolute terms, but declined in proportional strength throughout the period. Together, respondents in the No Religion, Agnostic and Object to State categories accounted for 5.06% of the population in 1936. These probably included a fair proportion of individuals sympathetic to Rationalist ideas. Nevertheless, they remained a numerical minority.

Jesus featured prominently in Rationalist discussions, reflecting the importance of Jesus for religion and the fundamentally religious

53   See *Census*, 1936, p.1 (Religious Section).
54   Bill Cooke, "'The Best of Causes": A Critical History of the New Zealand Association of Rationalists and Humanists', PhD thesis, Victoria University of Wellington, 1998, pp.13-14, 33.
55   *TS*, October 1927, pp.7-8; *TS*, November 1927, pp.7-8.
56   These rose from 25,577 in 1916 to 71,302 in 1936 (from 2.33% to 4.67%), of whom 38% were in Auckland.

character of the Rationalist movement. Commentators note that Rationalism functioned as something of a surrogate religion for ultra-liberals, or even as a form of Protestant extremism. Certainly, many leading New Zealand Rationalists had intensely religious backgrounds and drew freely upon those resources. Many utilised the Gospel accounts of the life of Jesus because they believed these provided potent ammunition for their assault on Christianity. Ettie Rout grew up a devout Congregationalist, but experienced 'conversion' to Rationalism as part of a broader transition to radical politics and progressive social morality. Long after this had occurred, Rout claimed to draw inspiration from the Bible and the life and teaching of Jesus. In *Sexual Health and Birth Control*, she claimed that Jesus provided a useful tool for attacking contemporary Christians whose 'fat-headedness' impeded moral progress. The Bible was excellent value for money as a source to 'slay a few modern Christians intellectually'. To do this she would:

> turn up the references to what Jesus had to say nearly 2000 years ago about the Scribes and Pharisees and hypocrites and Sadducees and Lawyers; and I find that his sayings fit the Modern Churches absolutely. I am therefore enormously grateful to my Bible and *Concordance* and to Jesus himself for having supplied such permanently valuable weapons... because Jesus is one of the world's greatest philosophers and geniuses whereas I am only a humble writer.[57]

Rout's Jesus was a Freethinker: 'he thought freely and he spoke freely, and he attacked the Church, which is the same yesterday, to-day, and forever. That is why he was crucified'.[58]

Rationalists recognised that Jesus was central to the structure of Christian belief, and that his character was widely admired. Destabilising confidence in him was therefore a logical strategy for tackling Christianity. Considerable efforts were made to demonstrate that, if he ever existed, Jesus was not the person Christians generally imagined. Satire, like Frederick J. Gould's 'What Jesus Did Not Say' in the *Truth Seeker*, relied on the premise that Christian interpretations of Jesus were selective and muddle-headed.[59] Rationalism did not provide a single

---

57   E. Rout, *Sexual Health and Birth Control*, London: Pioneer Press, 1925, p.11; cf. Jane Tolerton, *Ettie: A Life of Ettie Rout*, Auckland: Penguin, 1992.
58   Rout, p.42.
59   *TS*, July 1933, pp.1-2.

view of Jesus. Positions ranged from denial of his existence through to accusations of dubious moral character. Nevertheless, these agreed that the churches' opinions concerning Jesus were erroneous – whatever they were. Moreover, the fact that a plethora of often-contradictory views of Jesus existed simply demonstrated that 'Man makes God in his own image'. People shaped Jesus to 'exactly fit their own political, social and religious leanings'.[60]

The Mythical Jesus theory was perhaps the most controversial yet distinctive view promulgated within Rationalist circles. Numerous writers propounded it during the early twentieth century, most notably J.M. Robertson, W.B. Smith and Gordon Rylands, who helped the idea gain a measure of intellectual respectability. The Mythical theory argued that there was no historical evidence to justify any claim for the historicity of Christ, whether as 'god-man' or itinerant Palestinian preacher.[61] Mythical theorists dismissed the biblical Gospels as sources on grounds of their late composition, conflicting narratives and lack of reliable eyewitness testimony. Furthermore, they argued that no reliable extra-biblical source corroborated claims of Jesus' existence.

The Mythical Jesus theory was articulated forcefully and frequently enough to be considered a dominant theme. Provocative and controversial, touring speakers and debaters found the theory well suited for use in public forums. J.S. Langley's tours in 1929 and 1930 were important stimuli for the Rationalist movement, and he was an ardent promoter of the theory.[62] Earlier, Scott Bennett had followed J.M. Robertson's argumentation, claiming that Jesus was a beautiful but not historical figure like William Tell. Reporting a debate between a Mr Nugent and the Presbyterian minister Lawson Marsh at the Strand Theatre on 15 April 1928, *The Truth Seeker* claimed that Nugent's arguments against the existence of Christ were clearly the strongest, at least to those of 'unprejudiced mind'.[63] Commentary in the *Truth Seeker* routinely expressed grave doubts about the historical Jesus, and popular pamphlets like the leading British Rationalist Chapman Cohen's *Did*

60   *TS*, August 1928, p.6.
61   Patrick Campbell, *The Mythical Jesus*, with an introduction by James O. Hanlon, Auckland: Waverly Publishing, 1963, pp.9-10.
62   On the influence of Langley's tours and beliefs, see Cooke, 'Best of Causes', p.33.
63   *TS*, May 1928, p.4.

Jesus Christ Exist? were widely advertised and circulated.[64] In 1939, James O. Hanlon's dialogue on the question 'Did Jesus Christ Ever Live?' restated the Mythical Jesus position, and was supported by a later piece challenging 'The Resurrection Myth'.[65]

Little wonder that Christian apologists argued the theory was essential to Rationalism. Their contemporary antagonists consistently rejected this, however, noting that Rationalism eschewed unitary creedal positions. The most important alternatives followed Joseph McCabe who accepted the historical existence of Jesus, but argued that he was simply 'a man who was gradually turned into a God'.[66] McCabe was a prolific writer and polymath. His speaking tour in 1922 was a critical factor in the reinvigoration of Rationalist organisation in New Zealand after the Great War, and there was some support for his approach.[67] For H.H. Pearce, the historical existence of Jesus might be accepted, but was not ultimately critical: 'The issue is not a question of evidence on the existence of the *man* Christ, but of the existence of the Christ as in the Christian *conception*'.[68] Echoing McCabe, he contended that the human Jesus' existence was not the essence of Christian teaching or faith. It was the nature of his existence that mattered. The 'god-saviour' of Christian proclamation was, like McCabe's later-deified-man, unhistorical, irrational and ripe for criticism.

The various Rationalist approaches to Jesus uniformly rejected Christian representations. In particular, they contended against belief in Jesus' uniqueness and sublime character. To challenge this was to attack what Christians regarded as a strength, since Jesus' exemplary morality was routinely advanced as proof of his divinity and the superiority of Christianity. Rationalists denied that there was anything exceptional about Jesus using comparative and evolutionary approaches. McCabe's *Sources of the Morality of the Gospels*, for example, elucidated the influences that he considered shaped the teaching attributed to Jesus. For McCabe, Christian elevation of Christ's moral teaching was simply a

64   Chapman Cohen, *Did Jesus Christ Exist?*, London: Pioneer Press, n.d.; cf. *TS*, February-March 1939.
65   *TS*, April-May 1939, pp.2-3; *TS*, August 1939, pp.6-7.
66   Joseph McCabe, 'Did Jesus Ever Live?', cited in Bill Cooke, *A Rebel to His Last Breath: Joseph McCabe and Rationalism*, New York: Prometheus, 2001, p.190.
67   The Auckland Rationalist Association formed in 1922. See Cooke, *Heathen*, p.13.
68   *TS*, September 1928, p.6 (original italics).

response to the challenges that modern thought posed to traditional dogma. Stripped of the miraculous, Christ's greatness depended entirely on his moral teaching. McCabe argued that this teaching had exhaustive parallels in Jewish, Greek and Roman religion, and presented 'no advance whatever on the later and finer teaching of the Old Testament'.[69] The moral principles, maxims and parables of Jesus in the Gospels were the common stock of the religious movements of his time. Jesus did not even synthesise them; the Gospel writers did, once exposed to cosmopolitan ideas outside Judaea.[70]

Critics repeated that Jesus' teaching was unoriginal, irrational and immoral. It also included numerous aspects untenable to the modern mind, such as belief in devils, angels and the supernatural. Moreover, Jesus' advocacy of 'the horrible doctrine of Hell' was cited as evidence of moral imperfection.[71] This argument was advanced in Bertrand Russell's *Why I Am Not a Christian*, and utilised as a standard argument in public debates. Addressing the same topic at a meeting in the Majestic Theatre, J.S. Langley pointed to the 'absurd gospel stories' like the cursing of the fig tree, the money in the fish's mouth and Jesus' belief in demon causes of illness. Jesus also taught 'one of the greatest, wickedest ideas that has ever stained the face of this world's thought – that of everlasting hell.' Furthermore, 'Jesus taught nothing new… he came into the world and said not a word about war, or slavery, or of women and their inferior position'.[72] Others claimed that Christ's teaching was morally culpable for the horrors of Christian history, and made no difference to people's moral behaviour. The latter point was advanced to counter Christian advocacy for religious instruction in schools. 'When and where', H.H. Pearce questioned, 'have these teachings of Christ produced a society of people socially and morally desirable from a modern civilised view'?[73]

Other criticisms suggested that even the lofty elements of Jesus' teaching were too obscure, unintelligible or unliveable to be of practical

69   Joseph McCabe, *The Sources of the Morality of the Gospels*, London: Watts, 1914, pp.15-16, 204-97, 302.
70   McCabe, *Sources*, p.22.
71   *TS*, September 1927, p.3.
72   *TS*, May 1930, p.2.
73   *TS*, October 1932, p.6; cf. Robert Stout, *The Bible in Schools: The Scriptures as Moral Teaching*, Dunedin: Otago Daily Times Print, 1927.

use. A.E. Carrington argued that the most unique of Christ's moral utterances were also the most impracticable: 'Resist not evil' and 'Take no thought for the morrow' would only place a civilisation 'at the mercy of its most evil elements, leading to utter ruin'.[74] Rationalist apologists argued that 'love your enemies' sounded fine in principle, but that even Jesus failed to do it. Langley claimed that Jesus' violence in the temple was directed against innocent workers, while Carrington catalogued his various 'cruel words'.[75] This was a step further than the claim that the churches simply failed to live up to their Master's teaching and example. Indeed, H.H. Pearce argued that fidelity was as much of a problem:

> In paganism there was a growing universalism of love and brotherhood, independent of race or creed, and the new meaning of the word given by Christ was to limit its application to *fellow believers in him*. Unbelievers, infidels, or heretics, received the undying and full-blooded hatred of Christ and his followers. Its new meaning has persisted now for nearly two thousand years, with the tears, blood, misery, and degradation that history shows us as its consequence, and we are now only gradually back to its old and *unchristian* meaning.[76]

Significantly, the challenge to Christian representations of Jesus included those offered by social Christians, whose political views were often sympathetic to those commonly held by Rationalists. Rejection of Jesus' ethical superiority effectively eroded the ground on which they stood. In December 1930, Ormond Burton debated Langley before an audience of about 800 people. Burton proposed that the means to solve the 'problems of international relationships and strife' were found in 'putting into actual practice the teaching of Jesus'. Langley responded that 'There was so much advertisement of Christ by professional clergymen that the majority had never seen the true Christ'. Jesus was a 'simple, fanatical, Galilean teacher with the one great idea that the world was shortly to end'. Neither he nor his teaching was moral, and it was essentially otherworldly. Jesus could never provide an ethical answer to modernity as Burton proposed.[77]

Therefore, despite considerable sympathy between socialist and Rationalist ideas, Rationalist approaches diverged from socialist attempts

74 *TS*, July 1930, p.4.
75 *TS*, May 1930, p.2; *TS*, July 1930, p.5.
76 *TS*, July 1930, p.8 (original italics).
77 *TS*, 6 December 1930, pp.1-3.

to enlist Jesus against the Church. Both challenged organised religion. Socialist language tended to present religion as part of a failed capitalist system. Recovery of the true Jesus could provide an avenue for the critique of religion, but also its reform. By contrast, the Rationalist press criticised the churches, but also implicated Jesus in the critique by questioning his morality and downplaying the value of his ethical teaching. Mediating positions were thus rejected in favour of a hard line against organised religion. This position was not only anti-Church but also seemed anti-Jesus. Though consistent, it probably had a detrimental effect on popular support for organised Rationalism. Conscientious myth-busting made good press, but was too extreme to remain broadly appealing at this time. It could appear rather confrontational and pompous. Moreover, it underestimated levels of popular devotion to Jesus. Commitment to the destruction of organised Christianity some-times led Rationalists to use Jesus against religion. Their willingness to attack him directly was simply too radical to be popular.

The rhetoric of religious reform

It is possible to make use of this language sound like an attack on organised Christianity by the forces of irreligion. Such an interpretation is only partially accurate. Some critics clearly appealed to Jesus in these ways in order to undermine the churches. Yet, potentially damaging as they were, many of these claims had their counterparts within overtly religious settings. In particular, suggestions that Jesus was unknown to the churches, or actively opposed them, were widely expounded in ecclesial contexts. In their own way, groups expressing these ideas were usually aiming to enliven the churches, and renew their effectiveness and reach into the community. The strategy was often a direct response to criticism, and presumed that the churches were weaker than they ought to be. Conflict between Jesus and the Church suggested the need for religious change, perhaps by purification, or by bringing the Church closer to the Christianity of the New Testament.

During this period, religious leaders often claimed that the churches were 'under fire', and that 'active and articulate hostility to religion' was widespread.[78] As early as 1911, Presbyterians were acknowledging that failure to implement Jesus' teaching provided a fundamental element in criticism of the churches. The General Assembly's Report on the State of Religion suggested that the Church was being judged by new standards, especially regarding its response to social conditions: 'Men are growing increasingly conscious of a contradiction between Christ's attitude to the masses of the poor, to the lapsed and the social outcasts, and the attitude of many who profess and call themselves Christians'.[79] The report accepted that there was considerable common ground between the churches and the labour movement, since prevailing concern for the downtrodden and demands for equity and justice originated in Jesus' teaching. In 1928, the Foreign Mission Convenor of the Presbyterian Church, G.H. Jupp, also noted the prevalence of heavy and general criticism. To counter this, he contended that the Christian message had to be delivered 'authentically, and warmly, out of the depths of a real experience and without the impediment of obscurantism, negativism or outworn dogma'.[80] Organised Christianity faced existential, doctrinal and ethical challenges, and needed to respond to each.

Denominational leaders were less likely to accept claims of Jesus' hostility toward religion than critics or more sectarian religious groups. Nevertheless, they did accept that the churches had failed in some way, and increasingly invoked the real Jesus and the Christianity of Christ as touchstones in their proposals for reform. The notion of 'Churchianity', so reviled by critics of organised religion, was equally disdained by many of its strongest supporters. Churchianity was presented as a failure of moral courage and commitment to the religion of Jesus. It featured prominently in expressions of social Christianity that emphasised fidelity to Jesus' teaching. J.T. Paul was a committed Methodist, and a leading trades unionist and social reformer. In a terse interchange with correspondents in the *Methodist Outlook*, Paul argued that socialism was a more Christian system than competition, since it enabled 'men to live lives and act towards their brothers in the true spirit of Christianity, not of Churchianity'.[81]

78 *NZMT*, 29 March 1924, p.12.
79 *PGA*, 1911, p.64.
80 *Outlook*, 13 February 1928, p.29.
81 Newspaper Clippings Book, 1903-6, J.T. Paul Papers, MS-982, Hocken Library, Dunedin.

Criticism of Churchianity came from a variety of political perspectives, however. In 1928, the *New Zealand Herald* reported an address of T.E. Ruth at Pitt Street Congregational Church in Sydney that decried the righteous, complacent and moralising Pharisees of the city. He contended that 'Sin is not always swaggering, blasphemous and coarse. It is sometimes gentle and mild-mannered, and comes in the guise of an angel of light in the church. How insidious is the temptation to substitute Churchianity for Christianity!'[82] Ruth was no social Christian. A colourful and controversial Baptist minister from Melbourne, he had been a leading British imperialist during the war and one of the controversial Australian Catholic Archbishop Daniel Mannix's sectarian opponents.

The notion of Churchianity appeared frequently among youth, for whom the appeal of whole-hearted and ethically demanding Christianity was especially strong. Attacks against it also provided one of few legitimate opportunities to challenge the practice of seniors. One contributor to the *Methodist Bible Class Link* contended against the popular saying, 'I believe in Christianity, but not in Churchianity', arguing that it was as fallacious as believing in healing but not hospitals, or education but not colleges.[83] That argument only partially addressed the criticism, but did highlight how popular the idea had become.

The idea of Jesus as a stranger was another important theme in anti-Church rhetoric. Indeed, it could become a devotional image as much as a prophetic one. The idea may have been used to rebuke religion, but it also had currency within the churches, albeit in more romanticised terms. Reference to Jesus as 'the Stranger of Galilee' seems to have become popular in the late nineteenth century, aided by Leila N. Morris's hymn of 1893. A Methodist from Ohio, Morris was active in the camp meeting movement and a prolific writer of popular gospel songs. Her hymn recounted imagined encounters with Christ during his earthly ministry, which become personalised when 'the Stranger' reveals his hand and 'riven side'. The conclusion was explicitly evangelistic:

> Oh, my friend, won't you love Him forever?
> So gracious and tender is He!

82   *NZH*, 2 February 1928, p.13.
83   *NZMBC Link*, 24 August 1924, p.1.

Accept Him today as your Saviour,
This Stranger of Galilee.

Reflecting on the popularity of Morris's song, the Presbyterian minister and writer of devotional booklets W. Bower Black remarked that the notion was lamentably widespread. It demonstrated a worrying lack of certainty about Jesus' identity, and also a truth that Jesus was indeed a stranger to the greater part of humanity. This was the Church's fault, because Christians had failed to adequately represent him:

> In some tragic way we have misrepresented our Master, so that many of those round about us have never really seen Him as he is. Neither our preaching nor our living as Church people have set forth Christ in all His strength and fulness of manhood. Men have not got the impression of the real Jesus, the Man Christ Jesus, when they have considered *us*.[84]

Like Morris's hymn, Black's discussion of Jesus as Stranger ultimately challenged readers to encounter him as Saviour, Friend and Lord. He argued that the familiar Jesus was a tepid fiction. If people saw him as he really was, rather than as Christians represented him, they would gladly accept Jesus. The real Jesus was not 'gloomy', but rather:

> possessed of a marvellous attractiveness for the ordinary man of His day. He mingled in all companies, and He did not criticise these men, though on the other hand He never condoned their sin. He was never demonstrative or gushing. He had the dignity of a strong man. His life was not narrow, but free, spontaneous and glad. He had in Him the constraining force of a great personality.[85]

According to Black's analysis, Christians' own insipid character obfuscated Jesus and impeded commitment to him. This limited support for the churches, which further diminished their influence.

Popularisers like Colin Scrimgeour also favoured the imagery of the Stranger. After his time with the Methodist Auckland Central Mission, Scrimgeour became best known as 'Uncle Scrim' through the extraordinarily popular non-denominational 'Friendly Road' radio church on 1ZR. In this, he sought to promote a simple, heartfelt but non-

---

84 W. Bower Black, *The House of Quietness*, Christchurch: Presbyterian Bookroom, 1945, pp.58-59 (original italics).
85 Black, *Quietness*, pp.59-64.

creedal form of Christianity based on friendliness and goodwill. The church he hoped for was one 'without creed, something that was built in the human heart, something that required of its members no doctrine other than that of love and kindness'. For Scrim, the only test for any creed, idea or philosophy was that urged 'by the Stranger of Galilee many long years ago', who said '"By their fruits ye shall know them"…. One man's meat is often another's poison, and so these differences are called creeds'.[86]

Scrimgeour apparently developed a profound dislike for the Bible early in life. He later claimed to have once opened his mother's Bible, but found it an 'entirely useless piece of literature, tinted by superstition with a tone of reverence'. Scrimgeour's references to the 'Stranger of Galilee' avoided biblical parlance and fitted with the folksy and vaguely-defined style of religion he promoted. Quite deliberately, it also served to distance Jesus and true religion from conventional understandings. Scrimgeour constantly espoused the line that churches had veiled the real Jesus. This 'strong, healthy, happy, friendly Jesus' had been hidden for nearly 2,000 years 'beneath the dark Cloak of Orthodoxy and almost buried in the tomb of man-made creeds'.[87] Theology's crime was to obscure personality.

Notwithstanding the significant differences between Bower Black's evangelicalism and Scrimgeour's 'practical Christianity' they were agreed on a number of points. Not least, they concluded that Jesus was inherently attractive, especially when presented as a virile, well-rounded individual. According to Scrimgeour, Jesus was 'not the physical weakling we often see depicted in story books and stained-glass windows', but 'must have had sinews of steel to live as He did'. Neither was he a killjoy, but rather a gentleman who always went around doing 'charming things'.[88] Thus, the idea of Jesus as Stranger was allied to calls for more assertive forms of religion, but was also deeply sentimental. It exuded mystery and invited curiosity, maintaining that Jesus was knowable and worthy of a committed following. There was perhaps some irony in this use of the motif to promote religion given Scrimgeour's uneasy relationship with organised Christianity. However

86   *Hello Everybody*, 4, 1935, p.8; *Hello Everybody*, 2, 1935, p.26.
87   *Hello Everybody*, 2, 1935, pp.4-5.
88   *Hello Everybody*, 2, 1935, p.6.

94

much the Fellowship of the Friendly Road criticised established forms, it still aimed to promote Christian religion rather than abolish it.

Restorationism and primitive Christianity

Use of this kind of language was aided by a revival of primitivism within contemporary Protestant Christianity. Primitivism, or restorationism, describes efforts to recover a Christian faith believed to have been practiced in the first century. These attempts to restore New Testament Christianity generally presumed a fall from primordial rightness that could be reversed in the modern age. In this sense, the primitivist agenda was distinctively Protestant and harked back to Reformation principles. Richard Hughes has demonstrated the enduring impact of primitivism in North America, especially from the nineteenth century. The ideas were prominent in smaller sects like the Mormons and Churches of Christ, but also in dissenting Protestant groups like the Brethren, Baptists, and some Methodists. By the late nineteenth century, the primitivist ideal had become widespread. It was an influential force within the mainline denominations, and in Pentecostal and Fundamentalist groups.[89]

Jesus-centred religion fitted comfortably with this general move to recover pristine forms of New Testament Christianity. Jesus-centred primitivism reprised established themes for a new age and context, incorporating criticisms of the contemporary churches into a discourse of faithfulness. At the opening address to the United Christian Convention in Cambridge, A.S. Wilson, a prominent Baptist revivalist and leader in the local Keswick-influenced interwar revival movement, commented:

> We have no hesitation, but much sorrow, in saying that the average Christianity of the day is a caricature of that portrayed in the New Testament. Surely we are in the

---

89 Richard T. Hughes (ed.), *The American Quest for the Primitive Church*, Urbana: University of Illinois Press, 1988; Richard T. Hughes and C. Leonard Allen, *Illusions of Innocence: Protestant Primitivism in America, 1630-1875*, Chicago: University of Chicago Press, 1988.

Laodicean age, and it will be well for us to get out of the mind of the age, and get into Christ's mind.[90]

Divisions within Christianity were often blamed for the churches' failures, and provided impetus for greater cooperation. Early ecumenists argued that a weakened and divided Church betrayed the teaching of Jesus and Paul. In 1928, Lionel Fletcher's address to the Congregational Union presented Christian union as the best way to face an increasingly cynical 'Christless' world. The current position was one of strong Churchianity but weak Christianity:

> Organised Christianity was never so perfectly organized as it is to-day. It was never so wealthy. It was never so rich in scholarship. It never had such tremendous opportunities for carrying out Christ's commands. Yet it is facing a world seething with discontent at its seeming inability to do more than propagate its own separate denominations.[91]

A.L. Haddon, Principal of the Churches of Christ College in Dunedin, became a leading advocate for ecumenism. He spoke widely on the topic, and introduced a course of eighty lectures on 'ecumenics' to his students in 1941. In one popular apologetic for the World Council of Churches he declared, 'The church has been lost'. A divided Church was a defeat, and betrayal of Christian origins. For Haddon, ecclesiology and the doctrine of the Incarnation were closely allied. Thus, he argued, the invisible unity of the churches in Christ must be made manifest in order for the Church to become 'the bearer of His second incarnation, His mouthpiece, the bodily instrument of his will'.[92]

One way to repristinate religion was to make it less complex. Primitivism idealised simplicity, and often supported the widespread call for less dogmatic forms of religion. Commentators noted that Jesus' wisdom was practical, and confounded intellectual dogmatism and speculation. One writer in the *New Zealand Methodist Times* claimed that the school of life constantly confirmed Jesus: 'Time, which has tested and cast away a thousand theories, has but vindicated Him. The

---

90 A.S. Wilson, *Faith's Fight*, Auckland: Scott & Scott, 1933, p.12.
91 *NZH*, 9 March 1928, p.11.
92 A.L. Haddon, *The Coming of the World Church: A Brief Introduction to the Ecumenical Movement*, Wellington: Youth Committee of the New Zealand Council of Religious Education, 1942, p.5.

heated eloquence of politicians, the supercilious certainties of the scholarly, the pompous platitudes of the Pharisees had their day.... From them we turn back to the Divine Peasant'. A concluding prayer invoked the simple religion of Jesus: 'We turn back to Thee from those experiences which have shattered the system of philosophers and turned the doctrines of the wise to nonsense. How refreshing has been Thy simplicity in those sad days of disillusionment!'[93]

Simplicity and anti-intellectualism were occasionally allied with appeals to Nature. Thus, Colin Scrimgeour advanced forms of simple, natural religion as an alternative to dogmatic Christianity:

> The God of Theology has caused many people to become discouraged, and to lose touch with the greatest things of life. It is perhaps because they have mis-read the orthodox labels. So, in the unfettered manner of the psalm of the birds and with the simplicity of the flower that grows on the garden wall, we seek to interpret the Great Law of Life.[94]

Devotional literature also frequently emphasised simplicity, and the spirituality of ordinary life. One prayer for housewives in the *Methodist Times* began, 'Jesus, teach me how to be / Proud of my simplicity'. The verse was an appeal for wisdom and spiritual renewal amid the mundane rituals and pressures of domestic life.[95]

Religious reform movements

Anti-Churchianity, representation of Jesus as a stranger and advocacy of simplified religion were all part of the rhetoric of religious reformism. The language did not connote a single approach, however, but was applied in support of remarkably diverse projects. Theological Modernism eschewed homely simplicity, but utilised tools of scholarship and biblical criticism to achieve a strikingly similar effect. H.D.A. Major was one of the leading figures in the Modernist movement in England.

93   *NZMT*, 13 March 1926, p.13.
94   *Hello Everybody*, 1936, p.3.
95   *NZMT*, 1 June 1929, p.6.

Though Modernism never gained a particularly strong following in New Zealand, his local connections ensured that Major's books were read and his career followed by at least some Anglicans and leading Rationalists. Modernist and Rationalist positions were similar in certain respects, with the latter's critiques often informing Modernist reworking of orthodox dogma.

Characteristically, Modernist approaches emphasised 'the historical Jesus'. Uncomfortable with a wholly transcendent or miraculous Jesus, notions of immanence were preferred. In *The Gospel of Freedom*, Major articulated a Modernist agenda for reforming the Church. He argued that a conflict existed in Christianity between those who regarded 'the Spirit of Christ as the supreme authority, and those who wish to elevate traditional dogmas, practices, and organisations to an equality with it'. Modernists were evidently the former, and felt duty bound to bring the Church up-to-date. To do so required rethinking dogmatic, institutional and miraculous encumbrances to Christianity, and more productive engagement with personality and ethics.[96] Like other critics, Major claimed that Church leaders, as Pharisees, were impediments to progress. Christ had condemned the Pharisees for not apprehending the signs of the times, and using education to hinder progress: 'they used it to stop development; they used it to quench inspiration; they used it to crush reform, instead, as they might have done, to help it forward'. According to Major, a return to the Christianity of Christ was now needed: 'not the Christianity of the great Church Councils. Not the Christianity of the mediaeval scholastics, not the Christianity of the Lutheran and Calvinist Reformation, but the Christianity of Christ'. It is 'our duty and our wisdom', he argued, 'to teach our people the Christianity of Christ'.[97]

Social Christians were seldom Modernists as such, but also honed in on ethics and the alleged neglect of Jesus' actual teaching. Groups like the New Zealand Christian Pacifist Society (CPS) were products of the churches, but critical of them. According to one leading member of the CPS, Ron Howell, churches perpetuated the half-truth that religion was an individual matter between 'a man and his God'. This 'debased the Gospel of Jesus Christ'. He argued that 'The Church, to whose charge has been committed the proclamation of a Gospel which was asociated

---

96   H.D.A. Major, *The Gospel of Freedom*, London: T. Fisher Unwin, 1912, viii-xii.
97   Major, pp.48-49.

[sic] by its Founder with the bringing of good news to the poor, healing the broken-hearted, freeing the captive and curing the blind, has been guilty of a tragic betrayal'.[98] For Howell, the idea of the Church as betrayer was closely linked to its performance on issues of social morality. It was also a matter of character, however, since the Kingdom of God required leaders of moral stature.

Theologically conservative Christians freely conceded that contemporary churches had failed. While their interpretations of the problem differed in some respects, Evangelicals also articulated anti-Church arguments as part of their critique. Poor theology, failure of Christian experience, and waning zeal and fervour were pinpointed as fundamental failings.[99] More specifically, claims of inadequate representation and experience of Jesus also featured prominently. Thus, A.S. Wilson quoted E. Stanley Jones: 'Our greatest difficulty is not *anti-christianity* but this sub-christianity. It takes the facts of Christ's life, His death, His resurrection, but not the living fact of Christ'.[100] Hence, correct theology did not necessarily produce 'true Christianity'. The Congregationalist Lionel Fletcher held that common disgust at double-faced Christians was positive since it showed that 'men of the world' understood that these were not true followers of Jesus.[101] Revivalist spirituality promoted uncomplicated, accessible religion. According to Fletcher, genuine, winsome Christianity simply followed from experiencing the person of Jesus, and appropriating his saving work in a personal way.[102]

Pentecostal Christianity emerged in New Zealand during the interwar years. Though innovative in some respects, the movement was also shaped by a primitivist impulse. Pentecostals were inspired by the New Testament church and interpreted their experiences as a new

---

98 Ron Howell, *Christian Pacifism and Social Change*, Auckland: Christian Pacifist Society of New Zealand (Auckland Branch), 1945, pp.22-24.

99 *Reaper*, March 1928, p.8.

100 A.S. Wilson, *Definite Experience: Convention Aids and Deterrents*, London: Marshall Morgan & Scott, 1937, p.53; quotation from E. Stanley Jones, *The Christ of Every Road: A Study in Pentecost*, New York: Abingdon, 1930.

101 Lionel B. Fletcher, *The Pathway to the Stars*, London: Marshall, Morgan & Scott, 1933, p.51.

102 Lionel B. Fletcher, *After Conversion – What?*, London: Marshall, Morgan & Scott, 1936, pp.9-10.

manifestation of earlier authentic Christianity. Early Pentecostalism emphasised Jesus as the means of atonement, but also the centre of the devotional life and source of power for victorious living. Fresh encounter with a personal and living Saviour opened the way for dynamic Christian experience. Early Pentecostalism also gained support, and validity, by criticising more established forms of organised Christianity. Claims that 'dry rot' had infected many churches and leaders were commonly advanced by pioneering leaders. By contrast, Pentecostal faith offered a revival of old-time religion, and personal connection with Jesus and the energy of New Testament Christianity. Some of the movement's greatest influence came through reshaping the experience and commitments of existing churchgoers. Many early converts were drawn from evangelical backgrounds, but dismissed much of their former experience as mere 'churchianity and religiosity'.[103]

A.H. Dallimore was one of the most colourful and controversial of the figures associated with early Pentecostalism in New Zealand.[104] Having spent time in New Zealand in the 1890s, Dallimore was converted in Vancouver by Charles Price, a protégé of the American Pentecostal leader Aimee Semple McPherson. Persuaded to enter the ministry in 1920, he returned to Auckland in 1927 and founded the Revival Fire Mission. Dallimore's mission placed considerable emphasis on healing, and became outstandingly popular. By 1931, his meetings had transferred to the Town Hall. The Mission faltered, however, following public denouncements of his healing activity after investigations led by a committee of ministers, academics and medical representatives late in 1932.

Dallimore's religiosity made Jesus central, and his activities were framed as imitating Jesus' historical ministry. Healing was effected by the 'power of Jesus', and attributed to his direct working. There was also a sense in which healing represented the fulfilment of promises Jesus made. This required radical commitment to Jesus, which was juxtaposed with the faith of 'the Church'. Arguing against the medical establish-

---

103 James E. Worsfold, *A History of the Charismatic Movements in New Zealand*, Bradford: Julian Literature Trust, 1974, p.173; James E. Worsfold, *The Reverend Gilbert and Mrs Alice White*, Wellington: Julian Literature Trust, 1995, pp.25-27.

104 Dallimore has generally been regarded as a Pentecostal, though he insisted that his ministry was independent. See Laurie Guy, 'One of a Kind? The Auckland Ministry of A.H. Dallimore', *Australasian Pentecostal Studies*, 8, 2004, pp.125-45.

ment, he called for simple a Christocentric faith that contrasted with prevailing religious patterns:

> If the whole of New Zealand would renounce the entire medical system and turn to Jesus Christ and put a childlike, sincere and simple faith in him, NEW ZEALAND WOULD SEE AN ASTONISHING TRANSFORMATION IN ITS CONDITION OF APPALLING SICKNESS AND MISERY. BUT NOT EVEN THE CHURCH BELIEVES THAT FAR IN JESUS.[105]

The Church's claim that God had raised up doctors, nurses and hospitals was a lie. God had provided Jesus.[106]

Critics argued that Dallimore's use of biblical texts were 'so outrageous as to amount to sacrilege', and described his ministry as a 'vaudeville show under the cloak of religion'.[107] His approach to Jesus aroused controversy, too. Laurie Guy has noted Dallimore's anti-trinitarianism and adoptionist stance.[108] His presentation of Jesus as a controversialist and sectarian was also problematic. In 1932, at the height of the debate over his ministry, the *New Zealand Baptist* noted Dallimore's love of calling loudly on the 'wonderful Jesus' to heal people. Yet, it claimed:

> The Dallimore cult are heretics. They deny the central dogma of our faith. They deny the deity of Jesus. It is only by denying his deity and making Him a rebel against the world order, which is of God's appointment, that they can wage war against the use of medical means.[109]

Moreover, the article argued, 'His Jesus is a rebel against the world that God made.... We do not wonder for a moment that he does not believe in the real deity of Jesus. A man with such a creed could not believe'.

Reaction to Dallimore notwithstanding, the ministry of healing garnered broad support during the same interwar years. Evangelicals

---

105 *Revival Fire Monthly*, July 1937, p.3, cited in Guy, 'One of a Kind', p.131 (original emphasis).
106 *NZB*, December 1932, p.370.
107 *Press*, 13 December 1932, p.7.
108 Laurie Guy, 'Miracles, Messiahs and the Media: the Ministry of A.H. Dallimore in Auckland in the 1930s', in Kate Cooper and Jeremy Gregory (eds), *Signs, Wonders, Miracles: Representations of Divine Power in the Life of the Church*, Woodbridge: Ecclesiastical History Society, 2005, pp.453-63.
109 *NZB*, December 1932, p.370.

were impressed by the ministry of T.W. Ratana, which seemed to provide evidence supporting conservative theological belief in the reality of miracles, and therefore the reliability of the New Testament. Even some of Dallimore's most scathing critics claimed to believe firmly in divine healing and regard it as indispensable. The spiritual healing mission of James Moore Hickson in 1923 represented a less theatrical and more respectable approach. Born in Australia in 1868, Hickson's involvement in the ministry of healing grew greatly after he moved to England in 1897. In 1905, he founded the Society of Emmanuel and began publishing *The Healer* as vehicles to encourage the healing ministry. After World War One, he became an important figure in the revival of spiritual healing within the Church of England.[110]

Hickson's approach to healing emphasised its basis in gospel Christianity. He consistently highlighted that healing was part of the ministry Jesus exercised, and should therefore be part of Christianity. The argument implied that churches had failed to make it so, and on occasions these criticisms were explicit: 'The church had been "going slow" for 2000 years and it was high time now that something was done about it'.[111] The contemporary healing ministry was replicating Jesus' work, as true Christianity should: 'When Christ formed His Church He made it clear that He intended that the healing work should be continued.... The early Church was a healing Church. What a calamity has befallen the Church since that day'.[112] Perhaps most importantly, healing was held to mediate 'the living presence of the Man of Galilee'.[113] It converted the churches' Jesus from a shibboleth into a personality and 'living spiritual force'.[114]

There is evidence that this incarnational dimension helped to arouse sympathy for Hickson's mission. T.H. Sprott, the cautious and scholarly Anglican Bishop of Wellington, claimed to have been reluctant to receive Hickson for fear that his mission might induce 'undue excitement', disappointment and antagonism to the medical profession.

---

110 Stuart Mews, 'The Revival of Spiritual Healing in the Church of England', in W.J. Shiels (ed.), *The Church and Healing*, Oxford: Basil Blackwell, 1982, pp.299-331.

111 *NZH*, 8 October 1923, p.9.

112 *Dominion*, 6 November 1923, p.9; cf. *Parish Magazine* (All Saints' Anglican Church, Palmerston North), 4 October 1923, p.19.

113 *Manawatu Evening Standard*, 24 October 1923, p.4; cf. *EP*, 6 November 1923, p.8.

114 *Parish Magazine*, 8 November 1923, pp.20-21.

Persuaded against these concerns, Sprott noted that, theologically, the ministry of healing seemed a natural corollary of the recent recovery of Christ's conception of the Kingdom of God. Moreover, the emphasis seemed attuned to a postwar age that was less materialistic than its predecessor. Perhaps this was the route to a renewal of Christian influence in society:

> The Church confronts the new age, and she confronts it with her more adequate conception of the Kingdom of God. Is it mere fancy that it may be the purpose of God that, just as the first proclamation of the Kingdom by Christ and His Apostles was accompanied by a Ministry of Healing, so the re-proclamation of the Kingdom to the new age should be accompanied by a revived Ministry of Healing? I confess it seems to me more than fancy. I think that this may be one of the ways by which the Gospel of the Kingdom is once again to come with power to the hearts of men.[115]

In Christchurch, Bishop Churchill Julius commented that the mission had helped to break through the 'crust of our traditions and conventions', providing a fuller revelation of Christ as the 'Saviour of men, and not souls only'.[116]

The anti-Church Jesus was a mode of argumentation that gained much by referring to Jesus' humanity and personality and all that those terms connoted. Its primary focus, however, was actually the Church, religion and institutions. These were its subjects as much if not more than Jesus was. Nevertheless, it was significant that the personality of Jesus carried so much authority in these debates. The diverse contexts in which the image emerged, and uses to which it was put, were also striking.

The approaches to Jesus identified in this chapter must be seen as a discourse of reform. Proponents of 'unconventional' representations used Jesus to project alternative visions for the future of religion and society. Some anti-Church discourse used Jesus to bolster radical social and political reform. It was also used to seek the destruction of the churches, ironically using their own language. Similarly, for the churches, the anti-Church Jesus was a symbol of necessary change.

---

115 *Proceedings of the Diocesan Synod of the Diocese of Wellington*, 1923, pp.48-49, 56-57.
116 *Church News*, April 1924, p.3.

This was a search for influence on all sides in which notions of power were fundamental. Jesus was especially popular among groups that felt their agenda was marginal to the centres of power. Indeed, the smaller or more threatened the group the more intense and sharply focused the argument became. Definitions of mainstream religion could vary, and differentiation from it was always a matter of one's perspective. Nevertheless, positions of marginality and relative lack of power appealed to an underdog instinct. To be effective, the rhetoric depended on disaffection with organised religion. In some quarters, criticism followed from a perception that churches were bastions of power. Perhaps this was the greatest weakness of the critique, since the churches in New Zealand were never as powerful as the rhetoric suggested. Indeed, those who used anti-Church language as part of a process of internal reform were often motivated by a perception of limited and weakening religious influence within society.

Notwithstanding the social and political factors influencing the rise of Jesus as an icon of anti-Church sentiment, the language needs to be understood as a specifically religious mode of argumentation. The wide circulation of these prophetic images highlights the credibility attached to Jesus' life. Jesus was central to Christian identity and belief, which made the compulsion to incorporate him in reformist arguments significant. In some senses, the anti-Church Jesus represented the logic of Protestantism at work. It was an aspect of Jesus-centred religiosity and argumentation that cohered with Protestant values. The critique of church life it offered would scarcely have been imaginable within contemporary Catholicism. Perhaps the anti-Church Jesus also demonstrated that Romanticism supplied the primary alternative to more conventional religious discourse.

4. Social Campaigner

From the late nineteenth century, changing social structures led to widespread concerns about social problems and to the emergence of sociological analysis. Proposals for reform were debated in New Zealand as elsewhere, and Jesus was frequently invoked in these deliberations. This chapter assesses three main contexts in which this occurred. It begins by considering the place of Jesus in social Christianity from the 1890s to about 1920, before addressing discourses of labour, unionism and socialism, and reaction to these over the same timeframe. A third context concerns the Protestant social gospel of the interwar years.

The Jesus of social campaigning reflected the pressures that different constituencies felt amid widespread upheaval within society. Social disharmony threatened church leaders' visions of a Christian society, while some also feared the competing influence of labour. The labour movement's own position was far from assured, however, and attempts to enlist Jesus to the labour cause reflected its need of internal stability. A socialist Jesus provided a retort to conservative critics. He was also attractive to religious workers. While appropriation of him in these debates did not always amount to Jesus-centred religiosity, it did cohere with the religious tone in society. In general, Jesus was enlisted as a moral symbol, particularly through discourses of brotherhood, ethics and righteous opposition. Jesus lent moral strength to competing social ideals, and was a prime cultural reference in the contest of values.

Social Christianity

Attempts to Christianise the social order incorporated a range of strategies. Social Christianity, which had become a feature of Protestant Christianity in the late nineteenth century, included engagement based on traditional principles, as well as efforts to reinterpret the Christian message in more sociological terms. Though informed by secular social thought, it was primarily a religious movement, animated by religious concepts and given coherence by a distinctive religious vocabulary.[1]

Jesus featured prominently in this common language. The doctrine of the Incarnation was a fundamental tenet, even if the emphasis did not produce a consistent Christology.[2] It often led to emphasis on Jesus' humanity, but not always. It could entail questioning or reformulation of Jesus' divinity, but not necessarily. The fatherhood of God, the humanity of Jesus and the brotherhood of humanity, however, were all central concepts. The Incarnation was viewed as having established a kind of kinship between God and humanity. Heightened sensitivity to God's immanence blurred the line between sacred and secular and encouraged a sense of social responsibility.

The Kingdom of God also featured prominently. The concept was drawn from Jesus' teaching and that provenance lent it moral weight and credibility. Echoing ideas developed by the English Christian Socialists Charles Kingsley and F.D. Maurice in the mid-nineteenth century, the Kingdom was interpreted in ethical terms and the Sermon on the Mount given special status. Social Christians prioritised the human element in society, anticipating that this focus would improve social harmony. Applied socially, Christ's teaching provided a means to more fully Christianise communities and realise the Kingdom of God. All of this was thought achievable in the immediate future. Christ was an optimist, and the Church's history of social endeavour inspired confidence about its prospects.[3]

The ideas informing social Christianity were not only derived from religious sources. A new world context of nationalism and expanding states helped shape the intellectual climate. Social Darwinism, the sociology of Auguste Comte and his 'religion of humanity', and Hegelian idealism and notions of organic unity were also important. Together, these elements strengthened interest in society as a unit of analysis rather than humanity as an aggregation of individuals. Jesus

1   Paul T. Phillips, *A Kingdom on Earth: Anglo-American Social Christianity, 1880-1940*, Pennsylvania: Pennsylvania State University Press, 1996, esp. xxiv-xxv.

2   Janet Forsythe Fishburn, *The Fatherhood of God and the Victorian Family: The Social Gospel in America*, Philadelphia: Fortress Press, 1981, pp.145-49.

3   A.H. Collins, *How Far and Why Have the Churches Failed?*, Auckland: Wright & Jaques Printers, 1899, pp.10-11; *YCU*, 1903, pp.50-51.

played a crucial role in connecting social thought with religion. He exemplified the ethical individual life, even as his life and teaching were cast as the means of redemption for society as a whole. As the leading British Wesleyan reformer Hugh Price Hughes had argued, 'Jesus Christ came into this world to save human society as well as to save individuals'.[4]

Social Christianity as a conservative force

The goals and social analysis associated with early twentieth-century social Christianity were characteristically conservative. Despite radical-sounding language, the social Jesus was often linked to social improvement through the individual rather than reordering of economic and political systems. Moral and evangelistic considerations were pivotal. On the one hand, the social Jesus encouraged conversion. On the other, he championed the personal ethics that would improve the social order. Social Christians sometimes added that the Incarnation created the Church, which was a great force for social good. Thus, the Australasian Student Christian Union was reminded:

> No doubt our Lord Jesus Christ was the highest example; no doubt He was the greatest teacher. No doubt His words ought to form the rule of life. But the Incarnation means a good deal more than that. It means, amongst other things, that Christ took human nature and perfected it, and in that perfect human nature all members of the Christian Church are united.... The life of Christ working in the life of men is the most effective force in social regeneration.[5]

Writing of the British context, David Bebbington has argued that the late nineteenth-century social gospel was grounded in evangelicalism and the difficulties of urban mission. It was an 'evangelistic strategy for reaching

4 Cited in K.S. Inglis, 'English Nonconformity and Social Reform, 1880-1900', *Past & Present*, 13, 1958, p.74.
5 *Jesus Christ and Social Need: Addresses Delivered at the Conferences of the Australasian Student Christian Union - 1911-1912*, Melbourne: Student Movement Press, 1912, pp.10-11.

the working classes'.[6] This influence was evident in New Zealand as in Britain, where the Protestant churches blended social and evangelistic concerns. The Rev. F.C. Spurr's call to 'proclaim the whole Gospel for soul, body, and society' also quite naturally urged Christians to 'receive Christ as our own personal Redeemer and Lord'.[7]

Social gospel language was utilised in local efforts to engage the working classes and increase church attendance. One series of meetings for working men in Dunedin was said to have been undergirded by mutual recognition of 'the Fatherhood of God and the Brotherhood of Jesus'. When Mr G. Laurenson, M.H.R., addressed an initial gathering, however, his message on 'The Supreme Need of New Zealand' was essentially evangelistic: true happiness proceeded not from legislation, but 'recognition of the saving power of Jesus Christ'.[8] Broader attempts to address social conditions also betrayed this evangelistic agenda. Addressing the Congregational Union in 1901, the Rev. J. Reed Glasson surveyed the characteristics of the age, and especially 'the growing social spirit'.[9] Glasson was generally considered progressive. Nevertheless, whilst affirming that 'The mission of Christ and of His Church' was both 'religious and social', he contended that it was primarily 'to save the individual man, to bring man to God, to reconcile the alienated and sinful child to his Father. It has been said that Christ discovered the individual'. Christ influenced society by taking a few 'simple' men, 'Not so much to lead in social reform, as to inspire and train the men.... All the age's need is included in this: God intoxicated men – Christ filled men'.

Conservative social analysis remained evident even where the evangelistic agenda was less explicit. Thus, J.J. North argued in 1905 that brotherhood and social reform were essentially Christian, deriving as they did from Christ's life and teaching: 'Social activities date from Nazareth.... Christ changed the world's climate. Ours is an age of wide philanthropies, of tender mercies, and of social sympathies. And this is of Christ'.[10] North was primarily aiming to counter perceived threats to the churches' influence. His apologetic claimed that the Church had

6   Bebbington, *Evangelicalism in Modern Britain*, p.212.
7   *Jesus Christ and Social Need*, pp.23-24.
8   *Outlook*, 2 June 1906, p.45.
9   *YCU*, 1901, pp.38-51.
10   J.J. North, *The Socialism of Jesus: An Argument*, Christchurch: T.E. Fraser, 1905, p.4.

historically led social reform because it followed Christ's teaching. Christ's own self-sacrifice was the best model for change: 'the world must either let go its social enthusiasms or return again to Jesus Christ. Selfishness is pressing very fiercely against the enlightened conscience'. Significantly, North's message also warned about the limits of humanising theology: 'It is not the manhood of a Jesus long since dead alone that feeds the fires of Christian love. It is His Godhead also'.[11]

A.S. Adams, another prominent Baptist and seven times president of the New Zealand Alliance, articulated similar views. He also celebrated the heroism and epoch-making reform led by forbears 'inspired by the spirit of the Saviour of men', affirming that 'There is no question affecting the social conditions of the people which cannot be explained and illustrated by the light of the moral teachings of Jesus'.[12] Yet, Adams' seemed more concerned with the churches' social influence than sociological analysis of structures and problems. He hoped for a revival of Christian citizenship based on Jesus' teaching. Democracy was practical brotherhood, but Christ's teaching was also conceived as a way to retain 'influence and power over men'. If Adams and North appeared progressive in some respects, their social analysis retained an emphasis on individual responsibility that was typical of older nonconformity.

Appeals to Jesus also addressed concerns about stability and social order, especially in response to the confrontational methods of militant labour and Red Fed-ism. In this context, Jesus' socialism was sometimes described in terms of the kind of even-handed moderation that would alleviate industrial conflict. Though describing himself 'a workman' and a 'unionist to the backbone, on principle', one apologist argued that Christians should remain impartial in the struggle between capital and labour. Jesus was 'the greatest socialist that ever lived'; in the principle of 'do unto others' he had given 'the highest ideal of socialism the world has known'. Whatever criticisms Jesus might make of modern industrial society, his teaching apparently boiled down to treating others well, doing a fair day's graft and taking pride in your work.[13]

11 North, *Socialism*, pp.6, 15.
12 A.S. Adams, *The Relation of the Church to the Social Problems of the Age*, Christchurch: T.E. Fraser, 1906, pp.5, 8-9.
13 J. Fuller, *Christian Socialism in the Industrial World: How We Can Abolish Industrial Warfare For Ever*, Auckland: Phipps & Hall, 1914, pp.8-11.

Similar arguments appeared in support of more definite political programmes. George W. Fowlds was a high profile Congregationalist who served as a Member of the House of Representatives for the Liberals from 1899. He gained a reputation as a left-wing member prior to his resignation in 1911. Frustrated at the slow rate of progress, he thereafter campaigned unsuccessfully for a programme of reform dubbed the 'New Evangel'. In an address to the Congregational Union, Fowlds argued that the social and political engagement of Christians was essential to social cohesion. Militant suffragists and the labour movement fought worthwhile causes, but their 'absurd and anarchical' methods and 'anti-Christian' spirit were socially disruptive.[14] On the other hand, Christians had departed from the 'the teaching of Jesus' and the 'Christianity of Christ', defined as 'justice and human brotherhood... an impartial equality of opportunity for all'. Political timidity had created a 'drift toward anarchy'. Fowlds urged the churches to include economic and political issues in their conceptualisation of morality, lest they 'degenerate into a pietistic social coterie'. Christ's moral teaching was necessary to prevent social disorder.

Social Christianity and progressive values

Some forms of social Christianity were more closely associated with progressive values and liberal theology. In these, Christianity was consciously adapted to cohere with contemporary thinking and conditions. Progressive forms exemplified the moral optimism of late nineteenth-century liberalism. Jesus figured prominently as principles of social thinking were related to his exemplary life.

The Forward Movement organised in Wellington by the Congregationalist minister the Rev. William A. Evans, with his counterpart the Rev. G.H. Bradbury, illustrates the flavour of late nineteenth-century progressive social Christianity. Begun in May 1893,

14   George Fowlds, *The New Evangel: An Address*, Auckland: N.Z. Land Values' League, 1911; George Fowlds, *The Drift Towards Anarchy: Its Causes and Cure*, Auckland: Wright & Jaques Printers, 1914.

the non-denominational movement was an attempt to respond to workers' needs along lines suggested by the settlement movement in London, and its institutions like Toynbee Hall. The settlements promoted social egalitarianism by encouraging wealthy educated citizens to live among the poor in order to help them. They also emphasised social and environmental causes of poverty rather than individual moral failings. Evans' Forward Movement was partly founded out of frustration at the limitations that conventional sectarian-based parish ministry placed on opportunities for service.[15] He described his movement as 'a faithful attempt to bring the cardinal principles of Christianity, as conceived and interpreted by its best exponents, to bear on the complex conditions of modern society'.[16] The organisation gathered momentum and briefly supported a journal, *The Citizen*, with the backing of civic leaders.

From the outset, Evans insisted that the Forward Movement was a modern form of evangelicalism. By this he meant that it considered 'man as a member of a body, and not as a mere individual', was humanitarian, and animated by 'the spirit of Jesus Christ'.

> The Forward Movement is the expression in modern times of the true Evangelical faith. It affirms the fatherhood of God, and the sonship of man, irrespective of nationality or sex. It maintains therefore the brotherhood of man; it accentuates the law of service as the law of life; it asserts that rights and duties are correlative terms, either of which cannot be separated from the other without the essence of both being destroyed; that man is above things, and should control and determine them, not be controlled and determined by them. It comprehends, therefore, all spheres within which man operates, and claims that all thought and action should be determined by the spirit of Jesus Christ.[17]

Jesus' 'supreme authority' was ethical and personal rather than doctrinal; true evangelicalism meant conforming to his spirit and teaching.[18]

Evans' Christology owed a debt to Hegelianism. Thus, Christ's genius lay in his ability to coordinate the 'energies of personality' and harmonise himself with the facts of the world, to discover the unity between subject and object. Assessing Jesus' ministry, he argued:

15 *The Cyclopedia of New Zealand*, vol. 1, Wellington: Cyclopedia Company, 1897, p.407.
16 *Citizen*, September 1895, p.1.
17 *Citizen*, September 1895, p.1.
18 W.A. Evans, 'The Basis of Authority', *YCU*, 1903, pp.45-57.

In the days of Christ, as to a very great extent in our own times, that unity was lost.... Jesus Christ reversed the process. Instead of analysis he employed synthesis. Instead of emptying the world of its meaning by the process of excluding all differences, he grasped in one conception all these differences and brought them under one supreme principle.[19]

The relationship between religion and the state was interpreted using Hegelian conceptions of the state as organism, which fitted comfortably with trajectories in liberal-labour politics. Recognition of humanity's essentially social nature marked a transition from individualism to socialism, conceived as a revolutionary emphasis on 'the common life'. For Evans, religion and state were complementary players in a moral project. The state organised social relations, creating the conditions where people could realise 'the moral ideal'. The Church simply embodied and articulated religion 'as unfolded and realised in the person of Christ'.[20] As 'the highest concrete embodiment of will', the state was based on the authority of Christ. Christian participation was necessary to 'make Christ's authority supreme in all its institutions'. Contemporary industrial conflict was merely a transitional period in the process of moralising property. Moreover, Christ was in the labour movement, which obliged Christians 'to sympathise with it, to understand it, and in His Spirit to guide it in the line of man's highest good'.[21]

Evans hoped the Forward Movement would forge a new, unified, and distinctly Christian view of society. This search for a broad consensus embraced some rather unorthodox positions. There was little interest in espousing creedal Christianity, and the movement included Rationalists, Unitarians, and others with few obvious religious commitments. In its short life, *The Citizen* published an eclectic range of essays. One, by Evans' sister-in-law Lilian Edger, for example, sought to combat criticisms that Theosophy was too abstruse to aid social reform by pointing to its central teaching: 'the universal brotherhood of man, a brotherhood which depends on unity of essence, all being animated by the same spirit, all being, as it were, rays from the one Divine Source'.[22]

19 *Citizen*, January 1896, pp.203-4; Evans, 'Basis of Authority', p.50.
20 *Citizen*, January 1896, pp.207, 210-11.
21 Evans, 'Basis of Authority', p.56.
22 *Citizen*, February 1896, p.248.

112

The movement was initially conceived as an non-sectarian body of workers and a society of 'mutual helpfulness'. A Mutual Help Society offered some assistance, but most of the philanthropic social work of the movement fell to Evans himself.[23] The most popular activity was a Literary Society and Evans clearly delighted in the 'literati' who gathered around him, and the classes which were effectively a forerunner to the foundation of a university college in Wellington. In 1904, Evans returned to parish ministry in the working-class community of Newtown where he served the Congregational Church until 1921. This move provided greater financial security, since the role with the Forward Movement had not been salaried. Despite earlier reservations about such ministry, he exercised considerable influence there and within the wider Church. This influence, and the growth of his parish, suggests that a significant constituency existed for his ideas. His endeavours demonstrated that concern to reach the working classes provided an important motivation, but also that notions of social morality were a central priority for social Christians of various kinds.

Moral campaigning and the alcohol question

This moral priority was most clearly reflected in the alignment between social Christianity and moral campaigning. David Bebbington has noted that British nonconformists became preoccupied with tackling social problems, often perceiving moral malaise at the root of social evils.[24] The tendency to mobilise on social issues where moral causes could be ascribed has led to identification of moral campaigning as a central religious response. According to James Belich, 'moral evangelism' was a feature of broader harmonising processes within New Zealand from the later nineteenth century.[25] It rested on the perception that social problems

---

23   Tim Beaglehole, *A Life of J.C. Beaglehole: New Zealand Scholar*, Wellington: Victoria University Press, 2006, p.34.
24   David W. Bebbington, *The Nonconformist Conscience: Chapel and Politics, 1870-1914*, London: George Allen & Unwin, 1982, pp.37-38.
25   James Belich, *Paradise Reforged: A History of the New Zealanders from the 1880s to the Year 2000*, Auckland: Allen Lane, 2001, pp.121-25, 157-88.

reflected moral failing. The social fabric was woven from private virtue, which suggested that these problems were also religious ones.

The campaign for the prohibition of alcohol was the most prominent social campaign of the early twentieth century. For its opponents, the liquor trade was the central vice of the age. Indeed, the prohibition movement has been convincingly interpreted within a social purity framework, wherein elimination of intoxicating substances from the body presaged analogous processes within society.[26] Campaigns had been conducted previously. The 1881 Licensing Act, which gave effect to the principle of local control, provided the crucial fillip to temperance supporters and marked the beginning of an era of significant agitation. Spurred by the rise of 'gospel temperance', Protestant churches took the leading role, though secularists like Robert Stout also advocated prohibition on grounds of the public good. The movement also held together disparate theological and political strands that fitted within the rubric of social Christianity. Support was strongest in the denominations with a heritage of independent activism, however, and where evangelical and pietistic traditions were most marked. Presbyterians, Methodists and other smaller Protestant churches were largely favourable, while there was less support among Anglicans and Roman Catholics.

For supporting churches, prohibition promised to improve morality and social conditions, and help Christianise society. Temperance campaigning was often hailed as spiritual work, since alcohol and its associated vices hindered the work of the gospel. Some emphasised that it was harmful to salvation, others that prohibition would improve the churches and uplift the moral tone in the community.[27] Further claims bordered on the eschatological, such as one that prohibition's ultimate success would usher in a 'universal reign of righteousness'.[28]

Temperance campaigning was popular among evangelicals. Despite this connection, and a desire to justify the campaign on biblical grounds, Jesus occupied an ambivalent space in the movement's rhetoric. Anthony Grigg has argued that the biblical grounds for promoting prohibition were in flux by the late nineteenth century; a fashion for

26   Sarah Dalton, 'The Pure in Heart: The New Zealand Women's Christian Temperance Union and Social Purity, 1885-1930', MA thesis, Victoria University of Wellington, 1993, p.1.
27   *White Ribbon*, 13:161, 1908, p.2.
28   *White Ribbon*, 20:234, 1914, p.12.

differentiating between unfermented and intoxicating wines in the Bible was waning, while the teaching of St Paul became increasingly central.[29] In fact, later literature still contested the alcohol content of wine in biblical times, though Pauline teaching did become prominent. The principle of the 'strong and the weak' in Romans 14 explicitly included a reference to wine, and became an important statement of the case for total abstinence.[30] Though broadly applicable, the principle seemed particularly apt for the problem of liquor.

Prohibitionists referred to Jesus in ways typical of social Christianity, especially at the level of principle. Thus, the ideals of brotherhood, care for the weak, self-control and self-denial that funded social reform all derived from him. The Rev. T.J. Wills accepted the Bible as the 'Word of God', but deplored its abuse in prohibition debates: 'We marvel at the undue prominence given to Bible references to wine in support of the drinking customs of Society, while the deep, broad principles of God's being and government are so often forgotten'. Temperance principles, including prohibition, were based upon 'the broad facts of Divine-Human relationships. God is our Father: all we are brethren-Brotherhood.... Christian duty is binding; the stumbling-block must be taken up out of the way, the weak brother's burden must be lifted – all this in fulfilment of the law of Christ'.[31]

This appeal to principles became axiomatic. The New Zealand Alliance was founded in 1886 and became the prohibition movement's leading organisation and mouthpiece. Its *No-License Handbook* admitted that Scripture sanctioned the use of intoxicating drink, especially 'by Christ's example, by the miracle at Cana, by the Lord's Supper, and by St. Paul's advice to Timothy'. The Bible, however, was to be understood as a 'unique record of man's progressive apprehension of God'. Jesus did not issue direct commandments, like those of the old Law, but laid down principles to be applied. He had emphasised the infinite value of the human soul. Opposition to the liquor trade was therefore consistent

29 Anthony R. Grigg, 'The Attack on the Citadels of Liquordom: A Study of the Prohibition Movement in New Zealand, 1894-1914', PhD thesis, University of Otago, 1977, p.75.

30 George Dash (ed.), *No-License Handbook*, Auckland: Louis P. Christie, for the New Zealand Alliance, 1908, p.58; also *Outlook*, 22 July 1899, p.4.

31 T.J. Wills, *The Church and the Liquor Traffic*, Christchurch: T.E. Fraser, 1894, pp.14, 18-19.

with 'the mind and spirit of Him who said: "If any man will come after Me, let him deny himself and take up his cross and follow Me." Self-sacrifice for the sake of others is the norm of Christian ethics'.[32]

Opponents' appeals to Jesus posed significant problems for the prohibition cause. Catholic support for temperance did not extend to prohibition, which was opposed for various practical and doctrinal reasons. These included sectarian, demographic and occupational factors, as well as concerns about sacramental wine.[33] Whereas many Protestant groups used unfermented wine at the communion service, the Catholic position on Mass was less adaptable. Catholics argued that the 'fermented juice of the grape' was necessary to faithful observance of the tradition inaugurated by 'the Lord Himself'. Concerned that prohibitionists would ultimately deny the use of wine for sacramental and medicinal purposes, Archbishop Redwood petitioned Catholic clergy to urge parishioners to oppose national prohibition.[34] Those Catholics who supported prohibition, like Bishop Cleary of Auckland, typically based their arguments on alcohol's detrimental social effects.

In 1911, the national election included a national licensing poll for the first time. With this forthcoming poll in view, Professor William Salmond launched a withering attack on the prohibition movement in a booklet entitled *Prohibition: A Blunder*.[35] As Professor of Mental and Moral Philosophy at the University of Otago, Salmond's opinions carried weight. His writing stimulated a spirited response, including replies by A.S. Adams and the Rev. A. Wood for the New Zealand Alliance. The arguments on each side of the debate were exemplary.[36]

Salmond's attack incorporated moral, philosophical and practical objections, but his appeals to Jesus carried the greatest rhetorical force.

---

32 Dash (ed.), p.58.
33 Greg Ryan, 'An Undertaking Worthy Only of Fanatics: Catholic Opinion on Temperance and Prohibition in New Zealand, c.1870-1910', *Australasian Journal of Irish Studies*, 10, 2010, pp.16-36.
34 *NZ Tablet*, 30 November 1911, p.2409; *NZ Tablet*, 7 December 1911, p.2479.
35 William Salmond, *Prohibition A Blunder*, 3rd ed., Dunedin: Jolly & Braik Printers, 1911.
36 A.S. Adams, *Professor Salmond's Blunder. Prohibition: An Effective Social Reform*, Wellington: New Zealand Alliance, 1911; A. Wood, *A Reply to 'Prohibition a Blunder', by a Presbyterian Minister*, Wellington: New Zealand Alliance, 1911; cf. J. Cocker and J. Malton Murray (eds), *Temperance and Prohibition in New Zealand*, London: Epworth Press, 1930, p.106.

Indeed, he directly challenged the prohibition movement's evangelical credentials, both in its biblical foundation and attitude to Jesus:

> Seeing that Prohibition is extensively preached in the name of Christ and of Christianity... and is used by so many who regard Christ's personal life as the pure moral ideal of conduct, I begin with this affirmation: *The thought and sentiment prevalent in the prohibition-camp in regard to wine and its use is at variance with that which pervades the Old and New Testament.*[37]

Salmond agreed that Christians should be guided by Jesus' example, but considered prohibitionists' appropriation of him ill-founded. Christ's attitude toward wine was consistent with the 'attitude of ordinary men in all generations until now'. If Jesus had appeared 'wearing the garb of a Prohibitionist, or harping on any dogma of sectarian morals, He would have frustrated His own mission. He counted wine among the good gifts of God, none the less so because men abuse it, nor the less so because it is the product of human skill applied to the raw products of nature'.[38]

Wood and Adams' responses emphasised the biblical underpinnings of prohibition, and its consistency with historic evangelical reforms. Opponents were cast as anti-progressive, anti-scientific and anti-evangelical. They were even accused of naïve biblical literalism.[39] Salmond's use of the generic term 'wine' in biblical references was criticised for obfuscating the nature of alcoholic drink in biblical and contemporary times. Adams argued that alcoholic drinks were not sanctioned in the Bible, while Wood claimed Timothy and Paul as biblical proponents of abstinence.[40]

It was also impossible to avoid discussion of Jesus, since he figured so prominently in Salmond's argument and appeals to him resonated strongly in the community. Adams and Wood accepted that Jesus probably drank wine, but particularised his actions to their historical context. Accentuating the gulf between the ancient world and modern society, Jesus was presented as a moderate drinker of weak beverages in a temperate culture. By contrast, modern drink had much higher alcohol content, and New Zealand was awash in the consequences of

37   Salmond, *Prohibition*, p.12 (original italics).
38   Salmond, *Prohibition*, p.14.
39   Wood, pp.10-11.
40   Adams, *Salmond's Blunder*, p.96; Wood, pp.8-9.

intemperance.[41] Historicising Jesus' actions left the question of how he might act in contemporary New Zealand open.

Specific events like Jesus' miracle at Cana remained problematic, since they suggested encouragement of drinking to excess. According to Adams, the assumption that the wine at Cana was alcoholic was a 'perversion of the text'.[42] Wood agreed. Moreover, he also rejected common assumptions concerning the quantity of drink involved: 'Christ gives to a young married couple 126 gallons of alcoholic beverages! The very suggestion that He did so is a desecration of religion'.[43] On the Lord's Supper, Adams argued that alcohol was not necessary since the word 'wine' was never used in the text, only the 'fruit of the vine'. Wood added that Christians should no more be slaves to principle on wine than with unleavened bread. The emblems were historically contingent: 'If our Saviour had appeared in the Arctic regions as man's Redeemer, he would have used the common articles of diet as memorials of His death, and these might have been dried fish and water'.[44]

With Jesus contained historically, appeals became a question of principles. Prohibition was faithful to Jesus insofar as it adhered to the 'law of Christ' to 'love thy neighbour'.[45] This approach cohered with the wider language of reform, but created certain difficulties. After all, the argument could be turned the other way. In 1919, the Baptist minister J.G. Hughes claimed that prohibition violated man's moral nature. Moreover, it contravened 'the great law of love and the golden rule' by denying alcoholic beverages to those who desired them:

> It is untrue and un-Christian to hold that because a man drinks at all therefore he cannot, like Christ, drink to the glory of God. Christ was a moderate drinker, but the bigots of his day dubbed Him a "wine-bibber," as though he drank to excess. By all means let us have Christian Temperance, but may we be delivered from the bigotry, fanaticism, and intolerance which masquerade under that name.[46]

The teaching and example of Jesus remained a sensitive point during the interwar years. Isabel McCorkindale, a former Education Director for the

---

41 Adams, *Salmond's Blunder*, pp.9-11, 96.
42 Adams, *Salmond's Blunder*, p.13.
43 Wood, p.9.
44 Adams, *Salmond's Blunder*, p.13; Wood, p.11.
45 Adams, *Salmond's Blunder*, pp.21-22.
46 *EP*, 6 December 1919, p.9.

WCTU in Australia and temporary assistant with the Youth Movement Against Alcoholism in New Zealand, indicated that Jesus' lack of teaching on alcohol troubled some young people in the 1920s. Her response was that Jesus' general teaching indicated his attitude, and the appropriate solutions for contemporary social problems:

> It has been asked why Christ said nothing about alcohol, about child labour, slavery, and other customs.... What Christ did say was "Love the Lord thy God with all thy heart and thy neighbour as thyself." If you follow this advice the problems will be solved soon enough. We should be actuated by His will and not by consideration of things he did not say.[47]

Interwar religious leaders continued to proclaim that the prohibition movement was evangelical, and a likely corollary of religious revival.[48] Appeals to Jesus' teaching and principles still occurred. By 1930, however, the prominence of philosophical, social and moral arguments in Cocker and Murray's history of prohibition was striking. Prohibitionists had always marshalled evidence of the social ills caused by alcohol and the successes of no-licence districts. Nevertheless, they appeared increasingly sensitive about claims like William Thomson's, that restriction of alcohol infringed individual liberty and undermined morality.[49] Significantly, A.R. Atkinson's justification of prohibition in Cocker and Murray's history was entitled 'The Logic of Prohibition'. It drew on social and philosophical arguments from John Locke and Edmund Burke rather than the usual vocabulary of social Christianity.[50]

Despite the authority attached to Jesus, prohibition exemplified the difficulties of using him to settle social questions. The declining popularity of the movement may have worked against religious argumentation. After failure in 1911, and again under more favourable conditions in 1919, the prohibition campaign lost momentum. In 1928, the vote for National Prohibition dropped to 294,453 (40.2%), which was less than the vote for National Continuance (374,502, or 51.1%) and well short of a simple majority.[51] From that time, the movement drew from an

---

47   *Freedom*, January-March 1929, p.12.
48   *NZMT*, 18 April 1931, p.8.
49   William Thomson, *Prohibition Fatal to Liberty, Temperance, and Morality*, Wellington: Whitcombe and Tombs, 1911.
50   Cocker and Murray (eds), pp.15-19.
51   *ENZ*, vol. 2, pp.874-75.

increasingly narrow base of support from within the churches. Declining religious argumentation may have reflected this weakened position, and a concomitant recognition that the public battle could not be waged effectively on an explicitly religious basis. Moreover, prohibitionists faced the difficulty that they could not enlist Jesus directly without fear of contradiction. His example was particularised historically, and biblical principles invoked instead. The language of principle alone, however, did not prove to be especially persuasive.

Labour, religion and socialism

Much Christian social analysis therefore focused on social issues that could be linked to moral failure. The rise of labour and working-class interests also encouraged more direct engagement with social and economic structures. Socialism provided the crucial overall ideology, but there was no single agreed expression of it and therefore no settled approach. 'Moderate' forms, like Fabian socialism, encouraged progressive amelioration of society. These were sometimes understood as kinds of 'ethical' socialism, and on that basis attracted support among social Christians of various stripes. Conversely, the militant industrial unionism of the Red Feds and Marxist approaches encouraged direct confrontation. These garnered little support from within the churches.

Striking similarities have often been noted between the structures of socialism and Christianity. Socialist discourse also regularly utilised religious language and ideals. Studies on its local dissemination have highlighted the quasi-religious language that permeated socialist language during the late nineteenth and early twentieth centuries. Nevertheless, the question of whether socialism represented a rejection of Christianity, an alternative to it, or simply a practical expression of religious commitment remained a point of debate.

From the 1890s, the idea of the 'religion of socialism' circulated widely, but even this term was multivalent. It could indicate rejection of Christianity for an alternative, or the Christian quality of socialist ideals. In 1911, the *Maoriland Worker* cited Dora B. Montefiore's claim that, 'In its essence Socialism is a religion, standing for the harmonious relating of the whole life of man'.[52] For a small group, the religion of socialism supplanted all alternatives. The 1911 national census included 107 individuals who nominated it as their religion.[53] Similarly, John A. Lee proclaimed after World War Two that the labour movement had been 'the great religious movement' of his lifetime. For W.S. McClure, socialism was a religion in the sense that it was a 'vision of the Kingdom of Heaven come to earth' that allowed workers to rise above the struggle for mere animal existence.[54]

Some advocates were adamant that socialism was materialistic and therefore not religious. According to 'Deucalion', in the *Maoriland Worker*, 'All Gods have been and are but phantasms of men's brains.... To say that Socialism is atheistic is to utter a truism'.[55] Others agreed, arguing that socialism and religion should be kept separate. Progress was 'a record of the slow retreat of God before the march of Man.... Socialism means scientific industry and public ownership – that's all'.[56] Materialism did not require active hostility, however, since this could create unnecessary offence and division. Some Marxian correspondents were prepared to encourage cultivation of all aspects of life, including religion, as complements to the socialist ideal – so long as the 'barnacles of supernatural ghosts' were scraped clear. F.D. Baucke of Westport objected to attacks on religion because they lacked basic courtesy.[57]

Ethical socialism and practical Christianity

Left-liberalism, Fabianism, and other 'moderate' expressions of socialism were among the most important influences in the early labour movement. Some of these, like Robert Blatchford's Clarion movement, were not at all sympathetic to religion. Interpreted as ethical socialism,

52 *MW*, 12 May 1911, p.14.
53 *Census*, 1911, p.103.
54 John A. Lee, *Rhetoric at the Red Dawn*, Auckland: Collins, 1965, p.8; *MW*, 5 May 1911, p.1.
55 *MW*, 27 June 1913, p.5.
56 *MW*, 12 May 1911, p.3.
57 *MW*, 24 February 1915, p.7; *MW*, 12 May 1911, p.3.

however, other expressions attracted social Christians' support. Notions of socialism as an ethical system built on assumptions about a correlation between religion and morality, but also the supremacy of Christ's moral example. By 1900, the idea that socialism was the practical expression of Christianity had become a virtual cliché. Invariably, such assertions emphasised Jesus' life and teaching, and ideals of brotherhood and cooperation. Arthur Desmond's early tract on the socialism of Jesus, for example, related him to notions of duty and social equality. Jesus came from the 'toiling masses', and remained a champion of the underdog. He was the 'defender of all those who in the world's unequal battle are weary or wounded or sore'. The historical Jesus was also apparently a democrat: 'That He preached the very essence of democracy there is not the shadow of a doubt.... His aim was both religious liberty and social equality'. The Christianity of Christ was an ethic of brotherhood and simple virtues like being 'unselfish, kind, brave and true'.[58]

Trades Council leaders were seldom extremists and often supported causes like compulsory arbitration. Like J.T. Paul, many were critical of the churches, but urged them to more practical expressions of Christian faith. In 1903, Paul chided fellow Christians for making a bogey of 'socialism' without considering its meaning. The churches diligently taught Jesus' commands to 'Love our neighbour' and 'Do unto others', but condemned themselves by 'so much preaching and so little action'. It was no longer acceptable to preach 'the brotherhood of man' while upholding a system that was 'the embodiment of a selfish individualism'.[59] Paul replied emphatically to complaints that he was turning Jesus into a unionist:

> It is not new to me to hear that Christ was not a unionist. We live in different times, and perhaps had Christ's teaching been followed or applied to industrial affairs trades unionism would not have been needed. Trades unionism is an effect. "Individual Christian" should know the cause. Christ was a Communist, and that is the opposite of an Individualist. Christ was an agitator.[60]

---

58 Desmond, pp.8-9, 13.
59 J.T. Paul, *The Duty of the Church to the Labour Movement*, Dunedin: Otago Trades and Labour Council, 1903, pp.2-3.
60 'The Working Man and the Churches', in Newspaper Clippings Book, 1903-1906, J.T. Paul Papers.

Paul was not a Marxist, and his Christ did not propose class warfare. He was primarily pressing for a cooperative ethic consistent with Jesus' teaching. His use of Jesus in this context placed the onus of explanation on his opponents.

Conceptualisations of socialism as Christian brotherhood were expressed in influential international sources. Edward Bellamy's novel *Looking Backward* had an enduring effect in New Zealand from the 1890s. Bellamy eschewed the term socialism, but supported socialistic principles. His utopian vision imagined religious change rather than abatement, and a new democratic society in which 'The only coin current is the image of God'. According to Mr Barton, a favoured preacher in the novel, nominal followers of Jesus had been slow to recognise the importance of human brotherhood but that situation had changed: 'The dawn has come since then. It is very easy to believe in the fatherhood of God in the twentieth century'.[61]

The leading British Labour politician Keir Hardie was another crucial influence in early New Zealand labour, and also promulgated the notion that socialism was Christianity at work. In one widely circulated pamphlet from 1908, Hardie denied that socialism was a religious creed, yet still related socialism's merits to the Sermon on the Mount and the socialist-proletarian leaning of 'the Carpenter of Nazareth'. Arguments like these established Hardie's reputation locally as a leading twentieth-century witness to Jesus' humanity.[62] They also demonstrated the style and tone of Hardie's socialism, which Densil Morgan has described as 'above else a moral code rather than an economic dogma'. Others have emphasised the important relationship between religious faith, socialism, and welfarism during the early twentieth century on the basis that the latter were conceptualised as essentially moral doctrines.[63]

61   Edward Bellamy, *Looking Backward from 2000 to 1887*, (electronic version), Champaign: Project Gutenberg; NetLibrary, (1888), pp.53, 115.

62   Keir Hardie and Rufus Weeks, *Christianity and Socialism: Two Views: The Miner's and the Millionaire's*, Wellington: New Zealand Times, 1908; cf. North, *'Me a Christian!!'*, p.13.

63   Densil D. Morgan, '"The Essence of Welshness"? Some Aspects of Christian Faith and Identity in Wales, c.1900-2000', in Robert Pope (ed.), *Religion and National Identity: Wales and Scotland c.1700-2000*, Cardiff: University of Wales Press, 2001, p.147; Mark Bevir, 'Welfarism, Socialism and Religion: On T.H. Green and Others', *The Review of Politics*, 55, 1993, pp.639-61.

Such associations enabled some religious commentators to embrace the language of socialism whilst rejecting its political tenets. One Protestant apologist, for example, claimed to have come to appreciate socialism as a consequence of his conversion, and that socialism was part and parcel of authentic Christian faith:

> I was standing meditating, looking straight ahead of me, when I saw a round white face about five yards from me.... There was a great love went through my whole being, and I knew I had seen Christ face to face: and in that few moments He showed me the whole world governed by His Spirit – and it was Socialism. I saw all the world in Socialism, and every person was in his right mind, and foolishness had vanished.... I changed from that moment as regards Socialism.[64]

True socialism, however, was distinguished from prevailing counterfeits. Genuine forms cultivated virtue and sympathy, for rich and poor alike. It also required conversion. Socialism was 'the true state of the affairs of the world being manifested to some by the Spirit of Christ'. In these terms, it was effectively stripped of political content.

Overall, advocates of the Christian ethical tradition greatly outnumbered secularists in the early New Zealand labour movement. Even the Labour Church movement that appeared to promote socialism as an alternative to Christianity was not especially hostile. According to Henry Pelling, the movement emerged in Britain during the 1890s in protest at a recently established link between nonconformity and the Liberal Party.[65] Notwithstanding the strong nonconformist influence within British labour, Pelling interprets the labour churches as a symptom of religious decline. The movement appeared in New Zealand when H.A. Atkinson founded the Christchurch Socialist Church in 1896.[66] Atkinson claimed that it was partially formed in order to recognise that 'in itself the effort for betterment inherent in the labour movement was religious'. Overtly religious language was limited, 'but the feeling was similar, that the movement was deeply and in a very real sense religious'. The church provided fellowship, based on brotherhood

64 Robert Luke, *The Definition of Socialism and Democracy*, Dunedin: The Budget, 1914, p.8.
65 Henry Pelling, *The Origins of the Labour Party, 1880-1900*, London: Macmiillan, 1954, pp.149-51.
66 Herbert Roth, 'The Labour Churches and New Zealand', *International Review of Social History*, 4, 1959, pp.361-66.

and equality, and the principle that 'only as we learn to lead purer and better lives can we benefit by any measure of Social Reform'.[67]

Like Pelling, Herbert Roth viewed the New Zealand movement as more of a propaganda organisation than a church. He noted that the organisation faded after the Socialist Party formed in Christchurch in 1904, and was resurrected only as a Fabian Society in 1908. This secularist interpretation has been challenged of late, particularly in Mark Bevir's claim that 'The origins of the Labour Church lay not in the decline of religion and the rise of class but in a shift in the content of religious belief.'[68] Notably, Bevir relates this shift to the rise of immanentist theology, with its emphasis on the doctrine of the Incarnation and the humanity of Jesus. The movement promoted socialism by rendering social life a religious matter and emphasising the divine presence within humanity as a whole.

Bevir's argument has relevance for the Christchurch situation where the membership included committed Christians. Albert Métin reported that Atkinson's 'church' was partly designed to appeal to workers who were both very religious and distrustful of socialism.[69] Prominent members like James McCombs were involved in the Church of England Men's Society (CEMS), while others like Jack McCullough had complex attitudes. Melanie Nolan has noted that McCullough was an atheist and held to a materialist conception of history. His upbringing was devout, however, and he maintained close relations with his family and other socialist Christians. Moreover, he followed Keir Hardie in claiming that his socialism was learnt in the New Testament. Christian socialism marked a phase in his development toward secular class-conscious activism, but continued to shape his thinking. His protests against materialist denigration of socialism's ethical basis were consistent with Christian socialist precepts: 'To preach exclusively the economic basis is to put it mildly shortsighted, and unity, the ideal of universal love and Brotherhood, will never be built up upon selfishness'.[70]

---

67 Socialist Church, *Monthly Leaflet*, 1, February 1897, p.1.
68 Mark Bevir, 'The Labour Church Movement, 1891-1900', *Journal of British Studies*, 38:2, 1999, p.219.
69 Albert Métin, *Socialism Without Doctrine*, Russel Ward (trans.), Sydney: Alternative Publishing Co-operative, 1977 (1901), p.54.
70 Melanie Nolan, *Kin: A Collective Biography of a Working-Class Family*, Christchurch: Canterbury University Press, 2005, p.104, quotation p.63.

Furthermore, the growth of the Fabian Society in Christchurch was not proof of the complete collapse of religious feeling within the local labour movement. Many socialist Christians viewed Fabianism as a political expression of Christian principles. While organised Christian Socialism was weak in New Zealand, it is notable that Christians within the Fabian Society were largely responsible for founding the Christchurch Church Socialist League (CSL) in 1913.[71] This branch was one of few groups to transplant from the late nineteenth-century Christian Socialist revival in Britain, and participated in national politics in a small way. There were occasional references to it in the *Maoriland Worker*, and the Rev. H.C. Money acted as the League's delegate at the Wellington Labour Conference of 1913.[72] Nevertheless, the New Zealand organisation remained small, and there is little evidence that the CSL influenced local interest in Guild Socialism which advanced similar positions. Prominent labour figures like Ted Howard also suspected the CSL was merely a Church of England propaganda organisation.[73]

Christian expressions of socialism were usually highly generalised. 'Christian socialism' often simply meant commitment to cooperation, social amelioration and the reduction of inequality, or 'humanising' of the social order. Churchill Julius claimed to find socialism 'in every page of the New Testament', but even he was decidedly vague on the social and economic implications.[74] Julius disavowed individualism, and correlated socialism with social cohesion. Nevertheless, even before the advent of industrialism, disapproval of conflict led him to oppose unions which he considered exclusive and un-harmonious. In this tradition, Christian socialism focused on moral and spiritual concerns more than the economic ones. Class analysis was not a significant factor.

Some self-professed Christian socialists were prominent in the wider labour movement. Among these, J.K. Archer, Moses Ayrton and Clyde Carr were drawn from the Baptist, Methodist and Congregationalist ministry respectively. Others like Walter Nash and William Jordan were

---

71   E.W. Plumridge, 'Labour in Christchurch: Community and Consciousness, 1914-1919', MA thesis, University of Canterbury, 1979, p.223.
72   E.W. Cunnington, *The Lectures and Letters of E.W. Cunnington*, edited by her children, Christchurch: Lyttelton Times, 1918, pp.138-39; *MW*, 1 August 1913, p.7.
73   *MW*, 26 April 1913, p.6.
74   Cited in Gertrude Elworthy and Anthony Elworthy, *A Power in the Land: Churchill Julius 1847-1938*, Christchurch: Whitcombe & Tombs, 1971, p.129.

prominent laymen. Margaret Thorn recalled that Nash's Christianity, and the early Christian tradition of communal ownership, informed his socialism, though she was deeply scornful of it: 'I couldn't go along with Jesus and the "grand old book, we must all get everybody reading".... I really wondered how anybody as intelligent as Walter Nash could wrap himself round in it'.[75] On the other hand, Jordan and Nash were hardly precise in explaining the relationship between Christianity and socialism. Nash was not keen on theology, and claimed to disavow dogmatism. The content of his belief was notoriously obscure, but his 'practical Christianity' clearly correlated ideals like truth, equality, justice and mercy with the 'Social Principles of Christ'.[76]

Jordan, a Methodist lay preacher and Labour MP, was similarly vague. Christian socialism was essentially a mood or attitude: 'Socialism as I see it is a certain state of mind of the people, a realisation of our interdependence and a determination to be of service to society'. Religious supports derived from general principles: 'Man is a social being and we cannot consider a way of life for an individual apart from our organised society; the biblical adage "No man liveth to himself" is undoubtedly correct'.[77] Jordan held more specific theological and political views than this, of course, but broad and uncontroversial principles suited public discourse. The morality of Jesus' teaching was largely accepted and hence provided an ideal reference. Nash, for example, doubted Christ's divinity but claimed that Christ's methods were 'infallible' if obeyed literally. Divinity lay in Christ's wisdom rather than his person.[78]

New Zealand Christian socialists drew on eclectic sources. Charles Gore and William Temple were especially known among Anglicans, while politicians like Jordan possessed controversial works such as *Christianity and the Social Order* by the British Congregationalist R.J. Campbell.[79] However closely he was actually read in New Zealand,

---

75   Thorn, *Stick Out*, p.62.
76   Keith Sinclair, *Walter Nash*, Auckland: Auckland University Press, 1976, p.65.
77   'A Way of Life', in Sir William Jordan Papers A-178, Box 4 Folder 3, University of Auckland Library. Copy supplied by Carina Hickey.
78   Cited in Sinclair, *Nash*, pp.18-19.
79   R.J. Campbell, *Christianity and the Social Order*, London: Chapman & Hall, 1907; cf. Carina Hickey, 'Man in His Time Plays Many Parts: Life Stories of William Jordan', MA thesis, Massey University, 2003, p.144; Fowlds, *Drift*, p.3.

Campbell provided theological support for socialism that could be cited as needed. Though aware that primitive Christianity and contemporary socialism were not identical, Campbell associated socialism with the Kingdom and offered startling endorsements of the British Labour Party. His Christology linked divinity and morality. As Robert Pope explains, 'It was in living the perfect life of service and self-denial that Jesus had reached the heights of human personality and had thus revealed the divine life in himself.... any human being could emulate Christ's efforts and achieve divinity, for the truly human was also the truly divine'.[80] This was immanentist theology in full flower. It harmonised with optimistic humanism and moderate 'ethical' socialism, and was indistinguishable from most other expressions of social Christianity.

The radical Christ and proletarian gospel

More radical representations of Jesus as a socialist and controversialist also circulated. These were evident in the *Maoriland Worker*, especially during periods of unrest, including industrial conflict and war. That he characteristically appeared at such times suggests that his primary functions were to disarm criticism and frustrate opposition. Jesus provided moral stature and respectability in the context of threat.

New Zealanders appropriated radical images from various international sources. Admittedly, the milder utopian reformism of Leo Tolstoy, with its strong emphasis on Jesus, was a more influential source locally – especially during the interwar years. Nevertheless, some Russian Marxists and revolutionaries also displayed considerable interest in Jesus, his disciples and gospel Christianity, and were cited in New Zealand. These noted similarities between socialism, communism and a progressive Christianity that they considered died early.[81] Ideas were

80 Robert Pope, *Seeking God's Kingdom: The Nonconformist Social Gospel in Wales, 1906-1939*, Cardiff: University of Wales Press, 1999, p.14.
81 See discussion of these ideas in Jay Bergman, 'The Image of Jesus in the Russian Revolutionary Movement: The Case of Russian Marxism', *International Review of Social History*, 35:2, 1990, pp.220-48.

also imbibed from American and Australian discourses of socialism. Notably, the IWW presented Jesus as a muscular critic of capitalism and organised religion, while Marian Quartly has highlighted that labour cartoonists in Australia regularly invoked Christ in the name of class.[82]

The proletarian Jesus was especially evident during the period when revolutionary socialism was most active. Revolutionary socialists associated religion with 'the establishment', so that anti-Church critique figured prominently. Thus, Jesus' command to love God and neighbour was construed as 'Socialism, and nothing but Socialism... brotherhood, and nothing but brotherhood', but contrasted with the failures and self-absorption of the churches.[83] Some attempts to enlist Jesus were more light-hearted. The *Maoriland Worker* playfully used Reginald Heber's hymn to suggest a long history for the red flag as the emblem of internationalism:

> The Son of God goes forth to war,
> A kingly crown to gain;
> His BLOOD-RED BANNER streams afar;
> Who follows in his train?

The 'Carpenter of Nazareth' had apparently used the symbol for at least twenty years.[84] Ironic images like these teased alarmed Christians who viewed militant socialism as the only form.

In any case, radical images of Jesus utilised favoured themes. In particular, the crucifixion was emptied of doctrinal significance to become a symbol of suffering and struggle. Notions of righteous persecution, crucifixion and redemptive martyrdom all featured in labour rhetoric, and furnished a universal metaphor for socialism. Martyr language provided an important rallying point. In 1911, the *Maoriland Worker* claimed that 'the torch of capitalism has kindled the martyr fire', and that modern 'wage slaves' were only the most recent victims of tyrannical capitalist 'oppressors'.[85] Prior to 1913, however, martyr

---

82   Winters, pp.61-81; Marian Quartly, 'Making Working-Class Heroes: Labor Cartoonists and the Australian Worker, 1903-16', *Labour History*, 89, 2005, pp.167, 171-72.

83   See *MW*, 7 September 1921, p.6; cf. Harold Begbie, *Religion and the Crisis*, London: Cassell & Company, 1913.

84   *MW*, 5 May 1911, p.15.

85   *MW*, 20 April 1911, p.13.

language lacked any distinctive local feeling. The death of Fred Evans at Waihi changed this. H.E. Holland and R.S. Ross' account of the Waihi strike explicitly applied the redemptive lessons of Jesus' death to Evans in the book's concluding sections:

> The sun may go down in blood on what seems to us a lost cause – just as it is alleged to have gone down in darkness on a day 2000 years ago when the ruling-class prevailed and the foremost figure in what was then undoubtedly a movement of the working-class was nailed to a cross and done to death after the manner of the worst criminal.

Black night and blood-red sunset would soon give way to dawn and the 'radiant sun of working-class victory'.[86]

Jesus appeared frequently in the *Maoriland Worker* in the wake of widespread industrial conflict in 1913, often as the archetypal victim of brutal state authority. One recurring motif placed Jesus at the mercy of the justice system. In August 1913, a cover image placed him dolefully standing before a judge in court, where he embodied an imbalance in power between 'the authorities' and 'the people'. Jesus' harmlessness contrasted with the severity of the court, while an accompanying caption questioned, 'What chance would he have in a Court to-day?' Apparently the image struck a chord, for it was reprinted 'by request' the following February.[87] A similar cartoon by Ryan Walker from 1914 placed Jesus, a poor man, in a court representing the capitalist system. The judge was portrayed as a puppet of capitalism, presiding behind a bench emblazoned with the symbol of the pound.[88]

Themes of victimisation and corrupt authority were also played up. Writing as 'the Vag', Ted Howard cited the American Congregationalist and radical social Christian George D. Herron in contrasting the 'applied Christianity' of strikers on the waterside and at Waihi with the powers that be. Like Christ, they had forfeited work and 'sacrificed themselves' in sympathy with their brother-workers. They too were victims of unsympathetic, authoritarian state power: 'Jesus, the God of Love, the Carpenter, was crucified by the "best people" of His day, is hid away,

---

86 H.E. Holland and R.S. Ross, *The Tragic Story of the Waihi Strike*, Wellington: Printed by The Worker, 1913, p.193.
87 *MW*, 29 August 1913, p.1; *MW*, 18 February 1914, p.7.
88 *MW*, 8 July 1914, p.1.

and we have got instead the Deified Policeman with a stopwatch and measuring tape and hardwood baton in his hand'.[89]

Jesus was not merely a victim, however. He was also a resister. During the conflicts of 1913, some Christian ministers allegedly offered to act as strike-breakers. In response, the *Maoriland Worker* invoked Jesus in support of the labour position, asking, 'If Christ were upon earth at the present time, and an industrial upheaval took place, would he scab?' Apparently not. The Carpenter of Nazareth was a 'Friend of the poor and the outcast', and actively supported them: 'Stripped of mysticism, with all controversial aspects of Christ's life for the moment placed on one side, it is abundantly clear to any student that the Gospel Hero was a man who fought for the oppressed against the oppressor'.[90] A working-class hero, Jesus represented the strength of the people. His communitarian movement had traced poverty to its root, the evil of property, and appropriation by 'an idle and a privileged class' of the fruit of other men's labour.[91]

During periods of turmoil, the socialist Jesus appeared as a Judean agitator, and leader of a hobo army.[92] Yet, even as the Great Agitator, the threatening possibilities of the image were largely restrained. Jesus' radicalism was romanticised, and framed as a message of love. He was 'a dreamer of dreams a friend of the lowly, a lover of little children.... He taught that love, and not brute force, was God's great fundamental. He would not set up – as His peasant followers hoped – a kingdom founded on the sword'.[93] The 'rescued and real' proletarian teaching of Jesus provided strength and inspiration for the working class. It promised inevitable victory, and called for love, strength and sacrifice on the path to revolution – even if that revolution was essentially peaceful. It was neither destructive, nor hateful, but merely sought the conditions for true religion to flourish: 'The proletariat does not wish to destroy religion, but to give it real life'.[94]

89   *MW*, 15 April 1914, p.1.
90   *MW*, 26 September 1913, p.7.
91   *MW*, 11 July 1913, p.3.
92   *MW*, 20 May 1914, p.7.
93   *MW*, 5 May 1915, p.1.
94   *MW*, 9 June 1911, p.14.

Jesus was therefore an 'irreducible rebel', but also a 'gospel-bringer of justice'.[95] He exhibited creative genius and force of personality, but confrontation was softened by good character. As an apologetic for labour, the argument highlighted a dilemma. While rhetoric was often combative, the local movement was not strong enough for unqualified self-assertion. Traditions of righteous rebellion were employed largely as a defensive strategy in which Jesus was invoked to placate critics and win the equivocal. Opponents might balk at confrontation, but could hardly quibble with virtue.

Opposition to war and militarism provided another context for images of a radical Jesus. Passion imagery featured prominently in anti-war literature. The title of Harry Holland's study of pacifist opposition to World War One, *Armageddon or Calvary*, starkly posed the alternatives he believed young men faced.[96] This imagery had been popularised before the war in association with Government prosecution of pacifist objectors during 1913 and 1914. According to R.L. Weitzel, Friday became known in Christchurch as 'Crucifixion Day', because it was the day the courts dealt with cases involving breaches of the Defence Act.[97] Objectors to World War One were drawn in largest numbers from those opposed on socialist and Christian principles. Jesus bridged these constituencies. Some Christian opponents remarked that it was hard to imagine Jesus leading a bayonet charge, while the *Maoriland Worker* employed Christian imagery to express disapproval of the war.[98] Each contrasted Christ's gospel of peace with war's destruction.

Even before the war, Jesus had been invoked to oppose Christian militarism.[99] Criticisms were particularly pronounced at Christmas time. In 1913, one cover cartoon of cavalrymen carried the ironic caption 'Peace on Earth and Goodwill'. The same issue carried a half page review of work by the American socialist historian C. Stewart Barnes under the title 'Was Jesus a Revolutionary?' Inside, a translation from a German discussion of 'The Redeemer' claimed that Christian

95   *MW*, 11 July 1913, p.3.
96   H.E. Holland, *Armageddon or Calvary: The Conscientious Objectors of New Zealand and 'The Process of their Conversion'*, Wellington: H.E. Holland, 1919.
97   R.L. Weitzel, 'Pacifists and Anti-Militarists in New Zealand, 1909-1914', *NZJH*, 7:2, 1973, p.147.
98   *NZMT*, 8 July 1916, p.12.
99   *MW*, 11 July 1913, p.3.

redemption was initially materialist, and criticised bourgeois celebrations of 'the Redeemer of the poor' with their 'hypocritical fetes', 'insincere prayers', and 'sounding bells'.[100]

The Christmas message of peace became a particularly potent symbol during wartime. Nativity scenes were juxtaposed with the 'Hell going out from Bethlehem in the present day'.[101] Christian anti-militarists presented their message as the application of Christ's teaching. They were supported for this in the socialist press, which also berated the churches for betraying Jesus' teaching and rejecting the Christ of peace.[102] Jesus was also used simply to highlight the discrepancy between war and moral idealism. In September 1914, a cartoon credited to the *Australian Worker* placed Jesus beneath explosion clouds of 'war', with the commentary:

> Nineteen hundred years ago and Bethlehem, Gethsemane, Calvary. Heaven's message: Love, Peace, Brotherhood, Fatherhood. Is it all a dream? Is the Cross a failure? Can it be that the message has miscarried?... Oh, the tragedy of it! Oh, the blasphemy of it![103]

Interwar peace activism continued this tradition, and also often invoked Jesus at Christmas or moments of particular pressure. In December 1921, the *Maoriland Worker* published Catherine Markham's poem 'The Sorrowful Christ', in which 'The Man of Peace' appeared and witnessed the human devastation wrought by war. Suffering, injury and death were the folly of braggarts, lordlings and statesmen, against which Jesus responded as an outraged mother. In the same issue as Markham's poem, the recently appointed editor James Thorn invited contributions from J.K. Archer, Moses Ayrton and James Gibb on the grounds that many of the paper's most loyal supporters were Christian believers.[104] Each emphasised the compatibility of Christianity and labour, and called for closer relations. Thorn's decision to open space for religious com-mentary created a ruckus, but indicated a desire for rapprochement with

100 *MW*, 24 December 1913, pp.1, 6.
101 *MW*, 22 December 1915, p.5.
102 *MW*, 19 December 1917, p.1; *MW*, 12 August 1914, p.1; *MW*, 22 December 1915, p.4.
103 *MW*, 2 September 1914, p.1; also, *MW*, 22 December 1915, p.10.
104 *MW*, 14 December 1921, p.11.

religious supporters at a time of pressure for the labour movement. Divided internally, and under pressure from the Government, Thorn was adopting a moderate approach in an effort to stabilise the movement and broaden electoral support.[105] Correspondents recognised these electoral factors, with one complaining that 'Churchism' was infantile science but that 'votes are votes'.[106]

A tendency to cast labour leaders as Christ-figures formed another characteristic of interwar imagery. Patrick O'Farrell has noted that Harry Holland became estranged from organised religion after a breach with the Salvation Army in 1892, but retained a religious attitude and an abiding affection for Jesus. Both tendencies were apparent during his editorship of the *Maoriland Worker* between 1913 and 1918. Therefore, when he finally died in 1933, Eileen Duggan's association of Holland with Christ seemed strangely apt.[107] More strikingly, Holland's successor as leader of the NZLP, the first Labour Prime Minister Michael Joseph Savage, was similarly hailed when he died in office just after Easter in 1940. In a column in the *New Zealand Tablet*, Duggan once more compared his life and death with that of Jesus:

> Just before the last election he rode in state from his train to the Parliamentary Buildings, followed by a huge retinue. And who were in that procession behind his car? Artisans, toilers, wharf-labourers in their working clothes, as they left the saw, the ship, the anvil! The kind of crowd that would have followed the Man on the ass going into Jerusalem. He passed at the very season when the greatest Idealist of all died, on a gibbet.[108]

This kind of imagery could be applied variously. At the same time, and perhaps in response to such associations, John A. Lee interpreted his expulsion from the NZLP in similar terms.[109]

Appeals to a socialist Jesus and typological application of Christ's Passion served a variety of purposes. Association with Jesus and

---

105 See Bruce Brown, *The Rise of New Zealand Labour: A History of the New Zealand Labour Party from 1916 to 1940*, Wellington: Price Milburn, 1962, pp.46-48.

106 See the various letters in *MW*, 1 February 1922.

107 P.J. O'Farrell, *Harry Holland: Militant Socialist*, Canberra: ANU, 1964, pp.6, 85, 95; Eileen Duggan, 'A Leader Passes', *New Zealand Worker*, 8 November 1933.

108 Eileen Duggan, 'Requiescat', *NZ Tablet*, 3 April 1940, p.8.

109 See John A. Lee, *Expelled from the Labour Party for Telling the Truth*, Auckland: Grey Lynn Democratic Labour Party, 1940.

religious moral foundations was partly intended to boost credibility, indicating that the labour movement operated within a cultural flow in which religious symbols were deeply embedded. Even where the religious framework was used ironically to mock religion, underlying respect for Jesus persisted. His story provided an interpretive structure for experience. That the radical Jesus appeared so often during points of conflict and pressure indicated his role as a symbol of hope. Jesus validated the cause. To some extent he was also unthreatening and respectable. He provided a rebuke to the establishment, but was more often invoked against actual class conflict.

Religious opposition to socialism

Religious attitudes to socialism included voices of sharp disapproval. Evangelicals, for example, typically interpreted socialism in relation to politically revolutionary ideas, which were in turn perceived as virtually synonymous with an unconverted soul. Thus, the Methodist home missionary Herman Foston's novel, *In the Bell-Bird's Lair*, associated socialism with youthful naïveté and immorality. Conversion was marked by a desire to walk in the footsteps of the 'Man of Galilee', and led to repudiation of socialism, atheism and liquor. The true religion of Jesus was an alternative to unwholesome socialist enthusiasms.[110]

The most persistent public religious criticism of socialism, however, derived from Catholic leaders. Papal teaching provided the crucial framework. From the nineteenth century, successive popes had denounced socialism's anti-religious aspects, notably in Pius IX's *Syllabus Errorum* (1864) and Leo XIII's *Rerum Novarum* (1891). Guided by these warnings, Archbishop Francis Redwood became the most influential and outspoken local Catholic critic, attacking socialism in a series of pastoral addresses. In 1892, he cited Leo XIII's claim that socialist agitation was 'One of the greatest and most formidable dangers

---

110 Herman Foston, *In the Bell-Bird's Lair, or 'In Touch with Nature'*, Wellington: Gordon & Gotch, 1911, pp.63-64.

of Society at the present day'.[111] According to Redwood, radical contemporary socialism sounded attractive, but required the total overthrow of society. In particular, it threatened property, family and religion, the threefold foundation of the social structure.

Redwood repudiated the materialist basis of socialism, and its denial of the doctrine of Original Sin. He also appeared troubled by socialist references to Jesus in support of their cause, and challenged the 'impious audacity' of comparing the 'destruction of Society' with Christ:

> But Jesus Christ assailed nothing by violence, and destroyed nothing by force. He sowed truth in minds and hearts as the husbandman scatters seed on the furrowed soil. No doubt He spoke severely to the rich, or rather to the abuse of riches, to riches devoid of compassion, fellow-feeling, or affection; but He never stirred up the poor against the rich, while He set charity between them as a meek and powerful mediatrix.[112]

Redwood's reflections on Jesus were shaped by disapproval of socialist appropriation. Jesus was neither agitator nor revolutionary, but sought social harmony and amelioration; 'His divine work was a creation, not a destruction'. Jesus was an alternative to socialism, and correlated with the benefits of Catholicism and Christian civilisation. In this sense, the mystical Christ was crucial. Thus, in blaming secularisation for impending socialist catastrophe, Redwood argued that previous Christian generations found a 'common centre of love in the heart of Jesus Christ.... The love of Christ, or Christian charity, expelled that hatred and envy which is now a menace to social order'.[113] Later pastorals took up similar themes. In 1906, Redwood discounted differences between so-called Scientific and Moderate Socialism, judging that all forms were in 'open antagonism with the Catholic Church and true Christianity'. Only the Church that Jesus founded could solve the great social problem: 'She can change the present state of things by changing the hearts and minds of men, by bringing back society to the feet of the Restorer of mankind, Jesus Christ, the Incarnate Son of God'.[114]

111 Francis Redwood, *Lenten Pastoral on Socialism*, Wellington: Catholic Times, 1892, p.1, which refers to *Rerum Novarum*, but quotes *On Freemasonry in Italy*.
112 Redwood, 1892, p.2.
113 Redwood, 1892, p.3.
114 Francis Redwood, *Pastoral Letter on Socialism*, Dunedin: Tablet Reprint, 1906, pp.11-13, 15.

By 1912, growing industrial unrest, labour militancy, and Catholic workers' participation in it provoked another caution. Redwood reiterated that socialism would destroy society's foundations, including 'Church Authority'.[115] His pastoral sparked a riposte from Edward R. Hartley, an organiser and lecturer for the New Zealand Socialist Party.[116] Once described as a 'rabid critic of religion', Hartley assailed impotent 'Christian civilisation' for its failures: 'Socialism would make class hatred an impossible thing. Christianity has failed to do so!' Notably, he appealed to Jesus in condemning support for the prevailing system: 'By what part of the teachings of Christ can such robbery of your fellows as the foregoing be justified? It would be difficult to imagine the Christ of Nazareth a shareholder under conditions like these. It is equally difficult for anyone who professes to be his follower'. Hartley's attacks provoked extensive debate, and criticism. J. Bowater, a 'Christian Socialist' from Westport, chastised him for doing more harm than good.[117] In reply, Hartley reiterated that Christianity should mean 'living according to the life and teachings of Christ', something impossible under present social conditions. Moreover, he claimed, disingenuously, that he was merely attacking 'Churchianity', not true Christianity.[118]

Other early Catholic responses followed Redwood in emphasising the role of the Church. In 1908, Frederick Maples provided a sophisticated account of varieties of socialism, ranging from Marxist collectivism to milder theories of land nationalisation and state socialism. Maples contended, against them all, that inequality could be rationalised on industrial, intellectual, political and religious grounds. Christians should seek fair treatment for the poor, but inequality created the environment for practice of virtue, which was the 'immediate end of man'. The argument was based in Natural Law, but perfected by Christianity.[119] Maples' ultimate argument was really that Protestant individualism had destroyed a golden age of Catholicism, and the natural

---

115 Francis Redwood, *Pastoral on Socialism*, Dunedin: NZ Tablet Print, 1912, p.5.
116 See *MW*, 8 March 1912, p.7; *MW*, 15 March 1912, p.7; *MW*, 22 March 1912, p.7; reprinted as Edward R. Hartley, *A Catholic Pastoral on Socialism. An Open Letter to Archbishop Redwood*, Wellington: Maoriland Worker, 1912.
117 *MW*, 26 April 1912, p.5.
118 *MW*, 26 April 1912, p.5; cf. 'Organiser's Notes', *MW*, 29 March 1912.
119 Frederick G. Maples, *Socialism from a Catholic Point of View*, Petone: Hutt and Petone Chronicle Office, 1908, pp.13-16.

'Christian Socialism' of church life after Pentecost. History demonstrated that Catholicism met socialist aspirations: 'Liberty! Equality! Fraternity! They are grand and noble names, rightly interpreted; they have ever been the watchwords of the Catholic Church, and the text of her preaching'.

To some extent, Joseph the Carpenter fulfilled the role that Jesus the Worker did for Protestants, and significantly, devotion to St Joseph the Worker expanded considerably during the nineteenth century. Jesus did become more evident, however, especially in Catholic anti-socialist argumentation. At the height of the conflict between Hartley and Redwood, and in light of the increasingly anti-Christian sentiments of leading international socialists like Robert Blatchford, the editor of the *New Zealand Tablet* J.A. Scott sought to provide 'Catholic working men' with answers for their 'Socialist fellows'. In particular, he highlighted Catholicism's historical sympathy for the victims of social ills, citing Leo XIII and the German bishops as exemplars of Jesus' spirit and teaching: 'The Church, like her Divine Founder, "has compassion on the multitude." She loves her working man, and to-day, as ever, shows herself as the Good Samaritan to the wounded humanity'.[120]

In this combative context, Jesus was used to counter labour rhetoric and present Catholicism as the golden mean between the extremes of socialism and unrestrained capitalism. In 1920, the *Tablet* argued:

We are told from all sides that the revolution is coming quickly.... On Catholics, as followers of the Worker of Nazareth, lies the obligation of striving for the reform of social abuses. All the virtues that Socialism claims are the virtues of pure Christianity.... Our Lord set the world the highest example of tender regard for the poor and the unfortunate. In His own life He proved that the condition of the laborer is the true nobility, and He taught us to despise luxury and useless wealth. His voice is still as strong in condemnation of those who oppress His poor as it was when He walked by the Lake of Galilee.... Between the limits of Capitalism and Socialism the middle way is marked out by the law of Christ.[121]

Even some of Redwood's post-war pronouncements gave more prominence to Christ. Thus, he claimed, 'our present-day struggles... are very largely due to apostasy from God, and revolt against Christ and His

120 J.A. Scott, *The Church and Socialism*, Melbourne: The Australian Catholic Truth Society, 1912, p.29.
121 *NZ Tablet*, 6 May 1920, p.26.

138

Christianity…. Our alternative must be either "Back to Christ" or "On to Socialism."'[122] Communism emerged as a distinct foe in the wake of the Bolshevik Revolution in Russia, and continued to be a focus of criticism throughout the interwar years. In 1933, Redwood attacked communism as a new form of paganism. Reiterating the principles of Leo XIII's 'Worker's Charter', he argued that 'the only solution of the social question lies in a return to the principles laid down in the teaching of Christ'. Specific teachings were seldom identified, except that resistance to state supremacy followed the principle of 'rendering to God'.[123]

Catholic attitudes to socialism did soften in some respects. An improving relationship with the NZLP after 1916 was one important factor. A strong Irish and working-class base in New Zealand Catholicism contributed to support for the NZLP. This increased after the party began courting the Irish vote in the wake of the Easter Rising of 1916 in Ireland.[124] Other changes helped. Perceptions of the NZLP as a bastion of communism began to diminish after a New Zealand Communist Party formed in 1921. Labour also increasingly abandoned formal socialist positions from the mid-1920s. Moreover, Catholics increasingly differentiated between definitions of socialism based on the abolition of private property and milder expressions.

The latter development made Catholic social teaching appear compatible with the increasingly moderate socialism expressed in Labour Party objectives.[125] In 1931, Pius XI rejected 'Christian socialism' as a contradiction in terms, claiming that 'no one can be at the same time a good Catholic and a true socialist'.[126] His alternatives to socialism and capitalism, however, were sympathetic to labour. *Quadragesimo Anno* criticised exploitation of workers, and the failure to practice justice and charity by assisting 'brothers in need as Christ the

122 *NZ Tablet*, 26 August 1925, p.27.
123 Francis Redwood, *Lenten Pastoral Letter*, Wellington: Tolan Print, 1933; cf. *Month*, 1 March 1933, p.27.
124 Barry Gustafson, *Labour's Path to Political Independence: The Origins and Establishment of the New Zealand Labour Party 1900-19*, Auckland: Auckland University Press, 1980, p.125; Richard P. Davis, *Irish Issues in New Zealand Politics 1868-1922*, Dunedin: University of Otago Press, 1974, p.190.
125 Christopher van der Krogt, 'A Catholic-Labour Alliance? The Catholic Press and the New Zealand Labour Party 1916-1939', *Australian Catholic Record*, 78:1, 2000, pp.16-29.
126 *Quadragesimo Anno*, 1931, n.120.

Lord Himself'. The encyclical called for a 'full restoration of human society in Christ'. These themes were taken up locally, especially in the social study clubs formed later in the 1930s. Commending these, Father L. Brice of Wellington argued that much of the Labour Government's social legislation accorded with Christianity. Socialism was radically opposed to the teachings of Christ, but watered-down application of socialist principles was not.[127]

The Interwar Social Gospel

Social problems and social order continued to concern the Protestant churches during the interwar years. Conservative social Christianity persisted, though Jesus became an important touchstone in moderating expectations around causes like Sabbath observance.[128] In general, however, social Christianity became increasingly associated with liberal theology and left-wing political causes. Ronald White and Howard Hopkins have noted a distinction between evangelical liberalism and modernist liberalism within the American social gospel movement. The former, they claim, was thoroughly Christocentric: Jesus was the knowledge and saving power of God; the climax of revelation was found in Jesus; the moral and religious fruit in believers' lives validated claims about him. Modernist liberalism was less Christocentric: Jesus illustrated universally relevant truths, but was not the source of religious norms.[129] Interwar social gospel ideas in New Zealand tended more toward the former in being reformist but not theologically Modernist. The place of Jesus within interwar social gospel thinking highlighted how strongly evangelicalism had shaped New Zealand Protestant Christianity.

In the aftermath of the disruptions of industrial unrest and war, Christian social commentators often argued that application of Jesus' teaching was the only alternative to complete social turmoil. As the

127 *NZ Tablet*, 7 July 1937, p.8.
128 28 October 1930, Minute Book (11.11.25 – 24.3.32), Public Questions Committee, PCNZ/GA 21: Location AE 6/3, PCANZARC.
129 White and Hopkins, pp.246-49.

Methodist Annual Conference of 1921 noted, 'In this hour of crisis the only alternatives before the world are CHRIST and chaos'.[130] Crucially, such observations were often accompanied by comment on the severe pressure churches were experiencing. In many ways, the social Christ and emphasis on Jesus' social principles reflected anxieties about social order, and a potential waning of Christian influence.

Despite this, references often sounded optimistic, almost triumphal, in touting Jesus as the remedy for social problems. As the Methodist Social Creed of 1922 declared:

> in the message and mission of the Gospel of our Lord Jesus Christ – a message of goodwill and of brotherhood – will be found the only power for promoting effectively the reconstruction and regeneration of society. Hence we seek to secure the recognition of the Golden Rule and of the Mind of Christ, as the supreme law of society and the sure remedy for all social ills.[131]

Presbyterian statements exhibited a similar tone. In 1922, a report to General Assembly affirmed the centrality of the 'Gospel of the redeeming love of God' and the 'Message of the Kingdom'. Amidst social unrest, this gospel was 'the world panacea'.[132] Commentators observed threats, but also an opportunity. The Spirit of Jesus was confronting churches with the challenge of the Kingdom of God. Fresh application of eternal principles would settle the prevailing confusion: 'In the social realm the challenge of Jesus means the fearless acceptance and application of truth, justice, and service.... It is Christ or discord'.[133]

The social gospel arguably became associated with Methodism more than any other denomination. Methodists had a long tradition of social activism. However, concern about changed social circumstances and falling church membership encouraged a shift away from earlier more conservative approaches. Mass evangelism was re-evaluated and social gospel ideas strengthened; the Social Creed was adopted, while ministry training increasingly emphasised the 'actualities of human life and experience, broadened by instruction in modern literature, philosophical

---

130 *MAC*, 1921, p.49.
131 *MAC*, 1922, p.76.
132 *PGA*, 1922, p.179.
133 *Outlook*, 21 March 1927, pp.13-14.

thought, and economic theory'.[134] Jesus and the Kingdom became focal points in hopeful projections of the denomination's future. As one commentator noted, 'There is much active and articulate hostility to religion.... A little less insistence upon the dark side of things, and how much it might mean for courage and confidence and the Kingdom of God!'[135] Observations of this kind were often a précis to calls for greater dedication and more strenuous exertions by church members. M.A. Rugby Pratt argued, for example, that: 'Jesus never sought to dazzle men with glowing visions of life in a happy land "far, far away". He directed their gaze to the Kingdom of God on earth. In that thought Jesus embodied and expressed His social ideal'. Bringing in the Kingdom required devotion, but would be repaid because the world's welfare was 'wrapped up in the religion of Jesus'.[136]

Kingdom language was often associated with social gospel figures like Walter Rauschenbusch, though there is little evidence that New Zealanders actually read him much. Another liberal, Harry Emerson Fosdick, was sufficiently influential that he provoked P.B. Fraser's ire.[137] Less often noted, though at least if not more important, were the interpretations of Toyohiko Kagawa. A Japanese Christian, Kagawa became admired in New Zealand from the late 1920s, though interest waxed greatly during a tour in 1936. Kagawa was associated with the Kingdom of God Movement and revered for his practical social commitment. He was once described an 'Asian idealist and social reformer... and one of the few living men... who take – and live – the Sermon on the Mount literally'.[138] Kagawa's blend of conversionism and social action was particularly appreciated. Martin Sullivan later reflected that Kagawa's visit influenced many of his contemporaries, especially on account of his emphasis on ministry to both body and soul.[139]

New Zealanders were impressed by Kagawa's authentic faith, and delighted that his Christianity was 'modelled upon that of Christ rather

134 Susan J. Thompson, 'Knowledge and Vital Piety: Methodist Ministry Education in New Zealand from the 1840s to 1988', PhD thesis, University of Auckland, 2002, pp.76-77.
135 NZMT, 29 March 1924, p.12.
136 NZMT, 19 January 1924, p.8.
137 Biblical Recorder, August 1931, p.226.
138 NZMBC Link, 5 August 1929, p.4.
139 Martin Sullivan, Watch How You Go, London: Hodder and Stoughton, 1975, p.70.

than from any Western replica'. His vocabulary also resonated. Kagawa claimed to be socially radical 'because Christ my Saviour was very radical'.[140] He criticised Christian traditionalism that ignored the spirit of the New Testament, and was praised for humanising 'modern industrial, capitalistic society'.[141] There were also conspicuously evangelical emphases. In accounting for 'The Motive of the Kingdom of God Movement', Kagawa explained that Christ was the centre of the movement, and the cross the centre of Christ:

> The cross is the motive of the Kingdom of God Movement. The motive is that Christ died for us. We are unworthy of that precious fact. Pursued by that love, we cannot but become heirs of Christ's blood and death.... The Christ depicted by Paul is a Christ Who has paid the debts of the whole human race as if they were His own. And this sort of thing is necessary to genuine social organisation. The Kingdom of God does not actually get established anywhere without the working of this cross-principle. Christ says, "If any man would come after Me, let him deny himself and take up his cross and follow Me." [142]

Part of Kagawa's appeal, then, lay in the combination of social activism and evangelical faith. Jesus was exemplary, but also the source of regenerative life.

The social gospel, liberalism and the left

Kingdom language remained attractive partly because it offered broad and deliberately generalised principles. It connoted an ideal Christian society, and was applied formulaically to all kinds of issues. In 1925, even the report of the Presbyterian General Assembly Committee on Dancing concluded by affirming that 'the only solution of modern social problems lies in the positive preaching of the Gospel of the Kingdom'.[143]

---

140 *NZMT*, 27 June 1931, p.2; *NZMT*, 10 June 1933, p.2.
141 *NZMBC Link*, 5 October 1929, p.6.
142 *NZMT*, 22 August 1931, p.8.
143 *PGA*, 1925, in Dennis McEldowney (ed.), *Presbyterians in Aotearoa, 1840-1990*, Wellington: The Presbyterian Church of New Zealand, 1990, p.96.

Like their British counterparts, New Zealand evangelicals were interested in social issues, but became increasingly uncomfortable with the collectivist and theologically liberal connotations of social gospel Christianity. Isaac Jolly, for example, was adamant that Christianity was individual, and that Jesus' teaching about the Kingdom was intended to have a purely personal application.[144] As divisions between conservative and Modernist Christians sharpened in the late 1920s, conservatives reacted against exaltation of Jesus' humanity. At the height of the Great Depression, Bower Black contended as a 'plain matter of experience' that it was:

> not so much the Jesus of Galilee who binds up the broken in heart but the Christ of the Cross. It is not the Sermon on the Mount that brings healing to your soul, but the Sacrifice on the Hill. It is at the Cross of the world's Saviour that life's deepest needs can be met, and the wounds of the broken hearted find healing for evermore.[145]

The emphasis on Jesus in social gospel thinking became increasingly identified with the politics of the left. Percy Paris was one of the most influential Methodist figures of the interwar years, and a leading advocate of the social gospel. In 1924, he became editor of the *New Zealand Methodist Times*. Significantly, the lead article in the first issue of his editorship was simply headed 'Jesus':

> Jesus – this is the first word which we, the new Editorial Staff, write as we take on the task assigned to us by the recent Conference. Its place at the beginning of these notes is symbolical... We shall always put Jesus Christ first.... It is His Spirit, we trust, that shall be the inspiration of all our effort. It is for His greater glory that we shall write. On all sides to-day evidence is piling up that Jesus is the only hope of this world: Jesus Christ and Him crucified. There is no alternative.[146]

At this stage, Paris' agenda was relatively conventional, and addressed discontent with the social ills of drink, gambling and immorality that 'gripped our age'. Economic, political and educational solutions were all inadequate, he believed, without the new heart that Jesus could create.

---

144 *Outlook*, 15 July 1935, pp.5-6; *Outlook*, 29 July 1935, pp.3-4.
145 W. Bower Black, *The Waters of Healing*, Christchurch: Presbyterian Bookroom, 1933, p.10.
146 *NZMT*, 12 April 1924, p.1.

Through the late 1920s and 1930s, social gospel commitment to Jesus became correlated with the political ideals of the NZLP. Paris cited extracts from *The Socialism of John Wesley* with approval.[147] By the late 1930s, he was identifying distribution of wealth as 'The fundamental problem today, next to the conversion of men and women to God through Christ'. Competing vested interests and speculators blocked solutions to social problems and turned the world into a den of thieves: 'Oh, for the Master and His scourge, and the overturning of the evil system once more'.[148] Paris' inaugural address as President of Methodist Conference in 1938 was controversial, and highlighted major rifts within the denomination. It also provided an exemplary statement of late interwar social gospel thinking. Jesus featured prominently in what Kevin Clements has described as a theological justification for the Labour Government's proposed social security system.[149]

Anti-war sentiment after the Great War and the depression of the 1930s both aided the leftward movement of social Christianity. This was expressed in sympathy for bodies like the League of Nations from its earliest days. The Congregational Union remarked favourably on the League's 'vast potentialities as an instrument for the manifestation of the mind of Christ and the realisation of the Divine Kingdom on Earth'.[150] In 1935, the Rev. Harold Peat from Hamilton confidently claimed that Jesus was increasingly the inspiration for 'thinking men': 'Nationalism is yielding to internationalism under the urge of the doctrine of the brotherhood of man, which is the doctrine of the Christ'.[151]

As the tone of the churches' anti-war statements sharpened, their appeals to Jesus strengthened. In 1927, an interdenominational peace committee reported that 'war as a means of settling disputes between nations is utterly opposed to the mind of Christ'. It called on the various churches to make an 'outspoken and uncompromising declaration that the war system and the Gospel of Christ are diametrically and irreconcilably opposed'.[152] The rhetoric was taken up in most subsequent

147 A.N. Faulkner, *The Socialism of John Wesley*, London: Robert Culley, 1908; O.E. Burton, *Percy Paris*, Wellington: The Friends of Percy Paris, 1963, p.63.
148 Cited in Burton, *Percy Paris*, p.64.
149 Kevin P. Clements, 'Paris, Percy Reginald, 1882-1942', *DNZB*.
150 *YCU*, 1923, p.15; cf. *PGA*, 1922, p.33.
151 *NZMT*, 9 November 1935, p.219.
152 *PGA*, 1927, pp.198-99.

statements. By 1935, Presbyterian declarations were even more assertive, with Jesus operating as an intensifier. According to the Public Questions Committee, 'just war' was no longer conceivable. War was:

> a crime against humanity and contrary to the mind and spirit of Jesus Christ.... In view of the sanctity of human life implied in the Fatherhood of God, the slaughter of men, women and children involved in modern warfare is intolerable to the Christian conscience.... War does not fit into Christ's Gospel of love.[153]

The Christian peace movement was strongest among youth. Methodist Bible Class conference studies related Jesus' life and teaching to issues of war, while resolutions demanding unilateral disarmament became almost de rigueur from the mid-1920s.[154] In 1932-33, one Methodist camp reflected on what 'A Sermon on the Mount Christian' should be like.[155] A report of a later gathering noted 'times of heartsearching... spent in study and discussion, as the challenge of the Way of Jesus was reconsidered in the light of the standard of conduct set for the Christian by Jesus Himself'.[156] Bible Class magazines highlighted Jesus' attitudes, noting that Christians simply followed his teaching. The churches, however, denounced war more readily than they adopted specific alternatives. Pacifism was influential, but the position was more radical than the mainstream of church membership. Where opinion was sharply divided, Jesus provided a focal point for unity and a rallying point for what could be affirmed; namely, that war was undesirable.

Reservations about pacifism partly derived from discomfort with the idea, but also the connections between Christian pacifism and Christian socialism. Those constituencies overlapped, and applied Jesus' teaching to each doctrine in similar ways. Campaigning in the 1928 general election, Ormond Burton contended that competition and war were equally 'alien to the spirit and teaching of Christ'.[157] Defining politics as a branch of ethics, and Christianity as the highest ethical system, he therefore promoted 'the practical application of Christian principles' as

153 *PGA*, 1935, p.164.
154 David Grant, *A Question of Faith: A History of the New Zealand Christian Pacifist Society*, Wellington: Philip Garside, 2004, p.21.
155 *NZMBC Link*, 5 February 1933, p.13.
156 *NZMT*, 2 February 1935, p.11.
157 O.E. Burton, *Christian Socialism*, Auckland: Wright & Jaques Printers, 1940 (1928), p.3.

'the only right solution' for political problems. Burton's principles were drawn from three maxims of Jesus: 'Love Thy Neighbour as Thyself', 'To seek and save that which was lost' and 'Love Your Enemies'. These were supposed to form a policy basis for everything from industrial to international relations. Christian pacifists like Ron Howell urged for more activist Christian pacifism, agreeing with Burton's socialist orientation: 'To-day Capitalism is the greatest obstacle to human progress, its existence means, not the likelihood but the inevitability of recurring wars, and it must go'. Pacifists were urged to work towards its replacement by 'a revived and invigorated Socialism'.[158]

The Sermon on the Mount and loving self-sacrifice were essential elements of Christian discourse during the depression of the 1930s. Initial religious responses focused on improving community standards, solidarity and relief work, rather than structural change. Andrew Picard has noted that some denominations also viewed the crisis as an opportunity for gospel preaching.[159] In 1932, the Presbyterian Public Questions Committee claimed that spiritual and moral failure lay behind the economic crisis. The world had made 'a travesty of the principles of Christ', though Christ-like relief work was also praised. Writing to the *New Zealand Baptist*, Frank Brookbanks urged Christians to follow Jesus' example by comforting the needy.[160]

Responses to the depression changed after the riots of 1932. Serving the community remained important, but the churches increasingly emphasised structural issues. Even a usually tentative Anglican General Synod urged use of 'every effort to transform our social order so as to bring it nearer the mind of Christ'.[161] From mid-1933, Methodist leaders were forthright in challenging the unequal distribution of resources in the community. Paris blamed ruthless economic and political retrenchment, while A.J. Seamer further commended the principle of mutual sacrifice found in the cross as the means to improving conditions.[162] Some congregations invoked Christ in denouncing government policy. One church's statement, for example, chided political indifference which

---

158 Howell, p.11.
159 Andrew Picard, 'Church Responses to Social Issues in Depression New Zealand, 1933', *New Zealand Journal of Baptist Research*, 9, 2004, pp.35-36.
160 *PGA*, 1932, pp.98-99; *NZB*, June 1933, p.174.
161 *PGS*, 1934, p.50.
162 *NZMT*, 10 June 1933, p.1; *NZMT*, 1 April 1933, p.10.

defied 'the great Command of Christianity found in the sociology of the Good Samaritan and the Golden Rule.[163]

Jesus and the Kingdom became associated with the churches' prophetic function. 'Crisis' literature of the 1930s illustrated that themes connecting Jesus with protest and hopes for a revival of Christian influence became more prominent with increased political activism.[164] In 1936, J.D. Salmond's edited booklet *Christ and Tomorrow* was influenced by neo-orthodox writers like Karl Barth and Emil Brunner, and considered sufficiently radical that John Dickie pressed to have it withdrawn.[165] Some religious opinion-formers believed that Christianity could contribute by purifying 'Socialistic ideals' in accordance with their Christian aim.[166] Socialism was never completely popularised, but the main Protestant churches became more willing to work with moderate socialism as an alternative to the status quo.

By 1935, many religious leaders suspected that the churches would survive better by supporting Labour, rather than opposing its national project. The NZLP had also largely become reconciled to the value of religious support by this time, and had begun courting religious endorsement. Church statements during the depression created a sympathetic atmosphere, and the Party responded by presenting the 1935 election as a tussle between the Christianity of Labour and anti-Christianity.[167] Leaders like Michael Joseph Savage and Peter Fraser seemed more sympathetic to the Christianity of their respective upbringings.[168] John A. Lee even played up harmonious values, claiming

163 Cited in James Thorn, *Peter Fraser: New Zealand's Wartime Prime Minister*, London: Odhams Press, 1952, p.106.

164 J.D. Salmond and Alex Salmond, *The World Crisis and the Gospel*, Dunedin: Otago Daily Times Print, 1931; J.D. Salmond and Alex Salmond (eds), *Facing Vital Issues: A Study Book for the Times*, Christchurch: Presbyterian Bookroom, 1932.

165 J.D. Salmond (ed.), *Christ and Tomorrow: A Study Book for the Times*, Christchurch: Presbyterian Bookroom, 1936.

166 John A. Allan, *Christianity and Communism*, Wellington: Publications Committee of St John's Young Men's Bible Class, 1936, pp.37-65.

167 A.J.S. Reid, 'Church and State in New Zealand, 1930-35: A Study of the Social Thought and Influence of the Christian Church in a Period of Economic Crisis', MA thesis, Victoria University, 1961, pp.133-36.

168 Barry Gustafson, *From the Cradle to the Grave: A Biography of Michael Joseph Savage*, Auckland: Penguin, 1988, pp.212-14; Thorn, *Peter Fraser*, p.107.

that 'there is no antagonism between the Labour movement and the Church. Socialism has never been advocated as an alternative religion'. A 'radical Church', he claimed, 'makes few enemies in a democratic country, and a radical party advancing a policy which will humanize the machine age has more friends than enemies in Church congregations'.[169]

The language of Jesus and the Kingdom supported this rapprochement. It validated reform, principles of social action, and Christian engagement with social issues. It was also unspecific. Thus, reports to the Presbyterian General Assembly denied the possibility of a Christian social order, yet urged for social expressions of 'brotherly love directing and interpreting justice'. Assembly's role was to rouse the Church's conscience 'in regard to necessary social change in harmony with the Gospel of the Kingdom of God, rather than the formulation of specific economic and social proposals'.[170] Mid-1930s Labour humanitarianism harmonised well with these generalised principles. Savage's own renewed interest in religion during the last years of his life was partly aroused through reading the New Testament and discovering similarities between his philosophies and Jesus' teaching. His discourse of 'applied Christianity' traded on reverence for Christ, who he referred to in 1938 as the 'The greatest man that had ever lived'. He even framed some social policy in terms of helping to establish the Kingdom of God on earth.[171] In its own way, the discourse was as moralistic as the churches' social Christianity, though it provided a basis for Christian cooperation on particular causes.

In 1934, Clarence Eaton's address to the Methodist Conference bemoaned the fact that interest in Jesus was not translating into support for the Church: 'Our social reforms claim Christ as their leader. Philanthropists pay tribute to Him as their inspirer and example.... Yet the Church is treated with indifference and organised religion given the cold shoulder'.[172] Later interpreters have suggested that the practical Christianity of Labour became increasingly secularised, and that Savage supplanted Jesus as the Christ-figure of the movement. Michael Bassett

---

169 John A. Lee, *Socialism in New Zealand*, London: T. Werner Laurie, 1938, p.268.

170 *PGA*, 1934, p.182; *PGA*, 1937, p.242.

171 Gustafson, *Cradle*, pp.212-14, 216, 227, quote p.213.

172 *MAC*, 1934, p.8.

describes visiting a 'simple, Catholic, working class home' to receive a portrait of Savage from the elderly occupant: 'There he was in the hall next to the crucifix. She picked him down, kissed him, and told me that Savage was the nearest thing to Christ in her life'.[173] The anecdote demonstrates strikingly how established the ideal of a social Christ had become. For the point is not that Christ was supplanted by a secular alternative, but that Savage was held to approximate an image of Jesus that had become virtually unquestioned. His kindly humanitarianism was felt to embody Jesus' teaching and example. Thus, the portrait interpreted the crucifix, but both belonged together.

Jesus was invoked widely in the cause of social reform in the first half of the twentieth century. He was put to work for various ends, but provided a language that proved amenable to humanitarian concerns. The prevalence of the language indicated the extent to which Christianity still flavoured the wider culture. It may also suggest some success in Christian efforts to influence society. Malleability aided this success. For the churches, Jesus-centred social concern provided an acceptable but distinctively Christian framework. For the labour movement, the language supplied a tool for provocative critique, but also respectability and a moral tone. Nevertheless, there were problems. Not least, that the pliability of the social Christ meant that his image often lacked substantial content. In this sense, Eaton's observations were on the mark. Value and clarity were easily sacrificed to broad dissemination. On the one hand, the Jesus of social campaigning did provide a remarkable common language. On the other hand, the extent of real influence was harder to ascertain.

173 Michael Bassett, 'How Ideal was the Savage Ideal', M.J. Savage Memorial Lecture, La Trobe University, 4 September 1998. URL: http://www.michaelbassett.co.nz/article_savage.htm, accessed 2 June 2006.

5. Children's Jesus

In many ways, New Zealand's Jesus was the children's Jesus. First acquaintances with him came almost universally in childhood, and this was also the time when he was most regularly invoked. Children probably had more occasions to consider Jesus than any other group, and beliefs about the nature of childhood, religion and society ensured that these representations were enduring. Stated more forcefully, Jesus and childhood were strongly correlated. Jesus featured prominently in the religious idiom associated with children and became an increasingly important focus, especially in the religion of Protestant children during the first half of the twentieth century.

Jesus' prominence in the religion of childhood reflected the rise of Jesus-centred Protestantism, and the impact of long-term social and religious patterns. There is widespread agreement that more pluralistic urban societies favoured 'the gradual emergence of a prolonged version of childhood and adolescence'.[1] In the nineteenth century, childhood lengthened along with education. The twentieth century concept of adolescence extended childhood still further. Smaller families altered age relations, while the philosophies of Locke and Rousseau, Romantic ideals and psychological ideas about human development all encouraged gentler, more sympathetic, child-centred ideals. Religious values were also important. Christian concern for children was often inspired by the New Testament. The Gospels suggested that Jesus elevated their status within the family, and generally, by describing them as exemplary entrants into the Kingdom of God.[2] Later Puritan and evangelical traditions emphasised doctrine of Original Sin, though the implications for child-rearing practices were often less severe than the rhetoric. Belief

---

1   Colin Heywood, *A History of Childhood: Children and Childhood in the West from Medieval to Modern Times*, Cambridge: Polity, 2001, pp.19-20, 30-31, quote p.30.
2   Mark 9.37 and Mark 10.13-16; cf. Judith M. Gundry-Volf, 'The Least and the Greatest: Children in the New Testament', in Marcia J. Bunge (ed.), *The Child in Christian Thought*, Grand Rapids: Eerdmans, 2001, pp.29-60; David Archard, *Children, Rights and Childhood*, London: Routledge, 1993, pp.37-39.

in the convertibility of the child meant that it was equally permissible to frighten or reassure them. Horace Bushnell's *Discourses on Christian Nurture* encouraged a new aim in Christian education: 'That the child is to grow up a Christian, and never know himself as being otherwise'.[3] Child conversion was stressed alongside the gradual enlightenment of children from within Christian experience. Parents should rather 'teach a feeling than a doctrine; to bathe the child in their own feeling of the love of God, and dependence on him'.[4]

These broad influences were fashioned by local factors. In the colonial setting, children's fate tested the veracity of myths about the land's Arcadian abundance.[5] From the late nineteenth century there were initiatives to regulate working conditions for children and provide protection for them.[6] Religious communities shared these concerns, but awareness that children represented 'the nursery of the Church' also encouraged care for their moral, physical and spiritual welfare. Introduction of the Education Act of 1877 prompted an expansion of religious education facilities, which in turn helped concentrate religious activity in childhood. This influenced the extent and manner of Jesus' appearance, both in the state education system and within the churches.

This chapter assesses characteristic discourses and the importance of context in shaping images of Jesus for children. Specifically, it examines modes of domestic piety including family religion, prayer and religious literature for children, as well as the educational contexts of week-day schooling and the Protestant Sunday school movement. These demonstrate that attempts to improve the reach and efficiency of religious education influenced the kind of representations children encountered. Ultimately, they also reinforced a correlation between Jesus and children that was problematic in a number of respects.

---

3   Robert Bruce Mullin, *The Puritan as Yankee: A Life of Horace Bushnell*, Grand Rapids: Eerdmans, 2002, pp.99-126, Bushnell quote, p.117.

4   Cited in Margaret Bendroth, 'Horace Bushnell's Christian Nurture', in Bunge (ed.), p.353.

5   On Arcadian myths and New Zealand, see Miles Fairburn, *The Ideal Society and Its Enemies: The Foundations of New Zealand Society, 1850-1900*, Auckland: Auckland University Press, 1989.

6   See Jeanine Graham, 'Child Employment in New Zealand', *NZJH*, 21:1, 1987, pp.62-78; Bronwyn Dalley, *Family Matters: Child Welfare in Twentieth-Century New Zealand*, Auckland: Auckland University Press, 1998, esp. pp.64-90.

Lover of the children

Representations of Jesus were profoundly influenced by the idea that Jesus and children enjoyed a special relationship. This singular bond depended largely on Jesus. Warm and inviting, he was the Great Personality who especially loved children and to whom they were instinctively drawn. Jesus' special love for children was celebrated and recited from earliest ages. The ubiquity of music and its capacity to evoke and interpret experience made it particularly important in children's lives. So it was significant that the love of Jesus formed the simple core of many of the most popular songs for the young, including favourites like 'I am so glad that Jesus loves me' and 'Jesus loves me, this I know'.[7] At one level, this reflected a broader conviction that Jesus was the embodiment of love. But children held a special place in his affection and his love was especially directed towards them. As one early advocate of religious work among children observed, 'the lambs are so dear to the heart of the Good Shepherd'.[8]

As this observation suggests, the idea of Jesus' special love for children, and the images that conveyed it, derived in part from the New Testament. The most important ideas were those of Jesus as Saviour and as Friend, and each was reinforced through favoured metaphors. The idea of Jesus as Saviour was supported by the central corresponding image of the Good Shepherd. This became a favourite subject for stained glass windows, prayers, and songs like 'Saviour like a shepherd lead us', 'Jesus, tender shepherd, hear me' and 'The king of love my shepherd is'. The un-denominational school worship book edited by the leading Presbyterian educationalist and minister J.D. Salmond was a good indicator of popularity.[9] This was designed for use in the formal and controversial setting of the state school environment. Consequently, the bulk of the songs were either rousing and patriotic or asserted un-

7   Jesus' love featured prominently in collections for children like *Golden Bells*, London: Children's Special Service Mission, 1878, and *The Sunday School Hymnary*, Carey Bonner (ed.), London: National Sunday School Union, 1905.
8   *New Zealand Methodist*, 15 October 1887, p.5.
9   First published in 1936, it was later expanded and republished as *Services of Worship (Undenominational) For Use in the Public Schools of New Zealand Under the Present Voluntary System*, Wellington: Bible-in-Schools League, 1940.

contested themes like the splendour of Creation and the greatness of God. Significantly, songs that did refer to Jesus were mostly for younger children, or referred to him as Shepherd.

The Shepherd image had a long history in Christian tradition and reflected a range of ideas about the Saviour. Though widely utilised, it was particularly favoured in relation to children. Where the New Testament referred to sheep, popular usage more often mentioned lambs. The influential Romantic tradition idealised children and rusticity, which helped popularise the connection; children were weak and vulnerable, and Jesus' love for them reflected his sensitivity and goodness. But there were also soteriological and moral dimensions, since the Redeemer was himself the Lamb of God.[10] The Shepherd connoted tenderness, guidance and rescue. He ensured safety, and brought the 'lost' and wayward back to the fold. Use of Sybil Parker's well known image of 'The Good Shepherd' on a Rechabite calendar clearly signalled these protective and directive aspects of salvation.[11]

The other crucial image was that of Jesus as the Friend of little children. As one young contributor to the *Outlook* noted, understanding Jesus as Saviour should not obscure his relationship as 'Friend and elder Brother'.[12] Popular children's hymns indicated that the notion of Jesus' friendship was multivalent. 'What a friend we have in Jesus' emphasised that he was helpful, comforting and reliable in times of need. 'Jesus friend of little children' articulated childhood fear of abandonment, but implied that Jesus could be an intimate companion: 'Take my hand, and ever keep me close to Thee.... Never leave me, nor forsake me; ever be my Friend'. On the other hand, 'There's a friend for little children' asserted the eternal otherness of Jesus and the glorious promise of heaven. Jesus' warm presence could console and fortify. Friendship with him was necessarily unequal, since it rested primarily on his capacities. It always entailed a reciprocal obligation to love and service.

Children were often reminded that they experienced the love and friendship of Jesus in very tangible ways. Their lives were better for living in a country where the teaching of Jesus was heeded. In 1923, the

---

10   *Reaper*, February 1930, p.295.
11   Independent Order of Rechabites Friendly Society, *No. 86 District, New Zealand Central (Christ the Good Shepherd Calendar), 1908*. Eph-D-ALCOHOL-Temperance-1908-01, ATL.
12   *Outlook*, 12 May 1900, p.7.

special Children's Year issue of the *New Zealand Methodist Times* argued that 'Wherever the message of Christianity has been preached, the welfare of the child has been regarded as a matter of special concern'.[13] On occasions, the alarming implications of this were made explicit. The Rev. James Cocker invited children to remember the blessings of Jesus in their lives by contrasting the fortunes of the young elsewhere:

> In countries where Jesus is not known little children are often cruelly treated. Some are thrown into the rivers and drowned, and others are left in the woods and fields to die. But Jesus is the children's best Friend, and where His teaching is followed children are loved and cared for.[14]

As F.W. Frankland, the eldest son of the illustrious Victorian chemist Edward Frankland and a prominent Foxton councillor explained, knowledge of Jesus' teaching accounted for the kindness of New Zealand parents and teachers to children.[15]

Jesus' love was perhaps best exemplified in his blessing 'the little children' (Matt. 19.13-15). This action was memorialised in one of the most popular children's hymns of the period, 'When mothers of Salem'. Frequently used as a baptismal hymn, it contrasted 'stern disciples' with a kind and sweetly smiling Jesus. The Gospel words of Jesus, 'Suffer the children to come unto Me', formed the hymn's refrain and were inscribed on baptismal fonts around the country. Popular artistic renderings of the incident depicted adoring children surrounding Jesus, often accompanied by their mothers. Where present, men looked on critically from a distance. Invariably, Jesus was holding a baby, laying hands on an infant's head, or in some way touching a child.[16]

The element of touch was crucial, as it was in the Shepherd image where lambs lay quietly on the Shepherd's back or safely in his arms close to his heart. The children's missionary hymn, 'I think, when I read that sweet story', used these images to evoke yearning for intimacy with

---

13   *NZMT*, 20 January 1923, p.1.
14   J. Cocker, *Keep Climbing: Twenty-Five Stories of Great Men and Heroes*, London: H.R. Allenson, 1929, p.86.
15   F.W. Frankland, *Bible-Religion the Most Important Thing in the World*, Palmerston North: Watson Eyre & Co. Printers, 1909, p.3.
16   *NZMT*, 20 June 1936, pp.53, 57; *NZMT*, 15 July 1939, p.81.

Jesus. After recalling how Jesus 'called little children, as lambs to his fold' the singer exclaims, 'I should like to have been with them then. I wish that His hands had been placed on my head, That His arm had been thrown around me'. Physical touch betokened warmth and intimacy. It also indicated tenderness characteristically identified with Victorian femininity. Victorian differentiation between the love of mothers and discipline of fathers was often expressed through the presence or absence of touch between parent and child.[17] Indeed, the 'touch of Jesus' always connoted stereotypically feminine qualities like kindness, sympathy and compassion.[18] The prevalence of physical intimacy suggested that the children's Jesus was conceived in essentially maternal terms.

Children's love for Jesus

Just as Jesus loved children, it was anticipated that they would respond warmly to him. In this, the children of Jesus' day were set forth as an enduring model. As the Dean of Christchurch Martin Sullivan explained, 'They loved Him when He was here and trusted Him, and came readily to Him. *They* didn't crucify Him. He was killed by evil men who forgot what it was like to be as children'.[19] A.H. Reed, the Methodist layman and publisher, concurred that children had always loved Jesus and expanded upon the Biblical narratives to prove it: 'Jesus called a child who was playing about. "Come here a minute, will you, Son?" All children loved Jesus. This one ran to Him and was taken upon His knee'. Mothers and children 'flocked around Jesus. There was hero-worship in the looks of the boys…. The girls rested affectionately against him'.[20]

17 Meredith Veldman, 'Dutiful Daughter Versus All Boy: Jesus, Gender, and the Secularization of Victorian Society', *Nineteenth Century Studies*, 11:6, 1997, p.6.

18 *Christian Outlook*, 21 January 1899, p.616; *Outlook*, 3 January 1927, p.17; *Harvest Field*, February 1940, p.10.

19 Martin Sullivan, *Children, Listen: Talks to Boys and Girls*, Christchurch: Whitcombe & Tombs, 1955, p.100 (original italics).

20 A.H. Reed (ed.), *The Isabel Reed Bible Story Book*, Wellington: A.H. & A.W. Reed, 1944, pp.272, 285 caption to facing illustration.

Contemporary children were expected to respond to Jesus with similar enthusiasm. The Methodist religious educationalist C.T. Symons argued that children should respond to Jesus as they did in Palestine where they 'clustered about His knee in glad confidence, trust and love. They were "thrilled" to be in His presence. They loved Him spontaneously with joy and abandon'.[21] This was especially true of the very young. One Sunday school training manual argued that young pupils were very loyal, and would say 'I love Jesus' very easily. In view of this, teachers should encourage them to 'do the thing that is right because it is right and because Jesus loves the children'.[22] Love and good behaviour were always closely allied. Another Methodist children's writer and broadcast personality, T.T. Garland, explained how he witnessed modern children emulating their forebears. He described children's responses to an artistic rendering of Jesus being rejected by his peers. This showed the Master leaving a village at evening because nobody would allow him to stay, with only the children looking at him. Garland noted the profound effect this had; all the children viewing 'stood very quietly' before the picture.[23]

Children's love for Jesus was thought to be instinctive and universal. It reflected Romantic notions of the natural and of childhood innocence. As one Sunday school teacher's guide expressed, 'A child instinctively loves that which is good. Tell a child about an admirable man and he intuitively admires and reverences that character'.[24] Children were believed to be naturally religious. Instinctive love for Jesus confirmed that impulse. Since they were also relatively unsullied by the taint of sin, children's intuitive responsiveness to Jesus confirmed the truth of religion in general and Christianity in particular.

These assumptions influenced approaches to ministry. When Presbyterians were concerned about older children moving out of church life they prescribed more opportunities to learn about Jesus. General

21 C.T. Symons, *Junior Worship*, Wellington: Youth Board, Methodist Church of New Zealand, 1940, p.3.
22 *Sunday School and Bible Class at Work: Text-Book for Teacher-Training Classes, Study Groups, and General Use*, 2nd ed., Melbourne: Joint Board of the Graded Lessons of Australia and New Zealand, 1936, pp.114-15.
23 T.T. Garland, *Judy Carries On*, Auckland: Whitcombe & Tombs, 1936, p.112.
24 Cited in *Sunday School Teachers' Guide*, Christchurch: Presbyterian Bookroom, for the Youth Committee of the Presbyterian Church of New Zealand, 1928, p.3.

Assembly suggested that the Junior Bible Class should seek to bring Sunday school drifters back by offering Sunday morning meetings to 'study the life of Jesus Christ', in addition to regular afternoon meetings.[25] Decision Day was an annual event in most churches, and widely understood as a mechanism to promote church membership by assisting the transfer of children as they graduated out of Sunday school. Occasionally, however, more idealistic emphases were suggested. For instance, some Methodists felt it was better viewed as an opportunity for children to express 'their love and promise of loyalty to Jesus Christ', recognising that failure to sign decision cards 'does not necessarily mean that the child does not love Jesus'.[26] Because they already loved Jesus, Decision Day was for *expressing* commitments rather than making them.

Death and the child

The relationship between Jesus and children was especially evident in the context of death, when the deceased were commonly said to have 'gone to be with Jesus'. The lyrics of Fanny Crosby's popular hymn celebrated his motherly love for everyone, but 'Safe in the arms of Jesus' was also a quintessentially childhood epitaph. Robin Hyde's interwar novel *The Godwits Fly* described reactions to the death of a child, albeit in a household with mixed attitudes to religion: '"What did he die of?" asked Carley, awed. Her mother said, "He was just taken quietly away to Jesus," but John snorted behind a newspaper, and ejaculated, "Water on the brain."'[27] To say that a child was 'with Jesus' was to assert that they were 'at home' and secure in a place of comfort and care.

More sentimental images portrayed Jesus in terms approximating a spiritualised lover. The *New Zealand Tablet* described the exemplary life of Noreen, whose devotion was compared to the child saint Imelda. She took daily Mass while at boarding school, and was self-effacing, self-

25 *PGA*, 1909, p.132.
26 *NZMT*, 4 November 1939, p.222.
27 Robin Hyde, *The Godwits Fly*, Patrick Sandbrook (ed.), Auckland: Auckland University Press, 2001 (1938), pp.14-15.

sacrificing, and full of affection and cheerfulness. These virtues bade well for her future life ahead until Jesus intervened: 'But He Who feeds amidst the lilies, was enamoured of this soul and wished to take it to Himself, in its unsullied beauty'.[28] Similar stories about people who were so pure and good that after First Holy Communion they died and went to heaven apparently circulated freely among school girls of a certain age.[29] Titillation aside, to be loved by Jesus in this way was an affirmation of piety and character that elevated the memory of the child and provided a positive and comforting interpretation of their death.

Burial inscriptions for this period demonstrate the close association that existed between Jesus and children in death.[30] Children's graves often had religious inscriptions. Jesus featured prominently among these, and the references were shaped by a distinctive vocabulary. Examples in the Terrace End cemetery at Palmerston North include references to scriptural words of Jesus like 'Suffer Little Children' and 'Such is the Kingdom of God', as well as the statements like 'Called to Jesus' and 'Asleep in Jesus'. Another popular inscription made Jesus' unsurpassed love explicit: 'We loved him well, but Jesus loved him best'.

Children's graves at the small rural cemetery at Bunnythorpe in the Manawatu were much more likely to include religious epitaphs than those of other age groups. Furthermore, where religious references were present they usually referred to Jesus. By 1985, when burial inscriptions were published on microfiche, the Bunnythorpe cemetery had 254 graves, with some 411 bodies interred. Of these, 35 were children aged twelve years or under, with 22 children's deaths recorded for the years 1890-40. During the whole period, all religious references for all years amounted to just 58 out of 411 (14.1%), with only 22 (5.3%) referring to Jesus. Excluding children, there are 48 religious references (12.8%) and 14 to Jesus (3.8%) out of 376 burials.

Religious inscriptions seem to have been the province of the conscientiously devout or those with the financial means to pay for such embellishments, or both. They occurred on children's graves in significantly higher rates than the overall average, and among these

28 *NZ Tablet*, 13 April 1932, pp.18-19.
29 Jane Tolerton (ed.), *Convent Girls: New Zealand Women Talk to Jane Tolerton*, Auckland: Penguin, 1994, p.152.
30 The following data and discussion draws from *New Zealand Cemetery Records* (microfiche), 1985, L04.03 (Terrace End) and L04.01 (Bunnythorpe).

references to Jesus were very high. For the period 1890-1940, direct reference to Jesus was a feature of 6 out of 22 (27%) child burials. References to Jesus accounted for 6 out of the 8 religious references up until 1940, and 8 out of 10 for the whole period. When the large number of children buried in multiple graves with other family members is included, the relative incidence of religious reference is noticeably greater. Half of all children were buried in family graves with no epitaph additional to basic personal and family details. Religious references were evident for 5 of the 25 multiple graves for children up until 1985. Only 8 of the 25 had any inscription, and 4 of these referred to Jesus.

This admittedly small sample illustrates a striking differentiation between the frequency of religious inscriptions for children and the general population. The language also contrasted sharply. Jesus' name was much more likely to be invoked in relation to children, while adult references tended to quote Jesus, or cite Biblical references referring to him. Moreover, whereas children's inscriptions openly addressed Jesus, adult inscriptions typically preferred Christ and showed greater interest in the resurrection. The thought of being with Christ was evidently better after three score years and ten. The appeal to Jesus in relation to childhood death illustrated the importance of religious sentiment in the ecology of tragedy. It suggested comfort and promise in the face of uncertainty. Equally, it provided a salient reminder of Jesus' love for children, who were often called 'Christ's little ones'. Being linked with him in death was a reminder that children belonged to Jesus.

Domestic piety

Children's religious life was cultivated in a variety of settings. These contexts had a profound impact on the representations of Jesus that children encountered, and the manner in which his love, redemption and friendship were expressed. Of all these settings, domestic ones were considered the most decisive. Home and family were widely understood as the crucial elements in children's formation, and churches often emphasised their religious significance. One Presbyterian devotional aid argued that the family was the 'true unit of human society', and that 'it is the revival of a strong and pure domestic life that is to save the earth from a curse'. Similarly, Methodist parents were frequently reminded that they stood in closest relation to their children and therefore had the great responsibility and privilege of securing their allegiance to Christ.[31]

Jesus featured most prominently where activities were designed specifically for children, rather than in the formal structures of family religion. Family devotions, or family worship, were central elements in formal home religion though there were significant differences between Catholic and Protestant patterns. Family worship had not been especially common among Catholics until the late nineteenth century, though it was increasingly emphasised from that time.[32] Where practised, family devotions tended to use standard prayers since extempore prayer was not highly valued. These seldom addressed Jesus directly. For example, one widely-used publication outlined five requisite prayers for night and morning. Of these, the Confiteor and Act of Contrition made no mention of Jesus. The Lord's Prayer quoted him, while the Angelical Salutation acknowledged him as the fruit of Mary's womb. The Apostles' Creed was the only 'prayer' that concentrated on his life, though its essential focus was doctrinal.[33] Recitation of the rosary was the central element in home worship for many families, and encouraged through specific campaigns.[34] Twelve of the fifteen aspects for meditation concerned events in Jesus' life. Conceptually, however, the rosary emphasised the 'mysteries' of Jesus' birth, death and resurrection, rather than engagement with personality.

Protestants expressed considerable anxiety about domestic religion throughout the period. Concern that interest in family devotions was declining had been mentioned during the nineteenth century. By the turn of the century, there were real though somewhat exaggerated fears that these practices were on the verge of total collapse. This led to numerous

---

31 'Preface', *Prayers for the Home Circle. With a Selection of Bible Readings*, Dunedin: Presbyterian Church of New Zealand, 1917; *MAC*, 1901, p.19; *MAC*, 1906, p.27.

32 H.R. Jackson, *Churches & People in Australia and New Zealand, 1860-1930*, Wellington: Allen & Unwin, 1987, p.165.

33 A Parish Priest in New Zealand, *Conversations on Christian Re-Union*, Dunedin: N.Z. Tablet, 1924, pp.66-68.

34 Jim Sullivan (ed.) *Catholic Boys: New Zealand Men Talk to Jim Sullivan*, Auckland: Penguin, 1996, pp.118, 134, 163.

attempts to reinvigorate it. Methodist congregations were exhorted to make 'Family Religion, or Parental Responsibility' the subject of a special Children's Year service in 1923.[35] In 1917, Presbyterians produced a book of prayers for use in the home. Then, in 1927, the Life and Witness Committee of the General Assembly began promoting the Family Altar Card system of the Australian Presbyterian Church. This aimed to promote family worship and home religion through an annual cycle of prayers and readings and an 'examination of conscience' based on the Ten Commandments and the Beatitudes. The focus was not Christocentric, but highlighted beliefs about the relation between religion, morality and social order. By 1928, about 2,000 Family Altar Cards had been sold. This was a significant though not overwhelming response given that adult membership and attendance for that year were 83,869 and 52,121 respectively.[36]

Evangelicals were often great advocates for family worship. The Rev. Joseph W. Kemp of the Baptist Tabernacle in Auckland, and founder of the Bible Training Institute, was an ardent supporter. He believed in paternal leadership and advocated relatively formal methods. While children's participation was deemed essential, there was little sense that methods were recommended with children's needs in mind. Nor was Jesus' life a major focus. On the contrary, popular devotional books like *Daily Light* and *My Counsellor* were compendia of inspirational verses drawn from the Bible as a whole. The Bible was a valued element in most Protestant family worship. Kemp was personally enthusiastic about R.M. McCheyne's Bible reading plan, in part because it allowed 'younger members of the families [to] become familiar with every part of the Bible'.[37] Hence, Jesus was probably more conspicuous in prayer, where references to his lordship and the wonder of his saving death were continually reprised.

As the popularity of family devotions waned, Christian educators encouraged less prescribed forms of domestic religion. Home religion became more acceptably defined as fundamentally a question of

35 *NZMT*, 6 January 1923, p.5. Similar appeals were commonly made at Sunday school anniversary celebrations.
36 *PGA*, 1927, p.189; *PGA*, 1928, p.198.
37 *Reaper*, August 1926, p.158. McCheyne's plan included three or four Bible chapters a day, thus covering the whole Bible once, and New Testament twice, each year. From 1927, monthly readings from this plan were published in the *Reaper*.

atmosphere. By 1940, resources and guides still asserted the centrality of the home, but emphasised love and healthy activity in the initial stages of the child's life.[38] One important consequence was a prioritisation of maternal domestic influence. Praying and loving were the essential principles of religious life. Therefore, mothers were encouraged to let 'the beauty and simplicity of Christ's example' control their day. Such changes reflected the waning of formal home religion, and perhaps the shift of priority from words to action that characterised much social Christianity. The trend, however, was wider. By 1939, J.D. Salmond was affirming Horace Bushnell's dictum that religion never permeates the life of a nation until it becomes domestic. Though family worship was valued, it was not more significant than precept and example. Parents' own faith, growing religious thinking, and parental respect for children's personality were all important new emphases.[39] Expressing Christ's character was becoming as important as naming him.

Prayer was an important and persistent aspect of domestic religion. Bedtime prayer often endured even where other forms of religious activity were limited. It was particularly important for younger children, with whom simple and repetitive prayers were frequently used. Such rituals could have a profound effect. In later life, Martin Sullivan claimed that he could still recall the first prayer his mother taught him:

Jesus, tender shepherd, hear me,
Bless Thy little lamb tonight,
Through the darkness be thou near me,
Keep me safe till morning light.[40]

Prayers for children were often prayed to Jesus, and regularly contrasted the foolishness and naïveté of the child with his goodness and reliability.

Jesus' help and presence was invoked especially, though not only, at night. Indeed, protection formed the theme of the simplest and perhaps most ubiquitous prayer: 'Now I lay me down to sleep: I pray the Lord my soul to keep'. Associations with maternal tenderness and comfort

---

38 *God and the Little Child*, Wellington: Youth Department, Methodist Church of New Zealand, n.d., pp.1-4.

39 J.D. Salmond (ed.), *The Church and Her Young People*, Christchurch: Presbyterian Bookroom, 1939, p.19.

40 Sullivan, *Children, Listen*, p.39; cf. *Prayers for the Home Circle*, p.67.

made the bedtime Jesus intimate. Emphasis on his protection at night was common, but Catholic prayer seemed both more formal and overtly preoccupied with death: 'Into Thy hands, O Lord, I commend my spirit: Lord Jesus, receive my soul.... preserve me from a sudden and unprovided death and from all dangers, and bring me to life everlasting with Thee'.[41] After night prayers, the catechism instructed devout Catholics of all ages to 'occupy myself with the thoughts of death; and endeavour to compose myself to rest at the foot of the cross, and give my last thoughts to my crucified Saviour'.[42]

Day or night, children learned prayers that encouraged them to be good, kind and gentle like Jesus. They were taught to turn from selfishness to service. Material in religious periodicals reflected notions of what was appropriate, and the tenor of prayers that were often prayed:

> "All for Jesus" Good Lord! I ask that this short day
> Be spent for Thee and Thine;
> Beloved! grant its every hour
> May reach Thy Heart Divine.
> Let not my foolish love of praise
> Rob work or prayer from Thee.
> Jesus! from pride, from self, from sin,
> May this one day be free.[43]

Children's own efforts to construct prayers, though sometimes affected, revealed their impressions of the important ideas. Eileen Soper remembered that the first fruit of her father's encouragement to produce poetry took the form of a prayer: 'Oh Jesu, Oh Jesu, Majesty of Love / Look down on Thy people from Heaven above'.[44] This Jesus was exalted and rather romanticised, though belief in his love remained essential.

41   *A Simple Prayer Book*, Wellington: Catholic Enquiry Centre, 1964, p.13, cf. p.8.
42   H.T. Cafferata, *The Catechism Simply Explained*, rev. ed., London: Burns & Oates, 1954, p.164; cf. Sullivan (ed.), *Catholic Boys*, p.187.
43   *NZ Tablet*, 13 April 1932, p.24.
44   Soper, p.17.

The child Jesus and ideal childhood

Jesus' childhood was consciously set forth as an exemplar and ideal. Catholics tended to view the childhood of Jesus within the setting of the Holy Family, though this often focused on Mary's role. By contrast, Protestants were drawn more to Jesus in general, and by extension to his childhood. Yet, the New Testament provides little detail about Jesus' childhood and family. Consequently, representations of his childhood tended to be heavily shaped by contemporary values and assumptions.[45]

Images of Jesus' birth and infancy provided the most frequent references to his early years. Christmas was a major event in the Christian Year, and a popular cultural festival. The season encouraged reflection on the doctrine of the Incarnation, and reflections on the 'wonder' of his birth as a helpless baby. At times, this preoccupation was quite mawkish. 'Isn't it lovely when birthdays come', the Methodist deaconess Sister Mabel Morley mused, 'and Jesus' birthday is the loveliest of all. It is so lovely that He was a baby – for babies are so sweet, and such lots of people are so glad that Jesus wasn't born in a palace. Don't you think it's the sweetest story to hear about Jesus being born in a stable?'[46] On the other hand, more radical Protestants were often suspicious of festivals, and placed less emphasis on Christmas and Jesus' infancy. Bethlehem was merely a milestone on the road to Calvary.[47]

Images of the Child Jesus were closely tied to domestic expectations on children. For Catholics and Protestants alike the primary virtue of the child Jesus was his obedience, particularly as this was expressed in helpfulness around the home. Readers of the *Month* were informed that if 'Catholic children wish to be like the obedient Jesus, they must strive to be truthful, unselfish and obedient, watching for opportunities of doing things for others, as Jesus did for Mary and Joseph'.[48] The story of Jesus being lost in the Temple had the potential to disrupt the image of

---

45 Christopher van der Krogt, 'Imitating the Holy Family: Catholic Ideals and the Cult of Domesticity in Interwar New Zealand', *History Now/Te Pae Tawhito o te Wa*, 4:1, 1998, p.16.

46 See the 'Young Folks' page, *NZMT*, 23 January 1915.

47 *Reaper*, December 1926, pp.262-63; *War Cry*, 22 December 1900, pp.4-5.

48 *Month*, 1 November 1932, p.8, cited in van der Krogt, 'Holy Family', p.16.

obedient childhood. In practice, such tensions were usually resolved by explaining the incident as a lapse on Mary and Joseph's part. Despite parental failings, Jesus remained polite and courteous. As A.H. Reed explained, Mary 'must have been pleased and proud' of his 'gentle but straightforward reply'.[49]

Jesus' industry was another celebrated virtue that was often closely related to his obedience in home life. For many years, the *New Zealand Tablet* included a 'Family Circle' page, the title of which included an image of the child Jesus working alongside Joseph at a carpentry bench with Mary looking on. The Holy Family was an economic unit to which Jesus actively contributed. Despite increasing attempts to protect children and limit their employment in the twentieth century, Jesus remained a conscientious worker in the family enterprise.[50]

Perhaps the most illuminating exposition of Jesus' childhood was put forward by A.H. Reed, who was responsible for compiling what was probably New Zealand's first Bible Story Book for children. This genre has been described as a 'combination of social utility and soul-saving',[51] for while they seem authentic and authoritative, children's Bibles are actually highly selective. They typically use only narrative sections of the Bible and freely add other material. Reed's book fitted this pattern. It invoked Jesus to construct a portrait of ideal childhood that involved enthusiasm for nature, diligence in work, and virtue and responsibility in relationships.[52] Like a good New Zealand child, Jesus apparently loved outdoors play: 'Jesus loved the countryside, its birds, and beasts, and flowers.' Yet, his play was always contained to its proper time and place. Like industrious modern children Jesus had schoolwork to do: 'Jesus had to work hard at his lessons, just as boys and girls must do to-day, if they want to get on, and make themselves useful in the world, and bring credit to their parents and friends'. In addition, he diligently helped his father in the workshop and his mother in the home: 'we may be sure no job he was ever called upon to do would be scamped'. Perhaps the most impressive aspect of Jesus' childhood was his unerring virtue. He was a

---

49 Reed (ed.), p.199, though Reed goes further than others in attempting to exonerate Jesus; cf. Mathews, *Little Life*, pp.42-43, and Smyth, *People's Life*, pp.56-57.

50 *NZ Tablet*, 20 January 1916, pp.33-34; cf. Dalley, esp. pp.13-168.

51 Ruth B. Bottigheimer, *The Bible for Children: From the Age of Gutenberg to the Present*, New Haven: Yale University Press, 1996, p.4.

52 Reed (ed.), p.196.

'real boy' who held work and play, character and responsibility in consummate balance:

> He would not hesitate to stand up to a bully in aid of a smaller boy, and always had courage to say No to anything wrong. Though we know little about his boyhood, we do know that he was manly and true, kind and courteous, obedient to his parents, and always showed respect to women and girls.

Discussions of Jesus' childhood illustrated that religion was often conceptualised in ethical terms, since it provided children with valuable moral frameworks. Following First World War One, the churches worked hard to extend their reach into the home in order to strengthen religious life. One consequence was a significant increase in the volume of locally-written religious literature for children. In keeping with contemporary religious educators' expressed desire that children would 'consciously and unconsciously take Him as their model and judge actions by His standard', Jesus featured prominently in this material.[53] He was the Saviour and Friend, but also their chief moral guide. His example was the standard for kindness, service and love, while children received encouragement from his help and promises. Being 'kind and good' was also suggested as the way to procure Jesus' blessing.[54]

Four authors illustrate the tone of this literature and the images of Jesus that predominated. The Rev. John E. Parsons was a regular contributor of material for children to Christian periodicals throughout the post-war period. In particular, he was closely associated with the League of Young Methodist's (LYM), which began a page in the *New Zealand Methodist Times* in May 1921, replacing a 'Boys and Girls' of the Rev. A.C. Lawry.[55] Though more recent critics often find Parsons' stories moralistic, they were widely appreciated in his own time. In 1923, his story *The Splendid Quest* was reprinted from the LYM page 'by popular demand', while *Three Wonderful Keys* was published in

---

53 C.T. Symons, *Teaching Temperance: A Guidebook for Youth Workers*, Levin: Youth Department of the Methodist Church, n.d., p.13.

54 See Joan Gale Thomas, *If Jesus Came to My House*, London: A.R. Mowbray, 1941, which was endorsed in *God and the Little Child*, p.16.

55 Membership of the LYM had reached 2,235 by February 1923, and later surpassed 6,000. See *NZMT*, 3 February 1923, p.10; also the LYM pamphlet, *The League Emblem*, Christchurch: Lyttelton Times Print, n.d.

1931 from contributions there and in the Australian *Christian World*.[56] A Bunyanesque allegory, *The Splendid Quest* follows a faltering member of the LYM called Oliver in his 'Splendid Quest of finding the Love in everybody'.[57] After conversing in a dream with 'a Stranger', Oliver sets out gallantly on his journey dressed in knightly attire. Circumstances force him to lay his armour aside piece by piece until he reaches his destination bereft of all his possessions. Resting in a hut, the kindly-faced 'Stranger' returns and helps interpret his journey before revealing himself as Jesus: 'Then he heard the Stranger, who was no longer a Stranger, saying: "Love one another, even as I have loved you. Greater love hath no man than this, that a man lay down his life for his friends."'

The Jesus of the *Splendid Quest* is a personable stranger. Warm and kindly, affectionate and wise, he indulges misguided enthusiasm, and offers reassurance. He appears victorious and promises Oliver victory, too, yet he is also sorrowful and bears the scars of sacrifice. Parsons' Jesus was loving and optimistic, like the Jesus of social Christianity. He was a fellow sufferer, an example, brother and guide. Similar themes could be found elsewhere in Parson's stories. *Three Wonderful Keys* claimed that bearers of faith, hope and love would have the faith to know that God is like Jesus, the hope to see 'goodness and happiness' everywhere, and the love to 'fill his life with the strength and beauty of Jesus'. Jesus was good to everyone, saw the good in everyone, and helped children to do their very best.[58]

Rita Snowden and T.T. Garland were arguably New Zealand's most successful religious children's writers. Both presented Jesus as the benchmark for children's behaviour, though they tended to introduce him incidentally, in everyday situations. Garland was active in Methodist Sunday schools and broadcasting for many years, but was best known as 'Uncle Tom' on 1ZR and 1ZB's 'Friendly Road' radio. His immensely popular *Judy* books consisted of short homilies drawn largely from this radio work. They reflected the Friendly Road emphasis on practicality and helpful everyday morality. Garland avoided conventional religious expectations or overly-religious characters. One rare reference to Jesus

---

56   John E. Parsons, *The Splendid Quest: A Story for Children*, Auckland: Unity Press, 1923; John E. Parsons, *Three Wonderful Keys*, London: H.R. Allenson, 1931.

57   The 'League of the Splendid Quest' is a pseudonym for the LYM, the aim and motto of which were to 'find the love in everybody' and 'love conquers all'.

58   Parsons, *Wonderful Keys*, pp.15-17, 56, 98, 128.

presented him as the epitome of Christian neighbourliness. Thought-fulness was his essential characteristic: 'If I had to rewrite the Ten Commandments I would put in, "Thou shalt not be thoughtless".... anyone who reads the Bible must be struck with the thoughtfulness of Jesus. He was so careful about the feelings of other people.'[59]

Snowden was another Methodist, and also an internationally renowned writer of adult devotional books. She deliberately emphasised Jesus' humanity in her children's works because she wanted to produce a more rounded portrait than churches often provided.[60] Moral principles were drawn from all kinds of situations, but Jesus' character, empathy and love were particularly celebrated. Since Jesus was not a 'half-and-half measure' person, children were encouraged to emulate these in a spirit of quest and adventure. 'Christlikeness' therefore consisted in having 'His big love for men and women' and a degree of moral courage. Jesus' goodness also provided motivation, since the unbearable prospect of letting down the greatest Friend was a stimulus to give ones' best. As one poem in her book *Through Open Windows* suggested, imitation of Jesus, and loyalty and commitment to him were interrelated necessities:

> He has no hands but our hands
> To do His work today,
> He has no feet but our feet
> To lead men in his way.
> He has no voice but our voice
> To tell men how He died,
> He has no help but our help
> To lead them to His side.[61]

Two widely distributed booklets by Martin Sullivan highlight that, after the 1930s, religious literature for children seemed almost entirely concerned with Jesus. Sullivan was the Dean of Christchurch from 1952 to 1962, during which time he conducted radio broadcasts that were subsequently published.[62] Sullivan's Jesus was extraordinarily virtuous.

---

59   Garland, pp.285-86.
60   Rita Snowden, *Story-Time Again*, London: Epworth, 1951, p.26.
61   Rita Snowden, *Through Open Windows*, London: Epworth, 1940, p.25.
62   See Sullivan, *Children, Listen,* and Martin Sullivan, *Listen Again: More Talks to Boys and Girls*, Christchurch: Whitcombe & Tombs, 1956.

He was never unkind, but 'always saw the best in the people'. He was the best man that ever lived; the greatest teacher, a wonderful healer and storyteller, 'the Son of the Living God'.

Jesus' prominence in Sullivan's talks was particularly striking. His booklets contained 41 addresses, all but seven of which dealt with readings addressing aspects of Jesus' life and teaching. Indeed, all Sullivan's text-based talks were based on readings from the New Testament. While Jesus was mentioned in every story, he was less prominent in five of the seven stories not based on a Gospel reading. Significantly, Sullivan's talks were based on a syllabus produced by an interdenominational Children's Religious Advisory Committee.

Close attention to Jesus reflected the belief that he provided the highest example and moral guidance children needed. The cover blurb to *Children, Listen* commended the book, noting that it 'not only presents the challenge of Christian behaviour, but also touches on the life and ministry of Jesus'. According to Sullivan, Jesus was always helping and healing people, and 'if everyone believed in Jesus, and everyone prayed to Him and tried to follow His example, loving his neighbour as himself... we would see hundreds of miracles being performed'. It was not always clear how particular Biblical passages connected with the virtues espoused. In one story, Sullivan advanced the curious suggestion that Jesus was 'the most courteous person the world has ever known'.[63] Jesus was also honourable, restrained and sociable. He kept his promises, put people at ease, and never got angry or anxious. Endorsement of this set of values required a rather liberal reading of the biblical texts. At one level, this merely indicated the extent to which Jesus was utilised as a model of ideal childhood. It also demonstrated the malleability required to use him as such a comprehensive exemplar.

State education

Formal educational settings were an important part of children's lives and became an increasingly significant context for attempts to nurture

63   Sullivan, *Children, Listen*, p.23.

children's religion during this period. Following the demise of the provincial system of government, New Zealand's education system was nationalised through the Education Act of 1877. By making it compulsory and free, the state increased access to education whilst also strengthening its influence. Private church schools continued to function, but state schooling increasingly predominated. As a crucial element in New Zealand childhood experience, state education became an important site for contests over the place of religion.

State education was compulsory and free, but also secular. This aspect of the 1877 Act sparked considerable debate, but was ultimately accepted in the interest of national harmony provided it helped circumvent sectarianism and the impression of Establishment. The New Zealand legislation extended a pattern that had already existed in most of the provinces. Nevertheless, it spurred the churches to action. Catholic and Protestant responses diverged sharply. While the former expanded their independent schooling, Protestants sought to bolster the efficiency of their Sunday schools and strengthen voluntary organisations. They also embarked on an energetic campaign to provide religious instruction in state schools, especially from 1911 through a reinvigorated Bible in Schools movement. As these attempts failed, the Nelson system became more popular. This allowed for instruction, rather than uninterpreted reading, outside schools hours under the guidance of volunteers. Jesus occupied an increasingly important space within these debates. In particular, his life and teaching became progressively more prominent as part of the search for an acceptable curriculum.

Prevailing interpretations of the secular clause limited the forms and extent of religious material for children. Jesus was generally a casualty of these strictures. But secular education did not entirely banish religion from school. As Colin McGeorge has noted, the secular clause did not exclude God, the clergy, or incidental religion, but ruled out formal religious instruction.[64] Leonard M. Isitt, a Methodist and the leading parliamentary supporter of the Bible in Schools movement, once claimed

---

64   Colin McGeorge, 'Religious Aspects of the Secular System Before the Great War', in Roger Openshaw and David McKenzie (eds), *Reinterpreting the Educational Past: Essays in the History of New Zealand Education*, Wellington: New Zealand Council for Educational Research, 1987, p.167.

that it was illegal to mention Christ at school.[65] Though not technically correct, this scaremongering had some basis. McGeorge notes the absence of any Scripture paraphrase in use at this time, and that religious subject matter was confined largely to older prose. References to Jesus were rare, but they did exist. Over time, suspicion about public religion and diminishing reliance on British materials made even incidental references less acceptable. According to Archbishop Redwood, 'God and Christ' were 'locked out, crushed out of the schoolrooms'.[66]

The *School Journal* was established by the Department of Education in 1907, and quickly became the state's leading education publication. Designed as a basic reading resource for core areas of the curriculum, it was distributed free to all children. Consequently, it had a massive circulation and influence. By 1919, 175,000 copies per issue were printed, and it had become the chief reading matter in many schools. Even private schools were purchasing as many as 15,000 copies per month.[67] As the leading figure in the Department at this time, George Hogben was instrumental in its establishment. A Congregationalist, Hogben had been a controversial appointment as Inspector-General of Schools and Secretary for Education in 1899. He initiated widespread reforms within the Education Department, including the introduction of a new syllabus in 1904. The *School Journal* was supposed to support this syllabus in lieu of a uniform textbook. Religious education was not a part of the general curriculum, so despite Hogben's own religious convictions there was little room for Jesus within the pages of the *Journal*. There were occasional intimations of his existence, and his cultural and historical significance, but only when addressing the very young. For instance, the start of an article on the 'Children of the Holy Land' questioned junior readers about their knowledge of that place:

Have you heard of a country called Palestine, or the Holy Land? It was in that land that many great things of which we read in the Bible took place long, long ago. It was there that Christ was born, lived, and died, and that is why it is called the Holy

65   D.V. MacDonald, 'The New Zealand Bible in Schools League', MA thesis, Victoria University of Wellington, 1964, p.208.
66   *NZ Tablet*, 15 May 1919, p.22.
67   *AJHR*, 1920, E-1, p.11.

Land. It is only a very small place, and did not rule over other nations, but it has given us the great Bible which has ruled in the hearts of men.[68]

Christ appeared seasonally, in relation to special events. References at these times were similarly cautious and oblique, and mostly occurred early in the twentieth century. The November edition was always the last for the year. In recognition of impending Christmas celebrations, early editions of the *Journal* cited religious verse in its 'Quotations Worth Remembering'. During World War One, passing reference was made to the 'faith, hope and joy' of Christmas because 'a Child was born'.[69] However, by the 1920s, even such generalities had disappeared as religious aspects were supplanted by images of a present-laden Father Christmas and wishes of 'A Merry Christmas to you all'. There is no extant evidence indicating that the Christ-child's disappearance followed a conscious change in policy, though it is possible that wartime sectarianism contributed to hardening interpretations of secularity in the state system. In any case, the change appeared to be permanent.

The incidental references to God that McGeorge noted in the period prior to World War One continued in some contexts. As long as Empire Day endured it was marked in a special edition of the *School Journal* in which dignitaries recited 'patriotic' messages. These frequently utilised a sense of shared Christian identity to extol the virtues of Empire. This identity was defined only in generalised categories. It was more likely to turn on concepts of 'Christian civilisation' and 'faith and trust in God' than anything specific like the life and teaching of Jesus. By 1940, Methodists were campaigning to redress this exclusion of religion from the *School Journal* by having Bible passages included in its pages.[70] Their efforts were unsuccessful.

---

68 *School Journal*, Part 1, 5:9, October 1911, p.136; cf. *School Journal*, Part 1, 12:2, February 1918.

69 *School Journal*, Part 3, 10:10, November 1916, p.297.

70 *MAC*, 1941, p.82.

Bible reading and religious instruction in schools

Protestant commitment to children's religious instruction led to a long-standing campaign for Bible reading in state schools. Enthusiasts for this cause considered that the preservation of Christian civilisation was at stake. From the time secular state education was first mooted, the Bible was celebrated as an essential factor leading to morality and civilisation. 'What but the Gospel', one writer inquired, 'subdued the savagery and influenced the proud spirit of the Maori Chiefs of these islands, to cede the Sovereignty to the British Crown, without a struggle'. Public reading of the Bible was therefore supported as 'the only sure foundation of public virtue and prosperity, and the best guarantee of private morality, happiness and security'.[71]

Proponents highlighted the historical, literary and above all the ethical value of the Bible. Thus, P.B. Fraser argued that excluding the Bible from schools amounted to 'moral and intellectual mutilation' of the nation's children.[72] For Fraser, the very act of Bible reading was morally uplifting. One of the most widely distributed and influential tracts of the New Zealand Bible in Schools movement cited the views of the English Roman Catholic Archbishop Cardinal Manning as he articulated the outcome that Christian supporters most feared should their campaign fail. Manning had argued that, 'A Christian people can be perpetuated only by Christian education. Schools without Christianity will rear a people without Christianity. A people reared without Christianity will soon become anti-Christian'.[73] The religious education of children was inextricably linked not only with morality, but the persistence of a Christian society.

Proposed textbooks and syllabi for religious education indicated changing ideals. By the 1930s, they also provided a reasonably reliable guide to use under the voluntary system. Within these, a trend toward greater emphasis on Jesus' life and example was plainly evident. This

71 S. Kempthorne, *The Holy Scriptures, the Only Sound Basis for the Education of Youth*, Auckland: William Atkin Printer, 1870, pp.6, 8.
72 P.B. Fraser, *Mental Mutilation of the People's Children by the Exclusion of the Bible from Schools*, Oamaru: Andrew Fraser, 1892, p.9.
73 Cited in W.N. Willis, *Bible Teaching in State Schools*, Auckland: Wilson and Horton Printers, 1911, p.2. Manning died in 1892.

corresponded with general shifts in Protestant religious education and a move away from older imported textbooks. Textbooks and syllabi indicated, perhaps more clearly than any source, the increasing emphasis on Jesus in religion for children.

The earliest textbooks favoured for use under the 1877 Act were known as the 'Irish Scripture Books'. Compiled earlier in the nineteenth century, these emphasised Old Testament history, the prophetic and the miraculous.[74] In 1895, however, they were publicly savaged by Parliament's Education Committee and their reputation never recovered. In April 1903, a national Bible in Schools conference in Wellington led to the formation of a Bible-in-Schools Referendum League. Spearheaded by the leading Presbyterian minister the Rev. James Gibb, this League articulated a scheme for religious instruction and developed a potential textbook. The new book was highly derivative, since 402 of its 408 readings could be found in a textbook used in Victorian schools.[75]

Curiously, the proposed textbook of 1904 echoed the 'Irish' text in also relying heavily on Old Testament selections. Younger children were more likely to hear about Jesus than older children, but would also hear more from the Old Testament than the New, since selections for junior readers favoured the Old by 59 to 44. The Old Testament portions were largely drawn from narrative in Genesis and Exodus, but spanned from Creation to the conquest of Canaan. The entire New Testament selection came from the Gospels, the majority being from Mark. Intermediate-aged students had more New Testament lessons than Old by a margin of 55 to 45. Their New Testament lessons also focused on the life of Christ from Matthew and Luke, while Old Testament lessons focused on David and Saul. Senior classes had only 39 Old Testament lessons, and 65 from the New Testament. Of the latter, only the first 26 concerned the life of Jesus, drawn from John. The remaining majority came from the book of Acts. The Epistles were excluded on grounds that their dogmatic and theological content made them too susceptible to sectarian controversy. Though widely considered the most 'theological' of the Gospels, John was still considered valuable. Reserving these selections for older

74 Ian Breward, *Godless Schools? A Study of Protestant Reactions to Secular Education in New Zealand*, Christchurch: Presbyterian Bookroom, 1967, pp.32-33.
75 *Outlook*, 9 May 1903; *The Bible-in-Schools Text Book, As Approved by the Wellington Conference*, Wellington: C.M. Banks Printers, 1904.

children reflected the assumption that doctrine and theology were for adults. Narrative, including Jesus' life, was primarily for children.

Bible instruction had largely been rationalised as promoting public morality. The Old Testament, however, raised as many questions on these grounds as it answered. Its emphasis in selections for juniors was particularly perplexing. One critique questioned the appropriateness of beginning with Genesis 1-3: 'What meaning [is] intended to be conveyed by the chapters from which these extracts are taken? and what meaning will the lessons convey to the mind of a child?'[76] While some passages concerned Jesus' life, the lack of selections from his teaching seemed to contradict the stated concern for moral instruction. Aside from the Beatitudes in the junior section, the Sermon on the Mount was absent, as were many parables with obvious ethical overtones. By contrast, the textbook reflected widespread belief in the ethical and symbolic value of the Ten Commandments. Education Boards could permit posting of copies of the Ten Commandments on classroom walls, so it was significant that one of the few amendments to the original Victorian text involved inclusion of a second version of the Decalogue.[77]

By the time the Bible in Schools campaign re-emerged under the Rev. D.J. Garland's leadership in 1911, Jesus was becoming more central in the movement's discourse. Earlier convictions persisted to some extent, but there was greater emphasis on Jesus' teaching and example. By 1914, the Bible in Schools League had widespread support and appeared headed for success. In December, New Zealand's Anglican Bishops even agreed to 'put the Bible in Schools Question above all political party issues at the next General Election'.[78]

The Bishop of Wellington, T.H. Sprott, was an important advocate for the Bible in Schools campaign. He articulated the rationale for his support at the Wellington Synod in 1913.[79] Sprott argued that the Bible was the moral force underpinning a civilised Christian nation. Christian morality was the agreed form in New Zealand – even if it was

76 *The Bible in Schools: A Criticism of the Proposed Text-book by the Wellington State Schools' Defence League*, Wellington: Evening Post, 1905, p.5.

77 *AJHR*, 1909, E-2, p.46. See also, *AJHR*, 1905, I-14B, p.3; *Bible in Schools: A Criticism of the Proposed Text-book*, p.4.

78 'Pastoral from the Anglican Bishops to the Members of their Flock in the Present Crisis', Supplement to *Church Gazette*, December 1914.

79 T.H. Sprott, *Bible in State Schools*, Wellington: Wright & Carman, 1913.

imperfectly practised – and the Bible was the source of that morality. Crucially, the morality espoused in the Bible was the life and teaching of Jesus. His life and character were the 'highest and only exemplification' of Christian morality, and the Bible was necessary only as the context for encountering it: 'Now our Lord, by His own Life, showed what He meant by His moral teaching; and His morality cannot be effectively taught apart from the commentary of His life'. Sprott argued that there was some moral significance in the Old Testament, but only as distinguished by the 'Spirit of Christ'. This sole criterion should determine the passages used in any syllabus. Jesus had found a niche within the matrix of moral instruction.

The outbreak of World War One stripped the Bible in Schools campaign of momentum at its most promising moment. By 1923, however, L.M. Isitt was promoting his own Religious Exercises in Schools Bill in the House of Representatives. Isitt's bill marked a further change in the direction of Sprott's argument, since the main component was now clearly Gospel readings. The bill received support from groups like the Women's Division of the New Zealand Farmers' Union, who believed that it served the interests of 'good literature, morality, and charity towards all others'. They therefore endorsed its programme based on recitation of the 'Lord's Prayer and the Ten Commandments, by the pupils, and the reading (without comment) of the Gospel and Psalms for five or ten minutes'.[80]

Isitt's bill, like others before and a succession after, failed. But while legislative efforts stalled, the churches increasingly took up the opportunities for voluntary instruction that did exist. In effect, this meant utilisation of the Nelson system, the legality of which had already been upheld. In 1925, the Nelson System was limited to a handful of schools catering for not more than about 4% of primary school children. By the time the Religious Instruction and Observances in Public Schools Act of 1962 legalised the system, it operated in 80% of state primary schools.[81]

---

80 New Zealand Farmers' Union, Women's Division, to Minister of Education, 6 August 1926, 'Syllabus and Instruction – Bible in Schools, 1925-26', Education Department, Series 2: E2/1926/1a_8/4/32, ANZ.

81 C.J. Parr to L.M. Isitt, 5 October 1925, 'Syllabus and Instruction'; Colin McGeorge and Ivan Snook, *Church, State and New Zealand Education*, Wellington: Price Milburn, 1981, pp.24-25.

From the late 1920s, numerous revised texts appeared for use 'under the present voluntary system'. These were dominated by Bible passages concerning Jesus' life. In 1928, the Manual Committee of the Bible in Schools League presented a scheme written largely by the Rev. J. Paterson of Wanganui. The six-part syllabus for junior students was framed entirely around Jesus, even though the second section addressed the Old Testament: '1. The Childhood of Jesus. 2. Stories Jesus would have heard when a boy. 3. Kind deeds of Jesus. 4. Stories told by Jesus. 5. Great sayings of Jesus. 6. The story of His Death and Resurrection'.[82]

From this point, proposals for religious instruction in state schools increasingly aligned with developments within the Sunday school movement. Cross-fertilisation reflected conscious policy, and the practical reality that the churches' educational efforts were directed by a relatively small group of people. In 1929, the New Zealand Council of Religious Education sponsored a 'Unity in Education' conference in Christchurch to promote a more integrated approach to the churches' various education programmes.[83] In 1930, Mary Salmond, J.D. Salmond's sister, produced a book of lesson outlines under the auspices of the Women's Missionary Training Institute of the Presbyterian Church. This formed the basis of the 1933 syllabus produced by the Otago Branch of the New Zealand Council of Religious Education. By 1937, the New Zealand Bible in Schools League had adopted another amended version.[84] This cooperation led to increasingly similar materials. By the 1950s, the question at Methodist Annual Conference was whether religious instruction in state schools added anything useful for children already acquainted with Sunday school and church.[85]

An increased focus on Jesus was one fruit of this interaction. Lessons for younger children concentrated on the birth and childhood of Jesus, and his love for children. Material beyond his life was still

---

82 MacDonald, 'Bible in Schools League', p.142.
83 *Toward Unity in Education: Report of the First Conference on National Religious Education*, Christchurch: New Zealand Council of Religious Education, 1929.
84 M. Salmond, *Lesson Outlines for Christian Education in New Zealand Schools Under the Nelson System*, Dunedin: Women's Missionary Training Institute of the Presbyterian Church of New Zealand, 1930; *A New Zealand Syllabus of Religious Instruction for Use in the Public Schools of New Zealand Under the Present Voluntary System*, Wellington: New Zealand Bible-in-Schools League, 1937.
85 *MAC*, 1959, p.88.

interpreted by it. In the 1933 syllabus, 'Stories of God's care that Jesus Learned' introduced scholars to children of the Old Testament. Similarly, children learned to be kind, unselfish and obedient to parents through lessons on 'What Jesus Would Like Us To Do'. When in doubt, teachers were directed to Jesus. Those working with intermediate-age children were encouraged to study the book of Acts and a Gospel if they encountered problems. Teachers in the nation's numerous rural schools generally had to teach across age-groups. For them, the syllabus suggested that, 'Time should be found each year for a short consecutive course of lessons embodying an outline of the story of our Lord'. While actual lessons could be selected freely, a short 'revision course' should deal with '1. Christmas stories. 2. Wonderful Deeds of Jesus. 3. The Teachings of Jesus. 4. Jesus and His Friends. 5. The Stories of the Passion Week. 6. Resurrection and Ascension'.

In the 1940s and beyond, the Christological imperative was articulated quite self-consciously. The Methodist minister O.E. Blamires was a long-time campaigner for religious instruction in schools who had served as Secretary of the Otago Regional Executive before becoming Dominion Secretary of the Bible in Schools League in 1927. Writing in 1960, he expressed gratitude that the school system had been kept free from sectarianism, but lamented the blight of division within the churches and the want of true religion – that is, 'the religion of Jesus'. Jesus was the 'champion of the children' whose example could only advance the New Zealand curriculum's goal of character formation. Failure to impart knowledge about him undermined children's growth and development. It estranged them from their great advocate and robbed 'Jesus Christ of His rightful approach to children'. The apologetic sustained a correlation between Jesus and child, and associations between Jesus, religious education and moral formation.[86]

Blamires presented Jesus as the Children's Saviour and Guide, but added that ignorance of the historical Jesus was educationally intolerable. Avoidance of 'polemical theology' was one thing, but denying children knowledge of the historical Jesus was too high a price to pay. Blamires observed that one Professor of History in the University of Cambridge had recently been lecturing students on 'the historical

---

86   E.O. Blamires, *A Christian Core for New Zealand Education*, Auckland: Printed by Whitcombe & Tombs, 1960, p.20.

Jesus'. Earlier instruction would have given these students an advantage denied to them under New Zealand's secular system. Though hardly compelling, the argument was understandable in the context of ebbing participation in organised religion. It illustrated an underlying concern, and perhaps an unintended admission, that Christian faith was in danger of becoming an historical artefact.

Sunday school

In addition to influencing the state education system, Protestants also worked to strengthen their own facilities, especially their Sunday schools. Prior to World War Two, association with a Sunday school was a normal experience for most New Zealand children. Participation in the Sunday school movement grew steadily during the late nineteenth century, reaching a height in the decade prior to World War One when up to 70% of children were connected. Numerically, Sunday school rolls did not decline significantly until the 1960s, though the proportion of children in contact with a school had dropped to around 42% by 1960.[87] The most detailed investigations of attendance suggest that rates of about 75% were consistently reached, at least around the end of the nineteenth century.[88] By contrast, general weekly church attendance was never higher than about 30% in 1896. Thus, vastly more children went to Sunday school than came from active church-attending families.

For many parents who did not attend church, sending children to Sunday school was a way to fulfil religious responsibilities and inculcate socially-accepted moral values. Additionally, in an age of limited opportunities, the Sunday school was a locus for social participation and an important source of leisure. To an extent, it may have provided families a break from parental responsibilities. This factor can be easily

---

87 Geoffrey Troughton, 'Religion, Churches and Childhood in New Zealand, c.1900-1940', *NZJH*, 40:1, 2006, p.40.

88 David S. Keen, 'Feeding the Lambs: The Influence of Sunday Schools on the Socialization of Children in Otago and Southland, 1848-1901', PhD thesis, University of Otago, 1999, p.291.

exaggerated, however, since the break was rather limited and association with a Sunday school entailed further responsibilities. Whatever motivations encouraged involvement, Sunday schools could be influential in children's lives even where domestic religious influence was slight. Most children simply attended the nearest accessible school. These were organised denominationally, but for most people the fact of the school mattered more than its denominational allegiance. Children could quite happily change their association as circumstances required.

Despite the obvious numerical success of the movement, Sunday schools were under considerable pressure. Continual calls for reform reflected the sense of competition with an increasingly well-funded and professional state education system, as well as the difficulty of keeping pace with an expanding population. Sunday schools were supposed to help convert children and prepare them for life in the church. The growth of child-centred approaches in education and the waning appeal of austere commandment-based forms of religion led to important changes in approach during the early twentieth century. George Tiller's introduction of innovations like the Cradle Roll, sand table, and other forms of expression work to Methodist Sunday schools in 1900 provided an early indication of these trends.[89]

Catechism had been a central element in nineteenth-century Sunday school instruction. According to David Keen, the function of catechism changed and its use diminished. He argues that catechism was viewed more as a supplement for shaping converts than an aid to children's conversion by the twentieth century. While Keen rightly notes the move to a more 'Christological' rather than 'dryly catechetical' syllabus, catechism did have a strong Christological element.[90] It helped fix the boundaries of orthodox belief, which was viewed in some ways as a form of protection. Catechism was one way to learn about Jesus, though his personality was not the focus.

Modern teaching methodologies disparaged rote learning, which challenged catechism's value. In 1908, for instance, a sharp dispute erupted over its continuing usage in the new educational environment.[91] Nevertheless, catechism did persist, even if it was never as important as

---

89   *NZMT*, 11 April 1925, pp.8-9; also *NZMT*, 14 July 1928.
90   Keen, pp.164, 172.
91   *Outlook*, 11 January 1908, p.4; *Outlook*, 30 May 1908, pp.14-15.

in Catholic education. It remained a component of Presbyterian Sunday school examinations as late as 1932, although students were required to recall only half the questions they had at the turn of the century.[92] From 1923, examinable catechism content was reduced to make way for the inclusion of Scripture memory work. Though the syllabus changed frequently, selections were always based on pragmatic considerations. Junior classes learnt the first questions, while the overall aim was to ensure that children covered the whole catechism in the course of their Sunday school education. There was no indication that particular sections were deemed more easy or appropriate for different ages.

Despite its persistence, catechism was increasingly at odds with shifts in religious education, where the trend toward child-centred methodologies was accompanied by increasing focus on Jesus. Sunday school syllabi and notes indicate that the Gospels had long been prevalent, while examinations were dominated by questions concerning his life and teaching. Nevertheless, there was an increasing feeling that Jesus should be more prominent. Thus, in 1940, the Methodist Youth Department reported to Conference, 'That while recognising the value of certain O.T. passages for Sunday school Scholars, we recommend a much greater place be given to the life and teaching of Jesus'.[93] In some ways this resolution merely confirmed a well-established trajectory.

Jesus and developmental theory

In June 1926, the *New Zealand Methodist Times* printed an article by the leading American social gospel theologian Shailer Mathews on 'Present Tendencies in the Religious World'.[94] According to Mathews, the contemporary religious world was characterised by four key trends: a revolt from authority, a new emphasis on Christ, social reform, and new conceptions of religious education. In particular, Mathews argued that

---

92 See the examination sheets in 'Sunday School Exam Committee Minute Book, 1893-97', PCNZ/GA: Location AD12/4, PCANZARC.
93 *MAC*, 1940, p.70.
94 *NZMT*, 5 June 1926, p.9.

historical study of Jesus' life had laid the emphasis 'upon Jesus Christ and his teaching rather than upon dogma and the Bible'. Consequently, 'It was inevitable that such a change of emphasis from dogma to life, from the Bible to Jesus Christ, and from the individual to the individual in society, should have led to new conceptions of religious education'. Though written in America, the observations were pertinent in New Zealand. As Mathews suggested, social and theological factors helped shape these changes. Psychological notions of the self were also important, and became influential in Protestant representations of Jesus.

The growth of psychology was a particularly important characteristic of the post-World War One years, especially after psychoanalytic methods were employed to treat 'shell-shocked' soldiers. The attitude of religious leaders and leaders in religious education was generally positive, despite some anxiety over the potentially corrosive influence of the 'psychology of religion'. Initial interest was limited to a smaller educated group who had access to these ideas, but there were attempts to bring the basic tenets of psychology into the mainstream. As early as 1923, the *Outlook* carried an article that attempted to explain the ideas and methods of psychoanalysis, including discussion of Freud, Jung and Adler.[95]

It was more than coincidence that this *Outlook* article was published only a week before the launch of Children's Year in the Presbyterian Church. The interest in psychology partly followed from belief that religious education would be bolstered by a stronger scientific foundation. Thus, in discussing the merits of psychology one contributor to the *Australasian Intercollegian* enthused that education based on the 'results of experiment and trial' would soon replace 'haphazard inherited ideas'.[96] Psychology promised a more 'efficient', professional and scientific basis that would allow the Sunday school movement to compete with state education. Child psychology was a relatively new field. Though it incorporated a range of methods, techniques and approaches, the developmental model was perhaps the most influential aspect for religious education. Developmental theory posited that children were biologically propelled in a continuous and universal

95   *Outlook*, 5 March 1923, pp.16, 25.
96   *Australasian Intercollegian*, 23:1, 1920, p.18.

process through increasingly advanced stages to adulthood.[97] The essential educational imperative was to understand those discrete developmental stages, and ensure that teaching content and methodology was appropriately targeted.

While it often took time before new ideas were incorporated into teaching practice, opinion-formers in religious education circles were remarkably open to developmental ideas. Methodists introduced 'graded' Sunday school lessons in 1903, partly because of the system's scientific credentials.[98] In 1908, A.B. Chappell delivered a keynote address on 'Child Psychology' at the first Dominion Conference of Methodist Sunday School Workers. Delegates were urged to study William James and John Dewey, and the psychological and developmental basis of the graded system was highlighted as one of its chief advantages.[99] When a furore erupted over adoption of the Australasian Graded Lessons in the 1920s, the issue was no longer about grading *per se* but of the best graded lessons for New Zealanders. By 1936, the Rev. J.C. Jamieson was reaffirming that the great merit of the graded system was its adaptation 'to the child'. Grading recognised that life is composed of different 'stages or seasons' of the soul, each needing 'suitable food'.[100]

Sunday school teachers from the late 1920s were expected to have an elementary awareness of new psychological ideas. By 1939, a module on 'Youth Psychology' was also included in the Leadership Training Course for the Bible Class Movement.[101] Books on child psychology and religious education were frequently found among recommended reading lists. D.F. Wilson's *Child Psychology and Religious Education* and A.A. Lamoreaux's *The Unfolding Life* were the most commonly commended.[102] Wilson's book was particularly influential. Published in

---

97 Archard, pp.32-34.
98 See E.F.I. Hanson, 'The Relationship between Sunday School and Church in the History of New Zealand Methodism', DTheol thesis, Melbourne College of Divinity, 2002, p.148; cf. *PGA*, 1910, p.146; *PGA*, 1916, p.127.
99 A.B. Chappell (ed.), *The Church and the Children. Official Report of the First Dominion Conference of Methodist Sunday School Workers*, Christchurch: Lyttelton Times, 1909; *Sunday School and Bible Class at Work*, p.9.
100 *Sunday School and Bible Class at Work*, p.9.
101 See *NZMBC Link*, 5 May 1939.
102 A.A. Lamoreaux, *The Unfolding Life: A Study of Development with Reference to Religious Training*, Chicago: Religious Publishing Company, 1907; Dorothy F. Wilson, *Child Psychology and Religious Education*, London: SCM, 1928.

London in February 1928, it was recommended in the Presbyterian training guide for teachers published later that year. Revised often, the book was considered essential reading into the 1930s and beyond. To some extent, interest in this literature reflected the growth of interest in psychology in New Zealand educational circles generally from the 1920s. For, while psychological interpretations of childhood became particularly important after World War Two, the seeds of this change were planted much earlier.[103] As Bronwyn Dalley has indicated, scientific study played an increasingly important part in thinking about children's welfare in the interwar years, even if the psychology was rather superficial at times.[104]

Interest in child psychology and developmental theory shaped representations of Jesus for Protestant children. To take developmental theory seriously, Jesus had to be interpreted not only for children in general but for the different stages of childhood. While children would respond positively to Jesus, their response would vary according to the image offered and the stage of the child. The teacher's task was to match carefully the representation with the stage, in order that children might understand. As Symons argued, '"the Eternal" to whom children respond... is "like Jesus," and like Jesus as comprehended by the child'.[105] By the 1930s, this was outlined within a reasonably clear ideological framework, though details of nomenclature and grade definition varied between denominations and were subject to constant refinement. D.F. Wilson, for example, differentiated between Infancy, Early, Middle and Later Childhood, each separated by about three years up to the age of twelve. These roughly corresponded with the Cradle Roll, Beginner, Juniors and Intermediate Departments.[106] According to G. Hope Kane, as children passed through these stages they would have a different picture of Jesus – from first impressions of him as 'Friend and

103 Geoffrey Troughton, 'Religious Education and the Rise of Psychological Childhood in New Zealand', *History of Education Review*, 33:2, 2004, pp.30-44; D.G. McDonald, 'Children and Young Persons in New Zealand Society', in Peggy G. Koopman-Boyden (ed.), *Families in New Zealand Society*, Wellington: Methuen, 1978, pp.44-56.

104 Dalley, *Family Matters*, esp. pp.40, 98-99, 114.

105 Symons, *Junior Worship*, p.3.

106 Wilson, *Child Psychology*, pp.123-26; *Sunday School Teachers' Guide*, pp.9-18.

Helper', to the 'Greatest of all Heroes' in Junior years, and ultimately as 'Divine Master, the Incarnate Son of God'.[107]

Developmental theory suggested that the infant years and Early Childhood were characterised by appreciation of 'concrete' objects. Rita Snowden called this the 'Realistic' period.[108] Jesus was considered well-suited to the pedagogical needs of this stage. Being interested in tangible objects, young children's concept of God would be anthropomorphic. Therefore, it was important to present God as a 'Loving Father', 'Inviting Friend', 'Friendly Protector' and 'Creator'. Jesus functioned as the concrete representation of God. Representations for the very young emphasised readily apprehensible concepts, such as Jesus' friendliness and helpfulness: 'The concept which the child needs of Jesus is of His surpassing goodness, His unselfish courage, and His loving service. Ground the child in knowledge that is rich and fruitful, for it is making God and Jesus real to him'.[109] Jesus would be known through his character and deeds rather than his teaching. As Kane's comments suggested, Jesus was much warmer and closer than adult 'religion'. Religion would ultimately take root through the appeal of personality.

According to Rita Snowdon, Middle Childhood could be characterised as the 'Imaginative Period'. From about six to nine years of age, children learned to play together more freely and were fascinated by 'make-believe'. Development of their imaginative faculties was the major priority, which made exposure to stories essential. Wilson considered that this was the time for 'carrying the children away into the surroundings and events of the bible stories in a way which leaves an indelible impression on their minds'. At this stage, children could immerse themselves in the world of the Holy Land where they would meet a Jesus who 'went about doing good'. Jesus' character, or 'spirit', could be encountered in the Gospel stories. During Middle Childhood, children were prone to question incessantly, which made introduction of details of Jesus' life appropriate. Insights into his environment, ancient ways of life, and geographical and historical information would sate hungry minds and make Jesus appear lively and interesting.

---

107 G. Hope Kane, *Beginners' Department*, Wellington: Youth Board, Methodist Church of New Zealand, 1941, p.17.

108 Snowden, *Story-Time Again*, p.10.

109 *God and the Little Child*, p.10; Kane, *The Cradle Roll*, p.17.

Later Childhood, the Intermediate stage from eight or nine to twelve years of age, was dominated by love of adventure and interest in personality. Children were thought to be particularly active physically, and unhindered by the imbalances of rapid body growth. Their logical faculties were also developing to a point where real and ideal could be distinguished. For Snowden, this was the 'Heroic Period', characterised by a love for stories of 'courage, daring and action'. Children of this age were considered susceptible to 'hero-worship' as they developed out of more dependent forms of love and attachment to parents.[110] Because they were responsive to the heroic, all manner of stories and subjects were admissible – stories form the Old and New Testaments, as well as from extra-biblical sources. Heroic examples would excite similar endeavour.

Later Childhood was also a moment of opportunity. It was *the* period when children could be 'brought to consider decision for Christ'.[111] As parental attachment weakened, children sought ideals and models to aspire to. J.D. Salmond argued vigorously that religious educators needed to take better advantage of the crises in children's lives at this point, whilst avoiding the dangers of 'promiscuous evangelism'.[112] This stage was also challenging in some respects. The Intermediate Department was commonly considered 'the problem department' of the Sunday school, the age of 'leakage' when children drifted out of organised religious association. There were hopes that developmental psychology could provide solutions in addressing these issues.

To appeal to this hero-worshipping stage, Jesus needed to be the greatest hero: 'If the boys and girls of this age are hero-worshippers, then they need to have set before them Jesus as the Supreme Hero'.[113] As R.E. Fordyce argued, 'From the age of eight to fourteen or sixteen years the child readily responds to the call of the heroic. Should we not, during that period, try to win his love and devotion for Jesus Christ, "the world's Supreme Hero?"'[114] While developmental ideas were meant to be universally applicable, Jesus the Hero was primarily for boys, and constructed in masculine terms. Rita Snowden considered that heroes

110 See *Sunday School Teachers' Guide*, p.14; Symons, *Teaching Temperance*, pp.14-16; Wilson, *Child Psychology*, p.107.
111 *Sunday School Teachers' Guide*, p.18; Wilson, *Child Psychology*, pp.125-26.
112 Salmond (ed.), *The Church and Her Young People*, p.21.
113 Symons, *Teaching Temperance*, p.16.
114 *NZMT*, 3 March 1923, p.13.

could include scientists and social workers, but it was exceptional to find this given expression. More often, heroes were adventurers or military figures, and Jesus the epitome of knightly or soldierly virtues who laid 'the spell of His adventure' upon his followers.[115]

Evangelicals expressed some uneasiness about the potential hazards of applying developmental ideas too rigorously. Despite his enthusiasm for aspects of the graded system, J.C. Jamieson worried that an emphasis on 'good deeds' could undermine evangelical belief: 'Over-awed by psychologists, some of whom have only a sub-Christian faith, teachers have been teaching to boys and girls a religion of works instead of the Gospel of the grace of God'.[116] Though not a New Zealander, Hudson Pope was an influential thinker in the Children's Special Service Mission. He was similarly concerned at a tendency to draw deterministic conclusions from developmental ideas. Pope expressed particular alarm at one claim in a Sunday school resource that 'You must teach the children of Jesus as Helper, Companion, and Friend, but *not as Saviour*, for the child has no sense of sin'. According to Pope, this effectively denied the doctrine of the Atonement.[117]

Evangelical representations of Jesus tended to focus on his saving redemptive work. Furthermore, evangelical thought did not distinguish between levels of spiritual need. Especially in its more Calvinistic forms, it emphasised the total corruption of humanity, and redemption 'solely by the blood of our Lord Jesus Christ'.[118] In a sense, Jesus was conflated with the gospel of the cross, with children viewed as 'little adults' in terms of their spiritual needs. Evangelicals tended to be wary of any developmentally-based assumption that real religious commitment was located in later childhood. Abstract theological thought may have been greatest then, but Jesus could be known as 'Divine Master, the Incarnate Son of God' at any childhood stage. The evangelical kerygma was relatively fixed, centring as it did on sin, and redemption through the cross of Christ.

While they were arguably less concerned about defining childhood stages than other groups, evangelicals did also present Jesus in warm and

---

115 Rita Snowden, *The Wind Blows*, London: Epworth, 1939, p.146.
116 *Sunday School and Bible Class at Work*, p.19.
117 R. Hudson Pope, *To Teach Others Also*, London: CSSM, 1953, p.17 (original italics).
118 *Reaper*, June 1923, pp.96-97.

invitational ways. Evangelistic messages focused on the saving death of Christ, but children also learnt about a Jesus who experienced the same pressures and troubles as present-day children.[119] The children's pages of the *Reaper* affirmed that no child was too young to apprehend Jesus' love, especially as expressed in the 'terrible' meaning of the crucifixion.[120] Youngsters needed to be reminded of eternal realities, even if the details were alarming and at times quite graphic. The options, as one *Reaper* column described it, were simply to be 'burned or blessed'.[121] Stories like those of a six-year old becoming caught in railway tracks were morality tales, but they were also reminders of the urgent need for decision. Ultimately, such horrors were also a vivid contrast with the glory and goodness of the Saviour. Jesus was still their loving champion, willing and able to save.

By the time New Zealand children left formal education, most had become well acquainted with Jesus as a very human figure, a Great Personality who especially loved them. That aspect of personality was critical, for it provided a form of religion that cohered with attempts to move away from stricter, law-based, moral-commandment forms of Christianity. Yet morality was still a crucial factor. The value of religion was often related to notions of social morality, and this was true for children as much as any other group.

Representation of Jesus in such moral and personal terms was not unproblematic. One the one hand, it made the children's Jesus highly susceptible to simply becoming the supreme example of conventional values. Jesus was sinless and morally excellent, yet the virtues he purportedly exemplified often bore little resemblance to New Testament pictures of him. This could effectively strip Christianity of much that made it distinctive. Biblical claims concerning Jesus' divine identity and the more challenging counter-cultural aspects of his message did not fit comfortably within the paradigm. On the other hand, the ideal of Jesus as a moral guide ultimately rested on belief that he was faultless. In some ways this could actually make him less easy for children to relate to,

119 B. Clark, 'CSSM History, Answers to Questions. Folder: Early History of the Movement', pp.2, 6-7, Historical Documents from the 1930s Box, Scripture Union Archives, Wellington.
120 *Reaper*, January 1926, p.308.
121 *Reaper*, March 1928, p.23.

however much they might admire him. A perfect Jesus was potentially daunting, and therefore a strangely distant figure. Moreover, Ian Dixon recalls knowing that Jesus was 'wonderful' and 'perfect in every way', but that he experienced him as a snoop. Jesus' interest in every detail of a child's life was supposed to be comforting, but could be invasive and unsettling.[122]

Religious activity was heavily concentrated in childhood, but by the end of the years of primary education much of this dissipated. As Lauris Edmond observed, the disjunction between high rates of Sunday school participation and lower adult attendance reinforced the association of religion with childhood: 'God was apparently for children, like bread and milk when you were sick, or going to bed early'.[123] The great emphasis on Jesus during these years meant that he was linked with this pattern. In short, it was easy to 'grow out' of Jesus. Representation of him in overtly maternal terms suggested that one could outgrow Jesus as surely as one outgrew childhood dependencies. Furthermore, a heroic Jesus could easily become just another fictional character whose historicity was quite peripheral, while stories of Jesus could also strengthen perceptions that religion was too naïve, sentimental and sanctimonious for the adult world. Indeed, this may help explain why the human Jesus was frequently less important to adults.

If this is correct, why did children hear so much about a human Jesus that adults were less comfortable with? The disjunction reflects the influences that made personalisation attractive, as well as tensions inherent in the religion New Zealanders sought. The increasing centrality of Jesus in children's religion reflected a general pattern within Protestant religion, and was perhaps its most striking example. Yet, this buttressing of a correlation between Jesus and childhood also posed risks, since the children's Jesus often represented the kinds of moralising and sentimental religion that were coming under fire. In particular, he seemed to offer little for men, whose perceived irreligion was also a focus of attention.

---

122 *Growing Up in New Zealand Part 28: Sundays and Church Going Before 1925.* URL: http://www.nzine.co.nz/features/guinz28.churchgoing.html.
123 Lauris Edmond, *An Autobiography*, Wellington: Bridget Williams Books, 1994, p.19.

6. Manly Jesus

In late 1903, the Rev. George T. Marshall concluded an address to the Warkworth Literary Society with the proclamation that 'Jesus stands supreme as the Ideal Man.... At the same time he is not more supreme than imitable, and his life repeats in winning accents his own words, "Follow Me!"'[1] Marshall's belief in Jesus as the archetype and model of humanity was commonly held by a broad spectrum of Christian believers. From the late nineteenth century, however, claims that Jesus was the 'Ideal Man' connoted a more specific meaning. In particular, they affirmed his masculinity and exemplification of manhood. Interest in the masculinity of Jesus was closely bound to anxieties about the place of men in society, especially as it manifested in an apparent gender imbalance in religious activity. If colonial environments weakened the bonds of religion generally, the effect upon men seemed particularly pronounced. Attempts to redress this situation and increase participation in organised religion typically appealed to men's supposed dispositions. Responses included the establishment of groups for men, and association of male religiosity with heroic masculinity. As the Ideal Man, Jesus was the standard of both religiosity and manliness, so that attempts to improve the appeal of religion for men readily turned to him. Marshall's own exposition focused primarily on aspects of Jesus' character, including his piety, steadfastness and self-sacrificing service. These facets remained important, but were increasingly cast in heroic terms.

Men, women and religion

Attempts to project Jesus in more masculine terms were embedded in wider concerns about a purported feminisation of religion and society in

1   *Outlook*, 24 October 1903, pp.23-24; *Outlook*, 31 October 1903, pp.22-23; *Outlook*, 7 November 1903, pp.23-24.

the nineteenth century. Evangelicalism had promoted the value of domesticity for men, but by the later part of the nineteenth century women had a more prominent role in the moral and religious instruction of the family.[2] A preponderance of women among churchgoers had been typical in places for much longer, but by the 1890s it aroused reaction among those who claimed that women's undue influence was marginalising men from religion. In North America, such views were bolstered by church attendance surveys which revealed that the composition of churches was often only one-third male, or less. Similar proportions were evident through much of Western Europe.[3]

Some commentators have suggested that evidence of resurgent masculinism in late-nineteenth century Anglo-American culture was a direct reaction to broader processes of feminisation. The years from 1870 to 1914 have been characterised as a time of waning respect for ideals of male domesticity. In Britain, historians have suggested that altered patterns of work and the economic and military demands of Empire may have contributed to a 'flight from domesticity'. North American interpreters have linked the 'hyper-masculinity' of the Progressive Era to a range of factors including the Civil War, Social Darwinist ideas, the expansion of leisure and the encroachment of women on previously all-male preserves.

This wider mood was clearly significant. Ideals of masculinity were plural not unitary, and shaped by variables of class, sexuality, ethnicity and belief. Explicitly religious conceptions were similarly variegated, coloured as they were by the additional influences of theology and denomination. Nevertheless, concern about the role and place of men transcended those differences, and religionists of various stripes, from muscular Christians and revivalists to social gospel radicals, seemed eager to reconfigure religion in more male-friendly terms. Muscular Christianity was perhaps the best known nineteenth century model. It presented chivalry, austerity and physicality as a remedy for the chaos of urbanisation, and a counter to what Thomas Hughes called the 'strange delusion' of religious effeminacy. Hughes was a Christian Socialist. In

2   John Tosh, *A Man's Place: Masculinity and the Middle-Class Home in Victorian England*, New Haven: Yale University Press, 1999.
3   Hugh McLeod, *Religion and the People of Western Europe, 1879-1970*, Oxford: Oxford University Press, 1981, p.29.

1879, his book *The Manliness of Christ* depicted its subject as a courageous combatant against evil whose athletic and physical manliness counterbalanced his 'tenderness, and thoughtfulness for others'.[4] This general approach appealed to a broad constituency. The revivalist D.L. Moody famously cultivated sentimental forms of spirituality and expounded the nurturing aspects of Christ's nature, but was also a firm supporter of the YMCA and its physical brand of manliness and health. His successors at the Moody Bible Institute in Chicago encouraged Warner Sallman to produce paintings of a manly Jesus that became ubiquitous in the twentieth century.[5]

The man problem in New Zealand religion

Despite the difference in conditions between colonial New Zealand and the urban industrial north, many of these patterns were replicated locally. Uneven sex ratios were common in settler societies generally. In purely demographic terms, the gender balance in colonial New Zealand favoured men. In 1861, 61.67% of New Zealand's population was male. That imbalance evened with the inducements offered to single women and families during the migration boom years from the 1870s to 1890s. By the time of the 1901 census there was only a small differential, with the male population being 52.54%. Except during wartime, this small gap continued to narrow. It was sharpest in the country, and evened earliest in urban areas.[6]

4   Peter Gay, 'The Manliness of Christ', in R.W. Davis and R.J. Helmstadter (eds), *Religion and Irreligion in Victorian Society: Essays in Honor of R.K. Webb*, London: Routledge, 1992, pp.102-116.
5   Clifford Putney, *Muscular Christianity: Manhood and Sports in Protestant America, 1880-1920*, Cambridge: Harvard University Press, 2001, pp.2-3; David Morgan, *Visual Piety: A History and Theory of Popular Religious Images*, Berkeley: University of California Press, 1998, p.119.
6   E.J. von Dadelszen, *Report on the Results of a Census of the Colony of New Zealand Taken for the Night of the 5th April, 1891*, Wellington: Government Printer, 1893, pp.14-15.

This numerical advantage was not reflected in organised religion, where the churches' leadership was largely male but the flock seldom was. Anecdotal evidence suggesting more active church attendance by women is supported by a range of data. For example, women tended to be more evident in churches where attendance was most greatly valued. In the 1906 national census, 53.01% of the total population and 52.98% of those making religious profession were male.[7] This proportion was only realised, however, in affiliation to the three largest churches. Significantly, the Church of England (53.06%), Presbyterianism (52.49%), and Roman Catholicism (52.89%) in New Zealand were all derivative of 'national churches' where affiliation was least likely to translate into frequent attendance.[8] The smaller Protestant groups placed a higher priority on active membership, and attracted greater proportions of female support. In general, the smaller the sect, the less likely men were to affiliate. In the largest group, the Methodist Church of Australasia, 49.61% out of 31,554 affiliates were men; Baptists (8,537) had 48.10% men, the Salvation Army (4,024) 47.97%, Congregationalists (3,532) 47.99%, and the Churches of Christ (3,304) 46.79%. Among the fledgling Seventh Day Adventists (990), only 40.3% were men. Men still made religious profession, but their affiliation suggested lower rates of participation.

Some analyses of the gender composition of church attendance support the impression of greater participation by women. Caroline Daley's research on Taradale during this period demonstrates that women attended church more often than men. Participation was highest among single women, and lowest among single men.[9] Similar patterns existed in urban South Dunedin where women were more frequent participants across denominations, often constituting between two-thirds and three-quarters of active communicants or churchgoers.[10]

7   E.J. von Dadelszen, *Report on the Results of a Census of the Colony of New Zealand Taken for the Night of the 29th April, 1906*, Wellington: Government Printer, 1908, p.25.
8   Jackson, 'Churchgoing', pp.43-59.
9   Caroline Daley, *Girls & Women, Men & Boys: Gender in Taradale, 1886-1930*, Auckland: Auckland University Press, 1999, p.96.
10 John Stenhouse, 'God, the Devil, and Gender', in Barbara Brookes, Annabel Cooper and Robin Law (eds), *Sites of Gender: Women, Men and Modernity in*

The records of Knox Presbyterian Church in Lower Hutt confirm these trends.[11] Knox was well established by the turn of the century, but grew considerably during the period. In 1903, there were only 59 names on the communicant roll. Between 1931 and 1936 there were 323. In 1903, 61% (36) of the communicant roll was female. By the later period, the proportion of women had increased to 66.6% (215). Interestingly, while men were less likely to become communicant members, those who did so attended slightly more regularly than their female counterparts. Male communicants attended Quarterly Communion at 56.5% of their potential in 1903, which compared favourably with a rate of 51.9% for women. Single men attended most frequently at 61.5%. Between 1931 and 1936, overall attendance rates rose slightly and the differential between male (56.5%) and female (55.2%) narrowed. Despite the persistence of slightly higher male attendance rates, the congregation remained predominantly female. By the mid-1930s, there were still nearly two women for every man receiving communion.

Around the country, expressions of concern about this kind of imbalance were common, even if explanations for the situation varied. Some argued that men found church dull, though others regarded this as a symptom rather than a cause. In 1908, one Presbyterian discussion about the lack of ministerial candidates quickly broadened into a more general debate about men and religion. Contributors asserted that women's interests and tastes dominated church life. Men were different, and needed to encounter religion in ways that reflected this distinctiveness. The Rev. J. Clark's hypotheses on this subject were received sympathetically.[12] One columnist argued that the churches focused too much on children, the elderly and women. Comparing a plethora of men's groups abroad, they noted a paucity of local initiatives:

> How many churches have a meeting where the subject of the meeting is masculine, where the treatment is masculine in view point, and the conduct of the meeting is

Southern Dunedin, 1890-1939, Auckland: Auckland University Press, 2003, pp.326-27.

11   See Communicants Register and Attendance Book, 1903-26 (MSX-4214); 1926-31 (MSX-4215); 1931-50 (MSY-4071), ATL.
12   Outlook, 2 May 1908, p.6; Outlook, 9 May 1908, pp.6-7; Outlook, 6 June 1908, p.7.

adapted to masculine tastes? Generally speaking, the kind of subject and the style of meeting do not specially appeal to the every-day thoughts and likings of men.[13]

The Presbyterian Assembly's committee on the State of Religion also highlighted the issue. Its convener, the Rev. Dr Frank Dunlop, succeeded William Salmond in the Chair of Mental and Moral Philosophy at Otago University from 1913-32. His report in 1908 urged for 'A more robust and manly type of Christianity amongst the men of the Church', 'Organised work for men by men', as well as greater enthusiasm in proclaiming 'those elements in the Gospel which appeal to men'.[14]

The relative absence of men was the culmination of a widening gender gap that began with adolescence. While boys and girls attended Sunday school in reasonably even proportions, many boys' religious participation ended with childhood. According to the Anglican *New Zealand Church News*, young people's tendency to 'abandon Church as soon as they leave the Sunday-school' was symptomatic of wider spiritual malaise.[15] Even so, the loss of boys was problematic, not only as a failure in the work of the Sunday schools generally, but also in relation to the religious potential of late childhood. The problem of 'leakage' was widely recognised, but frequent references to a 'Boy Problem' made plain where it was particularly acute.

Concern about boys was not limited to religious communities. A rise in larrikinism associated with late nineteenth-century urban growth focused attention on younger males in New Zealand as it had elsewhere. Writing of the Australian situation, Martin Crotty has argued that the 'Boy Problem' was symptomatic of the declining authority of religion, as well as a tendency to project hopes and fears onto young men.[16] Various organisations had been tackling delinquency and irreligion abroad for some time. The YMCA was one of the earliest, but others were operating by the twentieth century. In 1893, the Rev. W.B. Forbush founded the popular Knights of King Arthur in America. His book of 1901, *The Boy Problem*, was widely cited in New Zealand and did much to consolidate the terminology.

13   *Outlook*, 13 June 1908, p.3; cf. *Outlook*, 5 March 1923, p.3.
14   *PGA*, 1908, pp.59-61.
15   *NZ Church News*, March 1900, p.11.
16   Martin Crotty, *Making the Australian Male: Middle-Class Masculinity 1870-1920*, Melbourne: Melbourne University Press, 2001, esp. pp.10-20.

Appeals to the heroic became a staple ingredient in attempts to redress the gender imbalance. Heroic masculinity was widely celebrated and applied deliberately to Jesus, especially in relation to the doctrine of the Incarnation. On the one hand, it implied the necessity of identification with male experiences:

> we shall save our boys as Jesus did the world, by incarnation. For them we must go down into the Galilee of simple-heartedness and the Samaria of the common-place, and dwell at the Nazareth of childish toil and struggle, and kneel in the Gethsemane of intercession, yea, and climb the sacrificial mound of Calvary.[17]

On the other hand, it meant making Jesus more masculine. As Frank Dunlop explained:

> the strongest man meets in Christ one who is beyond controversy his Master in Manhood. In all the essential constituents of active heroism Jesus stands supreme. Inspiration for forceful, virile character and energetic living is here in abundance. To give its due place in the Christ ideal to this muscularity of soul cannot but be helpful.[18]

The manly Jesus and the social challenge

Social unrest and the rise of working-class interests provided one important catalyst for attempts to make Jesus more masculine. This impetus derived from a perception that the churches had failed to connect with the working classes and working-class men in particular. According to Erik Olssen, Protestant laments about their failings in this regard became a refrain from the 1890s.[19] There is certainly evidence that some church leaders, especially those working in the inner city, felt there was a problem. In 1905, the Rev. R.S. Gray of Oxford Terrace Baptist Church, Christchurch, organised special meetings to elicit working men's perceptions of the obstacles between them and church attendance. From this he concluded that the leading complaints were

17   *PGA*, 1908, pp.66-67.
18   *Outlook*, 30 May 1908, p.5.
19   Erik Olssen, 'The "Working Class" in New Zealand', *NZJH*, 8:1, 1974, p.44.

Christian hypocrisy, difficulty with Christian doctrine and the anti-labour stance of the churches.[20] Some churchgoers agreed, though they added that unattractive services and a tendency to highlight class distinctions were problems.[21] In Dunedin, the Rev. W.A. Sinclair of the Methodist Central Mission organised similar meetings. His consultations also suggested that there were serious limits to working-class participation, but were less clear in attributing responsibility. Nevertheless, by 22 April 1906, Sinclair was organising Sunday afternoon meetings to provide a service where 'where men could meet with men, discuss the questions closely affecting men, and especially those who labour'. According to a report in the *Outlook*, 200 attended the initial gathering and they were 'working men without exception'.[22]

John Stenhouse has questioned how alienated from organised religion the working classes actually were.[23] Some contemporary Protestants also dissented from the majority view of a disconnection between working men and the churches. W.H. Uttley, the President of the Dunedin Trades and Labour Council and a Congregationalist, argued that workers were actually the backbone and mainstay of most churches, including his own which was 'all working men'.[24] Following the lead of the Chicago YMCA, New Zealand Presbyterians conducted a survey to ascertain whether working men attended church in the same proportions as others. According to 72 of the 97 responding churches, they did.[25] On the other hand, the very existence of a survey indicated less certainty than the results implied. Even Uttley grudgingly accepted that there was widespread apathy, indifference and criticism among working men, even if outright irreligion was highly unusual.

Rapid unionisation of manual workers and growth in the more militant expressions of unionism prior to World War One sharpened

20 *NZB*, August 1905, p.121, cited in Brian Smith, '"Wherefore Then This Thusness": The Social Composition of Baptist Congregations in New Zealand', *New Zealand Journal of Baptist Research*, 3, 1998, p.76.
21 *Outlook*, 13 June 1908, pp.2-3; *NZB*, August 1909, pp.391-93; *Outlook*, 5 March, 1923, p.3.
22 *Otago Liberal*, 9 September 1905, p.7; *Otago Liberal*, 16 September 1905, p.7; *Otago Liberal*, 23 September 1905, p.5; *Outlook*, 2 June 1906, p.45.
23 John Stenhouse, 'Christianity, Gender, and the Working Class in Southern Dunedin, 1880-1940', *JRH*, 30:1, 2006, pp.18-44.
24 *Otago Liberal*, 23 September 1905, p.5.
25 *PGA*, 1909, p.53.

concerns about working men. As Fran Shor has demonstrated, part of the ethos of radical organisations like the IWW included the assertion of 'alternative masculinism'. Syndicalism promoted virility and solidarity as alternatives to the encroachments of 'managerial capitalism and the servile state'.[26] The masculinity it projected was far more aggressive than that of the Romantic 'toiler', and was popularised during the industrial unrest experienced between 1911 and 1913. Standing up to employers became a new mark of manliness during the massive strikes at Waihi, Wellington and Auckland.

Confrontation with employers was just one part of a wider engagement with traditional forms of authority that included scoffing at religion. While a masculine Jesus could be enlisted in the revolutionary cause, correlation of masculinity with antagonism to religion was another powerful rhetorical strategy. Thus, anti-Church language was sometimes couched in gendered terms.[27] On the other hand, where church leaders made pronouncements sympathetic to labour they were characterised as 'manly and outspoken'.[28] Arguments in support of socialism often utilised a quasi-religious masculinist tone: 'We need Men', the *Maoriland Worker* declaimed:

> Men! Real men. Strong men. True men.... Men who are not afraid to die for what they believe to be the right.... We stand for the working class, for freedom, for the truth, for justice. We have nothing to fear. We are fighting the battles of the Almighty's own children and the gates of hell cannot prevail against us.[29]

Given the gulf in men's church attendance, religious communities were sensitive to this kind of language. Derision of Christian masculinity was not entirely new. A long Protestant tradition within Christianity had denigrated Catholicism as a form of 'corrupting effeminacy'.[30] This was sustained in radical De Leonite socialism, and continued in the John A.

---

26 Fran Shor, 'Bringing the Storm: Syndicalist Counterpublics and the Industrial Workers of the World in New Zealand, 1908-14', in Pat Moloney and Kerry Taylor (eds), *On the Left: Essays on Socialism in New Zealand*, Dunedin: University of Otago Press, 2002, pp.60-65.
27 *MW*, 1 July 1914, p.6.
28 *MW*, 22 March 1912, p.4.
29 *MW*, 20 April 1911, p.13.
30 See Tim Hitchcock and Michèle Cohen (eds), *English Masculinities, 1660-1800*, London: Longman, 1999, pp.57, 110.

Lee tradition in New Zealand. However, socialist application of this discourse against Christians as a whole represented a significant challenge. Radical attacks on imperialism, capitalism and religious masculinity were understood as part of a wider assault on Christian civilisation. The perceived scale of this threat partly explains the effort expended in reconfiguring ideal religious manhood. Strident groups asserted a necessary opposition between organised religion and political agitation, and then framed the divide in terms of masculinity. In response, religious communities attempted to overcome the stigma of effeminacy by connecting Christianity with manliness.

The manhood of the master

Social gospel Christianity was one of the most explicit religious responses to this context, and concerns about 'feminisation' were often expressed within the movement. According to Susan Curtis, social gospellers reconstructed the gentle Saviour of feminised evangelicalism into a hearty carpenter between the 1880s and 1920s.[31] By the early twentieth century, young audiences frequently heard about the authority and strength of Jesus' manliness. Thereafter, a stream of literature by American social Christians like Bruce Barton bemoaned Jesus' emasculation and rehabilitated him as a model of robust manhood. Paradoxically, then, social Christianity may have produced a doctrinally gentler Christianity, but a more forceful Jesus. Heroic formulations were often complemented, however, by emphasis on Jesus' practical goodness and the moral basis of religion, as well its benevolent functions.

The leading American liberal Protestant H.E. Fosdick's *The Manhood of the Master* was arguably the most important twentieth-century religious text framed by notions of Jesus' masculinity. The book was widely advertised and cited in New Zealand, and helped make

31 Susan Curtis, 'The Son of Man and God the Father: The Social Gospel and Victorian Masculinity', in Mark C. Carnes and Clyde Griffen (eds), *Meanings for Manhood: Constructions of Masculinity in Victorian America*, Chicago: University of Chicago Press, 1990, pp.67-78.

200

Fosdick popular. Crucially, it responded to a climate of collective unrest by casting Jesus as a social visionary. In the introduction to the 1958 edition, Fosdick reaffirmed that Jesus was the 'eternal contemporary' whose character and ethics made him 'a pioneer, still far ahead of us'.[32] Fosdick's interest in the relation between Christianity and social life was matched by an enthusiasm for personality, which he once declared to be 'the key to the understanding of all life'. He had been heavily influenced in his early career by Borden P. Browne's *Personalism*, and what he called the 'back to Christ' movement of nineteenth century liberal theology.[33] For Fosdick, the historical Jesus provided a way to avoid excessive literal Biblicism and metaphysical speculation. The notion of personality connected the individual to society, and proved amenable to the ideals of brotherhood and friendship favoured by social Christians.

The Manhood of the Master was essentially a devotional aid, intended more as a character study than a biographical 'life'. Each chapter focused on a particular quality that Jesus exemplified. Discussion was organised around daily readings and commentary, with each chapter providing reflection for one week. For Fosdick, Jesus' character was more important than creeds. His practicality put him in touch with ordinary men's needs, and provided a basis for tackling social problems. Fosdick's ideals affirmed the anthropocentrism of social Christianity, and its simple romanticised message of love. In 1925, the *Methodist Bible Class Link* carried an article entitled 'I Believe in Man' in which Fosdick argued that one could not believe in Jesus' God without his idea of humanity. Wrestling with Kant, Spinoza, and Hegel would not lead to the 'distinguishing characteristics of Jesus' God'. Painters like Millet who reflected on the 'love behind His love' were enabled to see the worth in the peasant. True Christianity was practical love in action. Wherever the 'Manhood of the Master' was taken seriously, friendship and solidarity abounded.[34]

Local 'Puritan fiction' picked up on similar ideas, but focused particularly on itinerant workers who were considered susceptible to anti-religious socialist agitation and represented the kind of 'manly men'

32 Fosdick, *Manhood*, pp.7-8.
33 Prothero, p.110; Harry Emerson Fosdick, *The Living of These Days: An Autobiography*, London: SCM, 1957, p.63.
34 *NZMBC Link*, 24 October 1925, p.5.

to whom a manly Christ would appeal.[35] Much of this writing was fanciful and overdrawn. Even a reviewer for the *New Zealand Methodist Times* expressed doubts about Herman Foston's *At the Front*, remarking candidly that he had 'some distance to go yet before he can take the rank of a first-class novelist'.[36] Nevertheless, the book illustrated the genre and the way that a masculine Jesus could be used to counter the 'Socialist threat'.

At the Front followed Ralph Messenger from his wanderings in the wilderness of socialism and irreligion to his regeneration in the railway construction camps and subsequent career. Messenger's rise was based on a combination of conversion and self-help, and marked by involvement in moral campaigning and eventual influence and fame. His religion – the 'religion of Jesus' – was defined in masculine terms:

> Ralph went into the subject more fully, and found that the present-day religion may be, and is too often, an effeminacy, a mere parody of the religion of Jesus Christ and the heroic obedience, self-sacrifice, and valour of His early and true disciples.

Contemporary Christianity needed greater militancy. Jesus was strong and vigorous, and the religion of his followers should be also. Through the idea of Jesus' sympathy, Foston related manliness with the solidarity of workers: 'Men, Jesus Christ was the Great Sympathiser. Let us look at Him as such… as we study His life from the "manger to the Cross" we find it to be one of intense sympathy'. This involved fellow-love and duty, but was paradoxically condescending. Jesus was the supreme example of manly brotherhood and camaraderie, yet he was never truly 'one of the boys'. His propensity to fix other men's problems always placed him above them. However, the religion of Jesus provided a model of social advancement based on 'pluck and industry'. Thus, 'manly self-reliance' was favoured over a political socialism that tended toward feminising dependency. Jesus' manliness was characterised by moral

35   The nomenclature and corpus of 'Puritan fiction' are adopted from Kirstine Moffat, 'The Puritan Paradox: An Annotated Bibliography of Puritan and Anti-Puritan New Zealand Fiction, 1860-1940. Part 1: The Puritan Legacy', *Kotare*, 3:1, 2000, pp.36-86; also 'Part 2: Reactions Against Puritanism', *Kotare*, 3:2, 2000, pp.3-49.

36   Herman Foston, *At the Front: A Story of Pluck and Heroism in the Railway Construction Camps in the Dominion of New Zealand*, London: Arthur H. Stockwell, 1921; cf. *NZMT*, 13 May 1922, p.3.

steadfastness, independence and entrepreneurship, and could be imitated through 'heroic deeds, bravery, and self-sacrifice'.[37]

Though set in the bush 'frontier' rather than the public works schemes, Guy Thornton's semi-autobiographical *The Wowser* worked with similar ideas. Its central character was Sinclair, a worker converted through 'plain, and unadorned' nonconformist bush service preaching, a Nature-inspired religious experience, and a vision of 'Christ blotting out the past by His death upon the Cross and now living to save and keep me'. Classical evangelical conversion led to Christocentric faith: 'Looking away from self to Christ, I found Him all-sufficient'.[38] On becoming a Baptist preacher, Sinclair learnt the value of rugged bush masculinity, including a handy pair of fists. Thus, conventional piety was transformed. In the most important sermon in the book, Sinclair preached from the favoured masculinist passage, 'Quit you like men', before speaking on 'the manliness of Christ'. This exposition highlighted Jesus' 'superior courage, allied with the utmost gentleness; His intense love for men; His burning desire that the men for whom He died should live lives that would prove a blessing and not a curse to their fellows'. This was manliness that issued forth in service.[39]

Jesus' heroic masculinity was often linked with more conventional priorities. In *The Wowser*, Christian opposition to the sly-grog trade became the forerunner to bush revival, and provided the immediate context for one panegyric on the 'heroism and mighty love of the Crucified One'. Christ's heroism was allied to moral reform, and stood alongside pity for those who ignored his love, death and 'precious promises'. The heroism of the Saviour's redeeming love made an impact, even on Ned, a South African War veteran and the archetypal hard-case against religion: 'A splendid rider, an absolutely fearless man, an out-and-out gambler, and a hard drinker, he was wholly indifferent to Christianity'. Faced with the plain testimony of other blokes, Ned repented, married, and embarked with his wife on a famous adventure for Christ.[40]

---

37 Foston, *At the Front*, pp.84-85, 110, 119, 229.
38 Guy Thornton, *The Wowser: A Tale of the New Zealand Bush*, London: H.R. Allenson, 1916, pp.57, 73.
39 Thornton, *Wowser*, pp.123-24.
40 Thornton, *Wowser*, pp.203, 210-14.

Such works highlighted the evangelistic and moral imperatives that drove so much Christian social reform at this time. In this context, the manly Jesus provided inspiration in the Christian battle against social vices. Hence, A.S. Adams' argument that Jesus' moral teaching illuminated social conditions, while the 'spirit of the Saviour' provided the fount for drawing the necessary heroism to respond.[41] The Christian masculinity of Puritan novels emphasised strength, which was allied to moral character, brotherhood and neighbourliness. The idea of Jesus as a strong man did not produce a distinctive Christology, but provided a trope to challenge the claims of the apparently irreligious. Jesus' strength was commensurate with 'definite religion', in which moral character and dogged persistence provided the basis for a good life and a good society. This vision of Jesus' heroism aligned neatly with notions of male reformers as guardians of the weak.

Religious organisations for men

The establishment of religious groups for men was another characteristic feature of this period. Significantly, the rise of male denominational organisations corresponded with periods of particularly sharp social unrest and economic hardship. The CEMS began in New Zealand in 1904 at a time of intense debate about working-class men's religiosity. In 1912, the *Church News* responded to the great strike in Wellington by deploring socialism's absurdity in the light of such violent and destructive unreason. By contrast, it hoped that Christian men would exhibit 'brotherhood as it is in Christ', 'not self-serving, but self-sacrifice', and that through friendship and practical work the CEMS might help bridge any labour-church divide.[42]

The Methodist Men's Fellowship formed some twenty-five years later in 1931, though the setting during a period of deepening economic recession was not too dissimilar. According to its constitution, the fellowship was designed to 'enlist the co-operation of Christian men in

---

41   Adams, *Relation of the Church*, p.4.
42   *Church News*, March 1912, pp.3-4.

the active promotion of the work of the Church... and especially to cultivate the social aspects of Christian life'.[43] Some hoped that the organisation would help invigorate provision of social services in the wider community. This happened to a limited degree, but social and educational activities tended to be more common. Indeed, the *Laymen's Handbook* highlighted that the Fellowship placed a priority on the 'culture of the spiritual, mental and social life of its members'.[44]

Interestingly, Jesus was not particularly central to the language or modus operandi of these organisations, but was for the Catholic version of the cult of manliness. Elimination of profanity against Jesus' name ostensibly provided the raison d'être for the Holy Name Society. However, the main focus was usually the Holy Name man, whose 'simplicity and rugged religiousness' was 'the unanswerable argument to any and all objections against his Christ and his Church'.[45] Even in this context, ecclesiology could trump Christology.

In general, men's organisations were more taken with 'practical religion' and 'brotherhood' than notions of heroism. Thus, it was a practical, benevolent Christ who featured most prominently. The chaplain to the Archbishop of York's contention that the CEMS should be a 'practicalizing' agent was ostensibly grounded in Christology. According to Mr Woollcombe, 'religion ought to appeal to every practical man', since Jesus did not address men's intellects, but went 'straight to their consciences and to their common sense'. Men needed more religion because they needed 'more of the inspiration and power of Christ'.[46] When debate erupted concerning the need for reform of the organisation in 1927, there was widespread feeling that the overly 'spiritual' basis of the CEMS was limiting its success. Members were required to affirm and adhere to the CEMS Rule: 'In the Power of the Holy Spirit: To pray to God every day; to be a faithful communicant; and by active Witness, Fellowship, and Service to help forward the Kingdom of Christ'. According to Archdeacon Russell of Oamaru, the CEMS

---

43   *MAC*, 1932, p.127.

44   W.A. Burley, *Laymen's Handbook*, Christchurch: Methodist Church of New Zealand, n.d., p.14.

45   *Month* July 1927, p.11, cited in Barry Buckley, 'The Holy Name Society: A Short History of the Society in Auckland', BA Hons research exercise, Massey University, 2001, p.25.

46   *NZ Church News*, April 1910, pp.11-12.

'Rule of Life' set the standard too high, stunting organisational growth. The Rev. W. Bullock concurred, arguing that it was only 'practical work' that kept the organisation alive: 'Our Lord was the Master of life because he was the most practical man who ever lived: Let us get the "spirituality" out of the Society, and express our spirituality through practical works'.[47]

Religious organisations for men were only moderately successful. Like the Wellington Congregational Men's League, many struggled for existence let alone continuity or strength. Denominational organisations provided fellowship and support in varying degrees, but were competing against more established groups offering similar rewards. Reform movements, including unions, had stolen the march as advocates for workers' welfare. A variety of other organisations offered tangible material benefits as well as social networks, frequently expressing their purpose in quasi-religious terms whilst avoiding accompanying religious restrictions. Friendly societies and workingmen's clubs offered sociability and financial services, while the Returned Servicemen's Association which expanded rapidly after World War One was built on similar principles of practical care. Their provision of social and material benefits competed for space with men's religious organisations. Friendly societies grew significantly during the social unrest of the early twentieth century. By 1915, at least a quarter of New Zealand men belonged, and one in five continued to do so till 1940.[48] Though strongest among 'upper working class and the respectable artisans',[49] they were also prominent in some working-class areas. Many were small, but cultivated a sense of community through mutual care. Their social security measures were often perceived as expressions of practical spirituality.[50] Workingmen's clubs offered leisure activities that ranged from drinking and cards to billiards and bowls, as well as much larger social events. By contrast with the 'practical Christianity' operating in these 'secular' organisations, the earnest (and temperate) attention to social, moral and

47 *Men*, 10, June 1924, p.1; *Men*, 20, July 1927, p.11.
48 David Thomson, *A World Without Welfare: New Zealand's Colonial Experiment*, Auckland: Auckland University Press, 1998, pp.38-39.
49 Heather Shepherd, 'The Nature and Role of Friendly Societies in Later Nineteenth Century New Zealand', BA Hons research essay, Massey University, 1976, p.17.
50 Jennifer Carlyon, 'Friendly Societies 1842-1938: The Benefits of Membership', *NZJH*, 32:2, 1998, p.132.

religious questions in Christian men's organisations could seem much less practical or desirable.

Martial Christianity

From the later part of the nineteenth century, attempts to correlate ideals of soldierly manliness with religion featured strikingly in discourses of men's religion. The Salvation Army provided perhaps the greatest example of association of religion with militarism. However, its use of martial motifs indicated that appeals to heroic soldierly manliness were essentially evangelistic. The Army adopted the nomenclature of militarism but not its essence, and only superficially harmonised Jesus with masculinist ideals. Its favoured imagery was designed to reach working-class men on the basis that military language asserted strength and brawny masculinity over effeminacy. In reality, the organisation opposed most aspects of distinctively working-class male leisure, and used military jargon as a way to assert the 'true manliness' of doing so. Salvationists opposed violence, and promoted self-restraint and religious conviction as the true marks of strength.[51] Jesus was used to support this subversion of conventional military values. True 'patriotism' was an echo of Jesus' self-sacrificing service of humanity, while 'true manhood' followed Jesus' example of 'tolerance and liberality of spirit'.[52] In many ways, this approach set the pattern for other Protestant groups.

Connections between religion and heroic manliness were strengthened during the South African War. In February 1900, the *Outlook* greeted news that a chaplain would be sent with the Otago Contingent

---

51 Pamela J. Walker, '"I Live But Not Yet I For Christ Liveth in Me": Men and Masculinity in the Salvation Army, 1865-90', in Michael Roper and John Tosh (eds), *Manful Assertions: Masculinities in Britain Since 1800*, London: Routledge, 1991, pp.92-112, esp. p.107; Laura Lauer, 'Soul-Saving Partnerships and Pacifist Soldiers: The Ideal of Masculinity in the Salvation Army', in Andrew Bradstock, Sean Gill, Anne Hogan and Sue Morgan (eds), *Masculinity and Spirituality in Victorian Culture*, Basingstoke: Macmillan, 2000, pp.194-208.
52 *War Cry*, 1 August 1908, p.7; *War Cry*, 17 March 1906, p.3.

with the headline 'Religion and Heroism'.[53] After that war, a review in the same newspaper commended one veteran's poetry for exhibiting the 'soldier spirit – the spirit of brave, strong, dauntless, dogged endurance'.[54] The militant and moral aspects of religious masculinity were often bound together. Writing around the same time, Frank Dunlop described the best way to attract men to the churches:

> Call out the active impulses towards the morally beautiful! Bring into play the chivalrous instincts and the lust of battle! Appeal to the latent heroic in men!... Say this to him: "There is a fight going on; come on." and you will come out very much the wiser with the heat of battle upon you.... Yes, there is martial music in Christ's voice, there is the shiver of the trumpet in His tones; and he who responds to its challenge will discover that the heroism of man postulates the inspiration of God.[55]

Association of military virtues with manliness continued to be important. In particular, World War One provided the context for a marked upsurge in efforts to construct manliness in soldierly terms. As these trends influenced religious communities it became common to represent Jesus in heroic-soldierly terms. However, as in earlier times, the post-World War One heroic Jesus remained conventional in many respects.

The crisis of the returning soldiers

The churches' support for war demanded religious rationalisation. Historically, however, Jesus' teaching posed a problem for Christian justifications. The essentially pacifist stance of the first Christians, for example, was based in part on their appeal to Christ's example. On the eve of World War One, some still denied that Jesus' teaching could be used to justify war.[56] Not, however, the Life and Work Committee of the Presbyterian General Assembly, which argued:

53 *Outlook*, 17 February 1900, p.4.
54 Review of Frank Hudson, *The Song of the Manly Men*, in *Outlook*, 9 January 1909, p.7.
55 *Outlook*, 6 June 1908, p.3.
56 *Outlook*, 4 August 1914, p.4.

The same message which proclaims peace to men of good-will implies strife and misery to all the rest. "I am not come to bring peace, but a sword," was the hard saying of Him of Whom the Gospels tell.... And the searching Gospel message, while it brings peace and healing on its wings to the good man, is a two-edged sword to the selfish, mean, and bad.[57]

The churches overwhelmingly cast Germany in the latter category, accusing it of pride and aggression. By contrast, the British Empire 'being, in practical righteousness, the largest instalment of the Kingdom of God that has yet arisen among men', was divinely charged to resist.[58] Indeed, Germany had initiated an essentially spiritual conflict by obscuring the 'onward path of evolution as pointed by Christ'.[59] A leading Presbyterian, the Rev. James Gibb, warned that the 'great malignant nation' had 'thrown down the challenge to Christ, and it was inexorably doomed'.[60] Others, more conscious of the difficulties raised by jingoistic association of man's war with God's, expressed ambivalence. The sense of an essentially spiritual conflict remained, however, and led to claims that a militant Christ was incarnate in war. Addressing the opening of Theological Hall, Dunedin, R.E. Davies announced that 'Christ has come to destroy the power of the devil and give the captives their freedom. He is here for war'.[61]

There were early hopes that war might help revive religion, both among the troops and at home. On the one hand, war potentially led to greater penitence and dependence on the Almighty, and could have a healthy, purifying effect. On the other, it provided opportunities to exhibit the sacrificial love of The Lamb.[62] Some even hoped that the righteous basis of the war would give rise to the blessing of a wider spiritual awakening. The Presbyterian Life and Witness Committee was more cautious. In 1915, its report to Assembly noted that historically war had not been good for the Church, but had led to indifference. Two years later, it expressed concern that patriotic causes were displacing religious

57   *PGA*, 1914, p.57.
58   *MAC*, 1915, p.117.
59   *Outlook*, 12 January 1915, p.5.
60   Cited in L.H. Barber, 'The Social Crusader: James Gibb at the Australasian Pastoral Frontier, 1882-1935', PhD thesis, Massey University, 1975, p.196.
61   *Outlook*, 6 April 1915, p.8.
62   *Outlook*, 3 November 1914, p.3, cf. *MW*, 12 August 1914, p.1; *Outlook*, 5 January 1915, pp.3-4.

activity at home, whilst there remained no evidence of a 'work of grace' among soldiers. It urged the church to therefore 'concentrate on her growing lads, in the hope that before they enter camp she may see them taking their stand for Jesus Christ'.[63] The YMCA's wartime magazine the *Triangle Trail* provided a realistic assessment. Answering the question 'Is the Average Soldier Religious?' it suggested that 'there were "keen" men, and there were hard cases – neither, however, a numerous class. The average man came in between'. It concluded that 'behind his indifferent, somewhat graphic, language, and his apparent coldness in spiritual matters, the average soldier has true faith'.[64]

By 1919, it seemed more certain that war had done little to revitalise organised religion. Books on life after death found a ready market, but many returning soldiers seemed disinterested in religious activity. This partly perpetuated an existing trend, and probably signalled general feelings of alienation from civilian society. Particular issues also rankled. A few chaplains and YMCA officers, though certainly not all, had alienated themselves by parading their officer status.[65] The churches' leading role in prohibition campaigning probably added to disaffection, especially given the role of servicemen's votes in preventing New Zealand from going dry by a mere 3,263 votes in December 1919.[66] As one observer ruefully noted, 'The fact must be faced that five-sixths of the men voted against Prohibition, and they know that the majority of Church people probably voted for it'.[67] Moreover, some felt the continuing scorn of religious attitudes to drinkers. Another factor was a rising sense that the war represented a failure of Christian civilisation. The *New Zealand Tablet* considered that it was a failure of Protestantism, not Christianity, but this simply highlighted the extent to which religion was held to be implicated.[68]

63   *PGA*, 1915, p.121; *PGA*, 1917, pp.55-56.
64   *Triangle Trail*, 2, 16 February 1918, p.7.
65   Jock Phillips, Nicholas Boyack and E.P. Malone (eds), *The Great Adventure: New Zealand Soldiers Describe the First World War*, Wellington: Allen & Unwin, 1988, pp.199-200, 206.
66   *ENZ*, vol. 2, pp.876-77.
67   H.W. Burridge (ed.), *When the Boys Come Home: The Problem of the Returned Soldier and the Church*, Christchurch: Presbyterian Bookroom, 1919, p.14.
68   *NZ Tablet*, 6 May 1920, p.33.

The churches recognised that returning soldiers faced practical difficulties, but their apparent spiritual indifference aroused great concern. Observers noted that experiences at the front and at home had left many men embittered, and religious communities felt this in the rejection of church life. In the early 1920s, the question of men's non-attendance at church activities appeared continually in denominational literature. Presbyterians were particularly active in addressing the 'problem of the returning soldier'. Seeking an informed deliberation, General Assembly commended the Rev. A. Herbert Gray's pamphlet, *As Tommy Sees Us*, for study.[69] This was one of many books by ex-chaplains relaying their impressions of church work among the soldiers and analysing returnees' needs. These frequently pointed to the estrangement soldiers felt from civilian society, and urged churches to replicate the sense of 'brotherhood' experienced on active service. For evangelical controversialists like P.B. Fraser, Gray's attitude to the Bible and call for simple religious teaching reeked of 'Modernism'.[70] Other reviewers like Lester Smith suspected that the book would shock many church folk, but encourage socialists. Gray's 'Tommy' had no respect for the Church due to its blots on civilisation and disregard for the Sermon on the Mount. Conversely, soldiers' discovery of cooperative and communal life portended imminent socialist rebellion.[71]

When the General Assembly convened at Christchurch in February 1919, it decided that the problem of returning soldiers required further investigation. H.W. Burridge coordinated this, and his findings were published later that year in *When the Boys Come Home*. The pamphlet candidly acknowledged the churches' failings and called for sympathetic treatment of returnees. For present purposes, the critical feature was the final section, where Burridge invoked Christ as the cord that tied his observations together. Burridge pleaded for a radical re-presentation of him as a man's man, to reach returning soldiers by showing them 'the real Jesus'. Tellingly, he bemoaned the fact that few returning soldiers associated their ideal qualities with 'the Man of Nazareth, the Head of the Christian Church':

---

69   A. Herbert Gray, *As Tommy Sees Us: A Book For Church Folk*, London: Arnold, 1918. The book was endorsed elsewhere, for example, by the Anglican military chaplain P.C. Davis; see *Church Gazette*, May 1919, p.80.
70   *Biblical Recorder*, January 1919, p.7.
71   *MW*, 31 July 1918, p.1.

They do not know that the very traits of character which go to make up a good soldier, a brave man, and a true gentleman – traits which they have seen exhibited in the fierce crucible of war, and which they admire at heart – such reached their highest in the life and character of Jesus. "He was a man, and a complete man – strong, virile, and courageous. He had all the great masculine virtues which men already love and admire – of loyal hearts the most loyal, of generous hearts the most generous, and of all hopeful and cheerful spirits His was the greatest. He had the dignity that comes from a quiet reserve. He neither paraded His emotions nor asked others to parade theirs." Such is not the generally accepted picture of Jesus of Nazareth. But the tradition that contradicts it is false, and must be broken through – by our preaching, and by our life.

The Church's great task was to persuade returning soldiers to follow Jesus, the ideal frontline 'cobber' and a fierce 'stunt':

His Church and her representatives may often fail to present in actual life this picture of our Great Leader, yet it still is true that He was the manliest man who ever walked this earth. And His cause calls for the display of just such qualities to-day, and is willing to enlist all men in its service who desire to make such a one their example.... There are deeper conceptions of Christ and His work, we know. But it is on these lines of hero worship that we can first appeal to many men and influence them to enlist in the service of Christ and His Church. They will respond to the call of such a Leader if they know Him as such. It is our task to so present Him.[72]

Burridge conceded that hero worship resulted in inadequate Christology. Nonetheless, the idealism and personalised basis of hero worship was seen as the most likely means to arouse religious sentiment. Not surprisingly, the manly Christ that Burridge advocated fitted neatly with the dimensions of the ideal soldier. This image was consolidated in the 1920s as the churches employed Jesus in their attempts to 'enlist' men.

Jesus and soldierly ideals

Greater focus on Jesus was potentially shrewd. There is evidence that some New Zealand soldiers found Jesus attractive even when they were

72   Burridge (ed.), pp.30-32.

uncertain about Christianity and its teaching on the afterlife.[73] Visions and apparitions were apparently common in wartime, and Jesus featured prominently in these. Some experiences emphasised the comfort Jesus could offer soldiers and their families.[74] Images depicting a mystical Jesus as the soldier's friend were plentiful at home and on the front. Of these, James Clark's *The Great Sacrifice* (1914) presented Jesus as a fellow-sufferer, while the Jesus of George Hillyard Swinstead's *The White Comrade* (1915) provided help amid trouble. By the early twentieth century, postcards had developed as a cheap and convenient form of communication. Reproductions of paintings like *The White Comrade* were used on cards that were designed to connect troops with families and friends at home.[75]

As opposition to the hostilities increased, Jesus' teaching was invoked against the war. On the other hand, the man himself was also taken to embody a form of masculinity that conformed to military values. Soldiers were widely honoured as the cream of New Zealand's manhood, and the manly Jesus reflected this image of the ideal soldier. Thus, World War One stimulated a process that made soldiers into Christ figures and Christ into a soldier.[76]

Association of Jesus with soldierly values was achieved in a variety of ways. One was through military titles. The idea of Jesus as Captain pre-dated World War One, but became more popular at that time. In one sense, the term was simply an equivalent to the more conventional title of 'Lord'. It connoted believers' deference, obedience and whole-hearted commitment. Thus, the inaugural issue of the Bible Class periodical *Four Square* contended that 'The nominal, luke-warm or half-and-half

73   Glyn Harper (ed.), *Letters from the Battlefield: New Zealand Soldiers Write Home, 1914-18*, Auckland: HarperCollins, 2001, pp.159-60.

74   Jay Winter, *Sites of Memory, Sites of Mourning: The Great War in European Cultural History*, Cambridge: Cambridge University Press, 1995, esp. pp.54-77; Joanna Bourke, *Dismembering the Male Body: Men's Bodies, Britain and the Great War*, Chicago: University of Chicago Press, 1996, pp.230-35; Lauris Edmond (ed.), *Women in Wartime: New Zealand Women Tell Their Story*, Wellington: Government Printer, 1986, p.51.

75   Allen J. Frantzen, *Bloody Good: Chivalry, Sacrifice, and the Great War*, Chicago: University of Chicago Press, 2004, p.159.

76   Stéphane Audoin-Rouzeau and Annette Becker, *1914-1918: Understanding the Great War*, Catherine Temerson (trans.), London: Profile, 2002, p.127.

Christian is utterly unworthy of his Captain'.[77] The term affirmed qualities of leadership and authority, but it also supposed more personal emphases, since Captains were in direct command of men and relied heavily on respect earned through example. Therefore, appeal to Jesus as Captain preserved a sense of his superiority and conferred qualities of courage, character and strength without the taint of privilege.

The concept of sacrifice provided a more important point of interaction, and formed the basis of James Belich's description of 'A cult of 18,000 Kiwi Christs'.[78] Representations of Jesus as a self-sacrificing leader appeared around the world from the outset of war, and were associated with manliness and soldiering.[79] In wartime, it was relatively easy for religious communities to align Jesus' sacrificial death with those of believers who had likewise 'sealed their sacrifice with their blood'. But the relationship between Christ and the soldier was never entirely parochial, since all were potentially agents of atonement. Thus, R.E. Davies suggested that 'On the battlefields of Europe to-day Christ is, in a mystical sense, shedding His blood for the sins of the world'. Indeed, the apparently irreligious were even occasionally exalted. One letter to the *Outlook* suggested that the average 'seemingly Godless, careless and thoughtless' solder often displayed 'Christ's spirit in the trenches' more than 'professors of religion'. Their love of neighbour was truly Christ-like.[80] It exemplified the sacrificial spirit articulated in John 15.13: 'Greater love hath no man than this, that a man lay down his life for his friends'. This text became widely cited in the context of later memorialisation of the war.[81]

Anzac Day provided opportunities to reflect on the suffering and sacrifice of New Zealand soldiers. The motif of the sacrificial life became a favourite theme in Anzac commemorations. For Pastor E. Nicholls, Anzac Day honoured those New Zealanders who had gone out with 'high endeavour to take their places in the deadly breach for others' sake', supplying 'heroic proof of their manhood'. Moreover, 'The

77   *Four Square*, November 1920, p.3; *Four Square*, April 1921, p.75.

78   Belich, p.116.

79   Stuart Owen, 'Great War', in Houlden (ed.), vol. 1, pp.323-25.

80   *Outlook*, 23 November 1915, p.5; *Outlook*, 6 April 1915, p.8; *Outlook*, 1 January 1918, p.25.

81   Chris Maclean and Jock Phillips, *The Sorrow and the Pride: New Zealand War Memorials*, Wellington: GP Books, p.106.

bereaved, the maimed, the mentally unhinged, are bearing still the cross that the war-makers cruelly fashioned and thrust upon their guiltless hearts'. If their self-sacrifice imitated Christ, the challenge to 'be an Anzac for Christ' presented the soldier as a type of the true Christian. Anzac soldiers were archetypes of submission to God, and standard-bearers of courage, sacrifice and love.[82] For some interpreters, even the form of the Anzac Day ceremony was – from Last Post to Reveille – symbolic of the death and resurrection of Christ.[83] Contrary to Maureen Sharpe's contention, such sentiments suggest that the Anzac story was highly amenable to Christian interpretation.[84]

Association of Christ with soldiering manliness was also mediated through notions of chivalry and crusade. Neo-medievalism had been widespread in the English-speaking world prior to 1914. In New Zealand, 'crusades' for social purity were well established, and chivalric language also permeated many organisations. The incidence of crusading imagery rose notably in the early years of the war, and the idea of a holy crusade against barbarism was arguably one of the war's central motifs. In New Zealand, Ormond Burton noted that this view prevailed among his contemporaries: 'We were convinced it was a righteous war.... We went to fight for the Kingdom of God and for the future peace of the world, in much the same spirit as that in which the finest chivalry of Europe followed Peter the Hermit to the Holy Land'.[85] The modern crusade incorporated notions of adventure, heroism, virtue and valour. The World War One soldier became the new crusader.

Interest in chivalry and crusade declined in some places following the war, but not in New Zealand religion. Alignment between the soldier-crusader and Christ was particularly evident in visual imagery. Medieval motifs were ubiquitous in memorial stained glass windows, and many of these interacted with figures of Christ. One example was the two-panelled memorial to the Wellington Regiment of the New Zealand Expeditionary Force at All Saints' Anglican Church in Palmerston North. In this, the right hand panel of a New Zealand version

82 *Reaper*, June 1923, pp.117-18.
83 Cited in Keith Sinclair, *A Destiny Apart: New Zealand's Search for National Identity*, Wellington: Allen & Unwin, 1986, p.184.
84 Maureen Sharpe, 'ANZAC Day in New Zealand: 1916 to 1939', *NZJH*, 15:2, 1981, pp.97-114, esp. p.109.
85 O.E. Burton, *Shall We Fight?*, Auckland: Clark & Matheson Printers, 1923, p.7.

of Clark's *Great Sacrifice* balances one of a crusader on the left. The crusader, also with helmet off, kneels deferentially before an altar, gazing upward to the altar cross and to Christ on the facing panel. The text below is John 15.13. The window cast the World War One soldier as a modern crusader, serving and imitating Christ. The severe losses suffered by the Wellington Regiment at Chunuk Bair, and in other conflicts, help explain the suggestion of Christ-like self-sacrifice even surpassing that of the soldiers' medieval forebear.

Alignment of Christ-like character with chivalry and crusade was especially evident in relation to young people. During the war, a guild for Ladies and Knights began in the 'Young Folks' pages of the *New Zealand Methodist Times*. The League of Young Methodists later expanded upon the metaphor. The Bible Class movement and the YMCA appropriated the language; one evangelical organisation even styled itself as the Crusader movement. Young people were expected to exhibit the zeal and self-sacrificing commitment of crusaders. The first volume of *Methodist Manhood* claimed that the Bible Class message was one of 'unselfishness, of chivalry, and of service'. Young Bible Class men were exhorted to exemplify 'The manliness which consists in self-control, a trained and self-disciplined will, a right heart with Jesus Christ enthroned within', resulting in 'chivalry, nobility, and Christian knightliness'. Christian 'knights of chivalry' exhibited Christ's character as they stood in the 'shadow of the Cross'.[86] According to the *New Zealand Methodist Times*, 'Real Christianity' was the religion of Jesus Christ, 'adventurous and purposeful, a gallantry that takes risks and exults in them, a chivalry that makes daring appeal to men's manhood and courage and foolhardihood'.[87]

Appeal to chivalric imagery provided a way to imbue militarism with heroic righteousness, and helped resolve any tensions inherent in martial depictions of Christ. Chivalry was connected with military values, but it also softened them by displacing valour into the 'safe haven of agreeable fantasy'.[88] Post-war alignment of Christ and chivalry

---

86   *Methodist Manhood*, 25 August 1922, pp.7-8; *Methodist Manhood*, 17 November 1922, p.8.
87   *NZMT*, 27 July 1929, pp.8-9.
88   John Tosh, 'The Old Adam and the New Man: Emerging Themes in the History of English Masculinities, 1750-1850', in Hitchcock and Cohen (eds), p.222; also Mark

made a Warrior Christ appear more dignified and respectable. It evoked a less demonstrative heroism than the toughness implied by muscular Christianity. It also embodied a compromise between the perceived femininity of self-denial and masculine assertiveness. The persistence and development of this Victorian neo-medieval ideal in the post-war context demonstrated the limits to heroic Christology. Chivalric and crusading tropes favoured notions of honour, adventure, duty, righteousness and holy restraint. In other words, the underlying ideals of 'Christ-likeness' still emphasised morality and purity. Ironically, for soldiers like Burton, it was precisely these associations that were most difficult to reconcile with their experience.

Youth, heroism and the masculinity of Jesus

Though there was much talk about reaching returned soldiers and men, most interwar attempts to project a masculine Jesus were actually directed at youth. This partly reflected the intense interest in children characteristic of the era, especially after World War One when provision for them formed a central focus of social policy. The churches had their own particular incentives. Perceptions of a 'boy problem' and the loss of older boys from religious association meant that reaching them was an important strategy for strengthening men's religion generally. These longstanding concerns sharpened after the war.

Fears about the female threat to male religiosity were reflected in debates about portrayals of Jesus for children. The tendency to portray Jesus in feminine terms had been observed previously, but received much more regular attention during the interwar years. Commentators argued that male religiosity was damaged through exposure to feminised images of Jesus in childhood. These created misperceptions in boys' minds that were carried into adulthood, predisposing them against religion. Thus, the young men of Dunedin's YMCA were challenged as to whether they really knew Jesus at all, since 'all the pictures ever

---

Girouard, *The Return to Camelot: Chivalry and the English Gentleman*, New Haven: Yale University Press, 1981.

drawn misrepresent Him. They have made Him out a weakling, a woman's features with beard'. But Jesus was a man's man, with 'muscles of iron, made strong by many years of labour and a spirit that never once knew fear'.[89]

Early in 1933, the *New Zealand Methodist Times* advanced the ideal of 'Christ as Hero' for youth.[90] It printed a fictional exchange between a minister's wife and a Mrs Maxwell, whose boys were more interested in Scouts and Rovers than churchgoing. The minister's wife expressed sadness at such 'weakening loyalty to Christ', and attempted to interpret the problem. Surely Christ ought to appeal especially to boys since 'He was a young man Himself and withal a young man of great courage and force of character'. This being so, the obvious remedy was to present Christ to the lads as the hero he was: 'Jesus versus the world, fighting the greatest of all battles, and moreover a losing battle, yet never giving in'. Adventurous boys would be attracted by being encouraged to join the in fray:

> We should explain to our boys that Christ no longer fights alone; He needs soldiers who will dare to stand and fight for His principles in the word. God's will cannot be achieved without the help of young men. When they realise this surely many who are indifferent now will be keen to serve in the army of Christ?

A little less 'Gentle Jesus, meek and mild' and the boy problem would be solved.

A short time later, the same paper covered a prominent debate in England concerning religious art for children. The controversy arose when several leading educationalists sent a letter to *The Times* arguing that children were exposed to too many sentimental and effeminate representations of Jesus. The writers contended: 'One glimpse of a picture of Christ which suggests that He was effeminate or weak or merely depressed may easily destroy a living interest in Him, and many discourses on the real manhood of our Lord will not restore it'. It called on teachers to use pictures that would 'win the hearts of the young', and on artists to remedy the situation.[91] Following this, from 14 to 17 March

---

89 *Dunedin Manhood*, October 1935, p.1, citing Bruce Barton.
90 *NZMT*, 27 May 1933, p.9.
91 Council of Christian Education (ed.), *Pictures of Jesus for Children: Addresses by Eight Leading Educationists*, London: Religious Tract Society, 1935.

1934, the Council of Christian Education in Britain organised an opportunity for religious publishing houses to exhibit their art in Euston Road, London. Each day religious leaders and educationalists were invited to speak giving their opinions of the works. The London exhibition of 1934 concluded with participants selecting their preferred portraits from the images available. The overall favourite was Harold Copping's 'The Saviour of Men', and his art was hailed as a triumph of virility and masculinity.[92] Copping was well known in New Zealand through various religious portraits and especially the Copping Bible – an illustrated edition of the Authorised Version published by the Religious Tract Society. This commendation only enhanced his reputation.

Youth movements

Much of the attention focused on boys during the years of transition to independent adulthood, since this was identified as the critical period of 'leakage'. As noted earlier, late childhood was also the stage when children were considered developmentally most ready for conversion. Emphasis on converting older children had been an important strategy since well before the war. Thus, when the Salvation Army prepared for an 'Extension Campaign' in 1911, it argued that it had a particular duty to 'go after the boys and girls just on the threshold of manhood and womanhood'. It especially sought the young men, among whom undeniably large percentages were 'without proper religious training'.[93]

Programmes for youth were not solely focused on conversion, but more broadly on socialisation. Mutual Improvement Societies, Young Men's Institutes and Literary Societies were characteristic nineteenth-century initiatives. By the end of the nineteenth century, churches were increasingly responding to contemporary interest in physical culture by incorporating it into their programmes. Endeavours along these lines occasionally proved successful. In 1899, the Anglican parish of St Mark's in Remuera reported a Confirmation service where 28 male and

92   *NZMT*, 9 June 1934, p.1.
93   *War Cry*, 4 March 1911, p.5.

12 female candidates were presented. The relatively large number of males in this group was attributed to the 'zeal and energy' of H.D.A. Major, at that time curate in the parish, and the interest he had shown in the parish's young men. Major had been running mid-week gymnastic classes for boys, in addition to more obviously religious pursuits.[94]

The YMCA and Bible Class movements were the most prominent and influential forms of church provision for youth by the beginning of the twentieth century. Indeed, the latter was often fêted as an 'indigenous' New Zealand contribution to worldwide Christianity, and nurtured generations of the churches' opinion-formers until the 1960s. Bible Classes were denominationally based, and promoted a 'four-square' programme that combined social, intellectual, physical and spiritual activities. The non-denominational YMCAs espoused a similar ideology – so similar, in fact, that the possibility of merging the two movements was raised. Following debate, both were retained in order to occupy 'the whole field'; Bible Classes would focus on young men within the churches, and the YMCA those outside.[95] Their increasingly diverse programmes, and emphasis on physicality and adventure, reflected shifting perceptions of young people's needs. Other youth organisations grew rapidly in the interwar years, including uniformed movements where notions of martial manhood were widely promulgated. School cadets increased in popularity as did the Scout movement, while the Boys' Brigade was reinvigorated in the 1920s and 1930s having nearly become defunct before World War One. Nevertheless, the Bible Class movement and the YMCA remained the most important religious organisations.

Bible Classes had been established in the leading denominations prior to World War One, but the Presbyterian Bible Class was easily the largest. Efforts to re-energise it after the war led to the creation of a new publication, *Four Square*, which replaced a supplement in the *Outlook* from November 1920. With a subtitle proclaiming 'Be Strong and Show Thyself a Man', the magazine gave the movement a voice in advancing its work among young men. The YMCA also expanded following its extensive involvement with the troops during World War One. Some hoped that wartime work could be extended by presenting religion 'in a

94 *Church Gazette*, January 1899, p.7.
95 *Young Man's Magazine*, October 1907, pp.397-98.

very primitive and naked form' to 'those who have not yet come into vital contact with it'.[96] Both the YMCA and the Bible Class movement were conversion-oriented, and blended devotion to Jesus with promotion of manly Christianity. In the post-war years, this was often expressed in terms of soldierly heroism and manly character. The values of muscular Christianity persisted, but were modified by the cult of personality.

In 1921, the Rev. R.M. Ryburn was appointed Director of Youth Work for the Presbyterian Church. Speaking at his 'Inauguration' the Rev. S.W. Currie, then Moderator of the General Assembly, delivered an address that was described in *Four Square* as a 'masterpiece' for its articulation of 'the ideals and basic principles' upon which the Bible Class Movement was built. For Currie, the Bible Class stood for 'an all-round manhood'. By this he meant the inculcation of 'right thinking and physical fitness; interest in the welfare of others, for we are social beings, and, finally, the development of their spiritual nature'.[97] This was the four-square gospel inspired by Luke 2.52.

According to Currie, Jesus was the link between 'all-round manhood' and Christian faith. Being an all-round man himself, Jesus would have approved of the Bible Classes wide-ranging pursuits:

> Jesus was interested in all phases of life, and we believe that to-day He would be interested in the same way. The straight-forward business dealing; the self-denial and discipline of the athletic field; the innocent pleasures of our socials, and the mental training in our classes, are quite consistent with our major aim of the training of the soul.

Bible Class work was modelled on Jesus' life, especially in a focus on service. If men were reluctant to serve, they must have misapprehended Jesus' true qualities. Jesus' manly attributes, especially his courage and idealism, were thought to be particularly appealing:

> Jesus Christ as "the man of sorrows" may not appeal to us; but we see the man of courage, the man of great ideals, combining every characteristic that appeals to young manhood. In His death, He showed supreme self-sacrifice and courage, so that His claim to Leadership must appeal to every type of young manhood, and His Divine claim is easily understood.

96   *CC*, November 1919, pp.163-64.
97   *Four Square*, May 1921, p.93.

In this approach, accepting Jesus' divinity remained essential to Christian identity, but faith was simplified by removing the emphasis on intellectual and cognitive aspects of doctrine. Jesus' divinity was proven through his lofty ideals, his embodiment of manliness and the appeal of his personality.

This manly Christianity was clearly shaped by World War One. Christian soldiers were held up as examples of Christ-like Christianity, and martial imagery was readily exploited. The image of Jesus as a 'manly man' was bolstered by the language of battle. As one minister explained:

> During the late war we were gratified at the splendid response of our young manhood to the call of duty. I feel that if our young people could be inspired with the selfsame sort of call, but as a call from Christ, they would nobly respond. The call of Christ is a call to war.[98]

One of the most explicit attempts to address the issue came from the Rev. H. Clark, who explicated the manliness of Christ in a homily to the young men of the Presbyterian Bible Class movement. Clark noted the many explanations proposed to explain the lack of men in the churches, ranging from dull services and out-of-date theology to the lack of a socialistic programme. More important, he claimed, was the sense that ideals of manhood and the Christian life were somehow in opposition. The manly Jesus was Clark's riposte to the 'misconception' that following Christ would 'draw the sap of their manhood'. Clark argued that churches had traditionally communicated a gentle manliness to the detriment of other qualities. Gentleness was discernible in Jesus, but only as the lily adorning the pillar. His masculinity was composed of sterner stuff. The primary definition of manliness was bravery. On that score, Jesus was unimpeachable. His disciples had distinguished themselves on account of their bravery, and only a manly leader could only have inspired this. With this credential in place, Clark addressed hypothetical kiwi males' definitions of the 'basic element of manhood', exalting Jesus as the supreme manifestation of each – physical courage, moral courage, and ultimately 'fidelity and loyalty to the truth'.

The climax of Clark's exposition turned the question of unmanliness on its head: 'An unmanly Christ! Unworthy of our allegiance is He? The

98   *CC*, October 1923, p.158.

fact is it is the want of real manliness in us and all who condemn Him, lack of real courage, moral and physical, lack of absolute loyalty to the truth that keeps us from His side and the battle He bids us fight'.[99] Jesus' manhood was shown in his ultimate manifestation of military virtues – physical prowess, courage and unswerving commitment to truth. The militant Christ deserved allegiance in the call to 'fight'. Non-alignment with Jesus was tantamount to rejection of true manliness. To eschew identification with the 'Man's Man' was the way of cowardice and disloyalty. It was the path of the 'shirker'.

Similar notions circulated within the YMCA. The concept of Christianity as a 'fight' was important, though notions of chivalry and crusade were less common than in other more churchly contexts. In principle, the notion of a balanced life was essential. In practice, physicality and robust religion were prioritised in the pursuit of self-improvement and personal responsibility. The YMCA had invested heavily in gymnasiums and organised programmes for physical exertion. In the interwar years, this coalesced with the continuing popularity of eugenic ideas and attempts to enhance national health and fitness. For one young devotee, the ideals of the YMCA could be easily summarised: 'Young, Muscles, Christian, Achievement of being a "real man."'[100]

Speaking and writing for the YMCA, Ormond Burton projected the principal soldierly values as characteristics of followers of Jesus: 'The bravest, the most loyal, the truest, the faithful ones and the steadfast ones have followed Him. The gentlest, the tenderest, the most saintly and beautiful souls have been at His feet and in His name have ministered to the weak, and the helpless, and those ready to die'.[101] Jesus inspired bravery, but also more tender ideals. True manliness required discipline and self-sacrifice, though in following the 'Master of Men' the connotations had to be adjusted: 'any man who would follow the Master must take on himself the three-fold vows of Poverty, Obedience and Purity.... Men real men – who count their lives nothing that they may win Christ are the only ones needed'.[102] Wartime ideals of camaraderie and brotherhood were important, too. Throughout the interwar years,

99 *Outlook*, 5 March 1923, pp.3-4.
100 *Wellington Manhood*, June 1934, p.2.
101 Ormond Burton, *The Master of Men*, Wellington: YMCA, n.d., p.12.
102 Burton, *Master*, p.21.

YMCA men were thus urged to 'leave room for Christ in the business, political, and economical life of the world', and pursue the brotherhood ideal.[103]

Proclamations of Jesus' masculinity for youth often reinterpreted commonly held ideas. This was evident in relation to the dimension of strength. Responding to the notion that Christianity was for weaklings, Lilian Pearce extolled the strength of Jesus in poetry.[104] She celebrated Jesus as a vigorous adventurer and pioneer who relished the physicality of rural outdoors activity. He was 'no weakling' when he 'climbed the hilly slopes of Galilee'. Yet, wandering the hills was a limited part of Jesus' known life, and scarcely justified calls for whole-hearted devotion to him. Hence, more traditional virtues were also invoked, and interpreted within a framework of masculine power. Thus, Jesus' mercy became evidence of his strength:

> And just because You were so strong
> > and manful
> You stooped to lift the lowliest to their feet

Perceptions of weakness and helplessness were also dismissed. Jesus' early death therefore merely ensured that neither 'pallid sickness' nor 'decay' sapped his masculine strength, of which self-sacrifice was itself the measure:

> And at the end in all Your fullest
> > manhood
> You gave Your life when at its
> > highest crest;
> Your strength, Your human life in all
> > its richness,
> Upon the cross You gave us of
> > Your best.

---

103 *Wellington Manhood*, February 1934, p.1.
104 *Four Square*, September 1921, p.174.

Manliness, character and personality

Constructions of Christian manliness provide a good context for testing the idea that a Victorian 'culture of character' was displaced by 'the culture of personality' in the early twentieth century. While notions of personality were a fundamental ingredient in interwar images, the development of character remained a hallowed hallmark of Christian masculinity. Thus, the YMCA was able to idealise the conditions of the Depression as a context for character building, and advertise itself as a centre for character development: 'Men in the Making.... YMCA specialises on Character Building!'[105]

Jesus was considered the preeminent model of manly character, which was an achievement as much as a status. Writing in 1906, the Rev. H.H. Driver of Dunedin reflected that the Apostle Paul's call to 'build up one another's character' was a call to construct an 'enduring temple of manhood'. Cultivation of character was the purpose of life, and worth more than doctrinal soundness. It was an 'advancement from infancy to manhood', an entire lifetime's project that should shape the Church's whole task: 'The purpose of all the ministries of the church of God is the ennoblement of our manhood, and, if the highest type of manhood is not found among these who bear the name of Christ, they have sadly misunderstood and misrepresented their Master'.[106]

Driver never clarified its meaning, but 'character' clearly concerned morality and was capable of being formed through education. The models used in nineteenth-century organisations for men were shaped around personal devotion and self-improvement. Later movements continued to encourage character formation, but in a context in which notions of the body and society were more prominent. These emphases were evident in programmes that incorporated social and physical pursuits. Nevertheless, manliness and character remained intrinsically linked in the Bible Class and YMCA ideologies. As one early issue of

105 Justine Smith, '"Dunedin Manhood: Official Organ of the Dunedin YMCA". The "Manufacturing" of Christian Men in Dunedin, 1933-1938', BA Hons thesis, University of Otago, 1999, p.48; YMCA (Wellington Branch), Programmes of Activities, 1932-42, MS-Group-0662, MSY-2928, ATL.
106 *Young Man's Magazine*, January 1906, p.77.

Four Square expressed succinctly, 'The aim of our Bible Class Movement is the complete development of the manly character'.[107] Jesus' example of self-sacrifice suggested that this character would be developed for and by service. Currie's 'masterpiece' asserted that the aim of the Bible Class was 'character building', and prescribed the avenues where the necessary service would be expressed – as leaders of classes, Sunday school teachers, managers and elders, ministers or missionaries. The churches' future depended on it.[108]

Continued concerns about 'anarchy' and 'unrest' helped encourage a focus on character formation in the post-war period.[109] Writing in the second issue of *Four Square*, D.G. Wilson drew attention to the problem:

> The Great War came near to destroying civilisation, and the flames it set alight are not yet wholly extinguished. Bolshevism, a direct result of the spirit that brought about the war, is still pouring the deadly taint of its poison into the very blood of civilisation. The resulting social and industrial discontent visible in every land is still a menace to the social order of the race.[110]

The Bible Class needed 'men, real Christian, all-round, red-blooded men to live down this spirit in this our own little country'. Character, citizenship and social order were therefore closely allied.

In a climate of greater frankness about sexual matters, personal morality was also a concern. Victor French was a prominent Bible Class leader in the years following World War One. A popular Travelling Secretary, French had a reputation for 'Quiet, winsome effective heroism' that was enhanced by stories of his wartime valour. While French promoted military heroism and manliness, he frequently enlisted those concepts in the cause of social purity. Thus, the moral needs of post-war society were compared with the exigencies of war. According to French, Christ's called men was 'to battle for clean standards in their country's life'. Such purity was needed because impurity was akin to emasculation: 'Nothing enfeebles manhood more than sin. Every time

---

107 *Four Square*, March 1921, p.56.
108 *Four Square*, May 1921, p.93.
109 Lewis A. Barnes, *Oh How I Love Thy Law: Reflections on the Life and Teaching of T.H. Sprott D.D. Vicar of St. Paul's Wellington 1892-1911, Bishop of Wellington 1911-1936*, Hamilton: John Walker Publishers, 1985, p.34.
110 *Four Square*, December 1920, p.19.

you commit a sin it makes you less a man, in your own sight and in God's'.[111] By contrast, the real man was one who, trusting the example and power of Christ, stood against the 'vile contagion' of impurity, 'hating all uncleanness, shrinking from every spot, thinking pure thoughts, forging strong friendships'.[112]

This emphasis on character formation was not inimical to the culture of personality. Indeed, the two were often allied.[113] For writers like Fosdick, Jesus' personality led to interest in 'His basic principles and His qualities of character'.[114] The emphasis also led in other directions. During the interwar years, New Zealand YMCA leaders often related the personality of Jesus to a spirit of adventure. Len J. Greenberg was General Secretary of the YMCA, and Honorary Secretary of the Wellington Youth Council at the time of the 'Youth for Youth' campaign in 1932. This campaign had a high profile and culminated in a 'Procession of Witness' in which 2,700 young participants marched to a 5,000-strong rally at the Wellington Town Hall.[115] For Greenberg, the 'real Jesus' – not the funereal religious portrait, but the depiction one might find in a modern 'life of Christ' – was the essence of Christianity. He was also the key to engaging young people. Jesus would challenge their life, stir their conscience and summon their devotion to the 'adventure of doing good' alongside Jesus their 'silent but ever-present Companion along the way'. By reaching out to non-churchgoers, Christian youth could recapture some of the thrill and adventure of 'those lusty young Galileans who, in the face of tremendous odds... grouped themselves around Jesus, and with great heroism pioneered the Christian enterprise'.[116] Similarly, Greenberg urged 'enquirers' to focus their religious quest in a single question:

---

111 *Four Square*, April 1923, p.266; *Four Square*, June 1923, pp.327-28; *Four Square*, April 1923, p.280.
112 *Four Square*, October 1923, p.417.
113 Mathew Thomson, *Psychological Subjects: Identity, Culture, and Health in Twentieth-Century Britain*, Oxford: Oxford University Press, 2006, pp.42-45.
114 Fosdick, *Manhood*, p.7.
115 *Four Square*, 11 October 1932, p.187.
116 Len J. Greenberg, *Personal Adventuring For Christ: A Statement of the Principles of Youth Evangelism*, Wellington: Youth Committee, N.Z. Council of Religious Education, 1934, p.39; also Len J. Greenberg, *The Great Adventure*, Wellington: Wright and Carman, 1932.

> What do you see in Christ?... Will you start with that, follow that as far as it carries you, and then go on as you see more? Interpose no objections based on your disbelief in this theological theory or that. Start where you are, and follow what you do see. Christianity is an adventure.

Interest in personality provided a way to marry social and evangelistic concerns. YMCAs combined active social programme with evangelism, and invoked Jesus constantly with respect to each. One of the YMCA's primary aims was 'To bring young men to Jesus Christ'. Boys were therefore expected to spend part of their time 'studying the life of Jesus Christ and the Truths of the Bible'.[117] Personality provided the method and the message. Greenberg described evangelism as the 'overflowing of consecrated personality', and encouraged members to be active in introducing not 'a code of conduct, nor a schedule of beliefs, but a programme for their lives, inspired and directed by the living Personality of Christ'. Jesus' love, victory and conquering spirit would inspire legions of lads to live heroically for God, rather than his wounds.[118]

Because evangelism and social activism were closely allied, Jesus' personality was the answer to social problems as well as the source of personal salvation. As one piece in *Dunedin Manhood* declared, 'Turn to Jesus – the belief is steadily gaining ground that in His message and Personality are unexplored resources of light and power, and the solution of many of our present-day problems'.[119] In this context, representation of Jesus as a Great Personality asserted that he, and therefore religion, was relevant. It was also a statement of significance. Personality betokened power, influence and the capacity to persuade. It linked with heroic affirmations of the power of the individual to effect change, which contradicted accusations that religion was effete, impotent or weak. As The Great Personality, Jesus epitomised qualities of practical action in which his followers might share.

The manly Jesus was primarily constructed to address concerns about the religiosity of youth, 'working men' and returned servicemen. Representations rested on a range of assumptions about masculinity – both of befitting Christian manliness, and the forms to which 'non-

---

117 *Dunedin Manhood*, September 1933, p.1; *Dunedin Manhood*, April 1934, p.6.
118 Greenberg, *Personal Adventuring*, pp.7, 10, 17, 40.
119 *Dunedin Manhood*, June 1934, p.1.

religious' men might aspire. Attempts to present a more masculine Jesus aimed to utilise the more appealing aspects of Jesus-centred Christianity in order to win men to religion. A manly Jesus affirmed men's experiences. Focus on Jesus' life rather than his death was supposed to make religion seem more adventurous and inspire heroic living. It also made religion seem simpler, non-sectarian and non-theological. That Colin Scrimgeour employed motifs of Jesus' manliness so freely suggests that these were probably very attractive to many men.[120] By the same token, on this evidence, the ideas did not necessarily lead to greater participation in established forms of organised religion.

Indeed, the project was fraught with difficulties, not least due to the tendency to cast masculinity in heroic terms. A heroic Jesus could be considered childish, and reinforce the perception that Jesus and religion were primarily for children. Developmental ideas were providing an ideology in which hero worship was linked scientifically with the needs and capabilities of older children. Employing such ideas among young men risked infantilising religion by extending adolescence. Moreover, there was an additional danger after World War One: that conflict arguably represented the failure of hero worship, since so many young men had died pursuing it.

As with the children's Jesus, correlation of a manly Jesus with ideal manhood risked promoting degree Christology. Thus, the heroic Jesus was celebrated as the 'supreme' example of every conceivable manly virtue, but these often simply reiterated prevailing cultural ideals. The problem here was that Jesus-centred religion aimed to make Jesus the source of authority, not merely a reflection of cultural values. There was also the danger that men's actual ideals could be easily misread. For example, militant expressions of manliness sat somewhat uneasily alongside the pacifism and internationalism that also influenced religious youth movements during this period. Moreover, a soldierly Jesus risked underestimating returnees' disaffection with many aspects of military life and values.

There were also ambivalences in relation to other Christian priorities. Despite the emphasis on robust religion by some evangelicals, others doubted whether staunch masculinity could be reconciled with spiritual regeneration. Popular revivalist piety continued to encourage

120   Reid, 'Church and State', p.142; *Hello Everybody*, 2, 1935, p.6.

sentimentality and emotion that could be regarded as suspiciously feminine. Thus, one minister challenged delegates at a Baptist Young Men's Bible Class camp at Maungatawhiri, saying, 'Look here. Maybe you fellows think that we were "sissies" to break down and cry. Mark my words – some of you who think that you are big he-men will be in tears before to-night is out, for I am convinced that revival will sweep this camp as well'. The meeting finished with songs that included one of the Sankey corpus, 'Pass me not, O gentle Saviour'.[121]

For all the emphasis on strength, virility and personality, moral manliness and character formation remained important priorities. Indeed, even heroism itself was often interpreted within an essentially moral framework. It was frequently used as a kind of shorthand for having the courage of one's conviction, and pursuit of Christian moral agendas. In some ways, the notion of character was gender neutral. Moral manliness was not primarily conceived in ideological opposition to femininity, but involved imitation of Jesus through combining the virtues of both sexes. This 'sexless' quality could give the impression that manly Christian character remained essentially 'feminine', especially when it sought to subvert supposed masculine values of strength and prowess by reinvesting them with new meaning.

The manly Jesus was fundamentally instrumentalist and utilitarian. He represented an attempt to reach men who were expected to be resistant to organised religion. The persistence of notions of character, self-discipline and decency highlights a high degree of consensus concerning the nature of Christian masculinity. There were concessions to other forms, but also considerable continuities between the manly Jesus and his predecessors. Thus, the Jesus of heroic masculinity was in many ways a new fashion that supported much older priorities. It was a presentation technique rather than a reinterpretation. The move entailed some striking paradoxes. In some senses, the manly Jesus was a popularising figure. Yet, as a figure constructed from evangelistic intentions, he subverted popular notions. Perhaps his most important function was as a source of confidence for religious men.

121 Cited in J. Edwin Orr, *All Your Need: 10,000 Miles of Miracle through Australia and New Zealand*, London: Marshall, Morgan & Scott, 1936, pp.31-32.

7. Conclusion

By the late twentieth century, Jesus still seemed to have a high profile in New Zealand religion. Widely publicised Jesus marches in 1972 provided one example of his prominence,[1] while the growth of Pentecostal and Charismatic Christianity was also accompanied by a more explicit devotional emphasis on Jesus. One hundred years after *In His Steps* first appeared, Charles Sheldon's question 'what would Jesus do?' was back in vogue, only remarketed for a new generation as WWJD with matching bracelets and assorted paraphernalia. While Sheldon's Jesus had been invoked on behalf of the social gospel, this late twentieth-century personality was overwhelmingly associated with evangelical forms of Christianity.

These later representations of Jesus were in some ways built on an earlier pattern. The Jesus of late twentieth-century evangelical religiosity was often highly personalised, and cohered with a tendency to downplay doctrine and theology. Despite these commonalities, however, there were also substantial differences. Most significantly, the early twentieth-century emphasis on Jesus was not simply indicative of an evangelical-isation of religion. Indeed, while it remained an important influence, most commentators rightly note that evangelicalism was fracturing and its influence waning rather than increasing at this time.[2] Jesus-centred religion was primarily shaped by a preoccupation with religion and its audiences. In particular, the churches embraced Jesus as a means for navigating their way through the social and cultural changes of the age. He was a tool for addressing the challenges of modernity in a mature colonial society.

As a religious idea and ideal, Jesus became more attractive within a particular context. Broad longer-term influences such as the rise of historical consciousness, modern science, Romanticism and ideals of

---

1   Trevor Shaw, *The Jesus Marches*, Auckland: Challenge, 1972.
2   Peter Matheson, 'The Contours of Christian Theology in Aotearoa New Zealand', in Emilsen and Emilsen (eds), pp.255-71; Ian Breward, *A History of the Churches in Australasia*, New York: Oxford University Press, 2001, pp.256-58.

personality contributed to a cultural emphasis on historicity and individuality. Making the humanity of Jesus more prominent clearly accorded with these priorities. For New Zealanders, peculiarly colonial experiences of social change were compounded with other forms of upheaval associated with modernisation. Together with war and economic fluctuation these altered the context in which religion operated. Changes upset the basis of connection with the community, and contributed to a sense that the churches' traditional influence was being eroded. In response, churches increasingly viewed secularity, rather than rival denominations, as the leading threat to religion. Indeed, the secular world became the primary target of a great deal of Christian discourse. Amidst these concerns, Jesus functioned as a symbol of all that was good in humanity and in religion. He represented the exemplary life, and the basis of morality that was true religion's gift to society. He was also increasingly identified as the essence of religion, and the focal point of religious sentiment and argumentation.

Broadly speaking, revivalism and the social gospel were two of the key international religious responses to the challenges of modernity. Both streams were also very influential in New Zealand, and shared important characteristics. Significantly, each approach made Jesus central to their discourse of religion. In these contexts, appeal to Jesus provided a language of change and of ideals that was more instrumental than doctrinal in orientation. Jesus language built upon assumptions of a shared Christian identity within society, whilst nonetheless summoning the community to greater religious commitment. It was also used to reshape religion to make it more attractive and meaningful in a rapidly changing environment. Crucially, personality-inspired Jesus language in the first half of the twentieth century was not primarily one of inner devotion, nor of liturgy or formal religious occasions. These forms of spirituality came much later with the shift to a less formal society, and alongside influences like the Charismatic movement. Earlier Jesus-centredness refashioned religion in order to enliven it and extend its influence. In this sense, it was focused on mission.

Two particular aspects of Jesus' attractiveness warrant comment here. First, whether conceptualised in terms of personality or not, the focus on Jesus seemed to make religion simpler. Peter Matheson has argued that the 'utopian and bluntly material ambitions of ordinary folk' created a distinctive religious landscape in New Zealand.[3] Distaste for creeds and suspicion about theology arguably reflected these ambitions. They were expressive of harmonising tendencies within New Zealand society that Jesus seemed to support. As a moral example and source of authority, he circumvented the divisive theological and denominational differences that certainly did exist. The great historical doctrinal cleavages associated with Arminianism, Lutheranism and Calvinism continued, but tended to be downplayed rather than accentuated, partly out of a desire to avoid replicating Old World divisions. Instead, Jesus was related to ideals of practicality. Criticisms of 'Churchianity' were multivalent, but suggested that religion was about action rather than association, and should be practiced with a minimum of pretension. The religion of Jesus was one of essences. It required no theological qualifycations, and could be practiced by all and sundry. Significantly, this simplification of religion was not only fostered by populist visions, but also by Christian leaders who actually did possess theological qualifications.

The second of Jesus' leading assets was his malleability. One feature of the representations discussed in this study is their use for strikingly different ends. Jesus was invoked in a wide range of contexts, and constructed according to the needs of the situation. Thus, he was at once compassionate and courageous, assertive and tender, a socialist and a capitalist, a revolutionary and a loyalist, a pacifist and a military hero, a prohibitionist and a supporter of the liberty of the individual. Moreover, Jesus appeared in support of markedly differing religious visions and competing theological agendas. As the debates about social issues highlighted, however, Jesus could be widely invoked though the precise effects of all those references remained hard to measure. Jesus became more central to discourses of Protestant religiosity. Yet, as the universal man, he was almost too malleable to provide an authoritative basis for particular frameworks of action. Moreover, formulations of his identity were often remarkably similar to ideals and practices that were generated from elsewhere.

On the other hand, that Jesus was invoked in such diverse ways and contexts indicates something about the permeation of religious ideals and values. It highlights that religious modes of argument remained

3   Matheson, p.260.

attractive. Jesus' malleability suggests that religion penetrated the fabric of New Zealand society more extensively than institutional markers like rates of church attendance might imply. In the general historiography, lower rates of churchgoing have often been taken to reflect the limitations of religious commitment among New Zealanders.[4] By contrast, the pervasiveness of Jesus language tends against assumptions that religion was a minor and increasingly marginal influence. Configurations might change, but religion continued to have an important function, especially in processes of attitude formation. This finding generally supports Melanie Nolan's argument that religion was a significant factor in the country's working-class culture. Her study of the McCullough clan demonstrates that, for some, these religious connections were expressed through ongoing participation in religious institutions. For others, religious modes of thought and ideals were formative influences that endured even as formal commitments waned.[5]

In the conclusion to his survey of images of Jesus, Jaroslav Pelikan observed that reverence for Jesus grew as respect for the organised church declined.[6] To some extent, this process was also evident in New Zealand. Jesus was increasingly differentiated from organised religion as the churches' standing in the community diminished. Within the churches, declining respect for religion could make Jesus seem all the more attractive. In the community at large, the pattern was perhaps one in which respect for Jesus displaced that for religious institutions. In other words, respect for Jesus was not always equivalent to reverence or devotion. Nor did invoking him always indicate religiosity.

Nevertheless, even the strength of prophetic and anti-Church images indicated that religious sentiments were often attractive when institutional structures were made less important. The extent to which such ideas circulated suggested that the churches were subject to considerable criticism during this period. The pressure was not all in one direction, however. As a criticism from detractors, the anti-Church Jesus still signalled that churches were viewed as important social institutions. Targeting them amounted to a tacit admission of their significance, and

4   Belich, pp.350-51; Keith Sinclair, *A History of New Zealand*, rev. ed., Auckland: Penguin, 1988, p.105.
5   Nolan, *Kin*.
6   Pelikan, p.232.

acknowledgement that any serious programme of reform needed to engage them. Furthermore, the extent of anti-Church language also signalled the strength of essentially Protestant modes of thought, including the principle of *semper reformanda*.

The enormous investment in religion for children was a crucial method for extending the churches' influence and retaining contact with the community at large. Jesus' prominence in the religious discourse of childhood was a distinctive and significant feature. Childhood experiences created a store of perceptions, emotions and correlations. While the enduring sentiments attached to organised religion were seldom positive, those associated with Jesus tended to be more generous. This shaped the tone of diffused religiosity, even if the particular images of Jesus did not always work to the churches' long term advantage. By the end of the twentieth century, religious communities invested less in children and their connection with them had greatly diminished. Some mainline Protestant churches even ceased running programmes for children.[7] In 1996, only about 15% of children in Auckland retained any association with Sunday schools in the region.[8] One consequence of this was a decline in shared religious understandings, masked only by the strength of religious activity among some more recent migrants from Asia and the Pacific. An attenuated common religious vocabulary altered the functions and meanings attached to Jesus as a religious icon.

In New Zealand, Jesus represented a simpler, adaptable and optimistic form of religion. Despite this, he never achieved the cultural prominence or celebrity status of Jesus in America. Writing of the United States, Stephen Prothero has argued that America became a 'Jesus nation' during the twentieth century, but not a Christian one. No consensus emerged around views of him, but Jesus achieved a status as a unifying cultural symbol: 'In a country divided by race, ethnicity, gender, class, and religion, Jesus functions as common cultural coin... his popularity only seems to have increased as he has become more human'.[9] Perhaps, in this religious and symbolic realm, American

7   Mary Petersen, 'The Future of Christianity in New Zealand: What is Happening with the Children?', in John Stenhouse and Brett Knowles (eds), with Antony Wood, *The Future of Christianity*, Adelaide: ATF Press, 2004, pp.88-101.

8   Hugh Dickey, 'The Kids-Count '96 Survey', in Bruce Patrick (ed.), *New Vision New Zealand Volume II*, Auckland: Vision New Zealand, 1997, pp.145-57.

9   Prothero, pp.300-1, quote p.300.

approaches were too brash and unrespectable for local cultural tastes. In any case, New Zealand did not become a Jesus nation. Furthermore, for all the diversity of representations, there were also striking points of consensus concerning Jesus during the earlier decades of the twentieth century. In particular, he was an example and symbol of morality, solidarity and cooperation, as well as a prophetic critic of the Church and society. As a mirror to society, these common perceptions of Jesus suggest an admiration for religion that was warm, personal, practical and unpretentious. The prevalence of heroic ideals reflected the hopeful and optimistic tone of a society that was still rather rough and out-backish, despite its increasingly urbanised character.

Language about Jesus was a weathervane that picked up trajectories in culture and society, including shifting priorities. For example, notions of personality, the rise of youth culture and flourishing masculinism were all signalled in this way. Some changes were more deliberate and self-conscious than others. Representations of Jesus' masculinity were among the most populist, in the sense that they were clearly shaped by ideals that seemed to have wide acceptance within the community. One potential advantage of this approach was that it appeared to affirm experience, and to adopt a sympathetic stance to prevailing social standards and values. It made Jesus quite literally a man of the people. In this sense, Jesus was a contextual creation, though he seemed most fully a cultural artefact when purposefully constructed to meet the challenges of the age.

Tradition and scripture were also in dialogue with culture, helping to shape, reinforce and challenge the images of Jesus that circulated. Despite these influences, the depictions of Jesus that emerged during this period confirm the sense of a very weak tradition of theological reflection in New Zealand. On the one hand, images like those of a manly Jesus were driven opportunistically, in response to genuine though essentially pragmatic concerns. They reflected a preference for effective action over reflection or formal theology. Moreover, they were subjected to limited theological critique. The difficulty, as the Scottish theologian P.T. Forsyth's critique of his fellow Congregationalist R.J. Campbell's New Theology highlighted, was that weak theology provided an inadequate support for devotion to the person of Jesus.[10] It was all very well being an enthusiast for Jesus, but the attachment could prove parlous if its basis was incoherent. The danger was that, in the longer term, either the theology or the devotion must shift or likely give way altogether. The target of Forsyth's observation had been liberal theology, but it had much wider relevance. In the New Zealand context, the rise and later decline of Uncle Scrim's Friendly Road Christianity demonstrated how prescient his admonition was.

This book has emphasised that interest in Jesus grew, and constituted a distinctive and increasingly pronounced feature of religiosity in New Zealand between 1890 and 1940, especially among Protestant Christians. It was not exactly that Jesus was discovered in this period. He had after all been central to Christianity for the best part of two thousand years. Nevertheless, particular understandings of him did become more important; there was a new discursive focus on Jesus, and his status as a source of authority changed. Notions of humanity and personality were central in this, even if these did not comprise the entire range of discourse about him. Indeed, cultivating a sense of historicity and personality was often more important than the specific dimensions of Jesus' life and teaching. Moreover, to those within the churches, and for many nominal Christians, Jesus was primarily humanity's Saviour and Lord. Together with belief in his divinity this conviction ensured that Jesus-centred religiosity was never entirely focused on his personality or human attributes.

Nevertheless, the rise of Jesus-centred religiosity was a critical factor in the transformation of images of Jesus during this period. To a certain extent, Jesus-centred religion arose as a conscious attempt to modernise Christianity and extend its reach in the light of wider transformations within society. Equally, it may also be seen as a less deliberate indicator of social and cultural change. In any case, the representations that circulated during these years testified to Jesus' continuing cultural and religious significance, as well as to the complex cluster of influences that shaped contemporary interest in him. To invoke Jesus was to say certain things about him, but perhaps equally – then as ever – about religion, culture and society.

---

10   B.G. Worrall, *The Making of the Modern Church: Christianity in England Since 1800*, 3rd ed., London: SPCK, 2004, pp.130-31.

Bibliography

Primary sources

Archives and manuscripts

Auckland Peace Association, Minute Book, MS-Papers-2530, ATL.

Brooklyn Methodist Church, Sunday School Minute Book, 1918-1932, Methodist Archives, Christchurch.

Charles Booth Scrapbook, Ms797/II/91/3. Charles Booth Papers, Special Collections, University of London Library, London.

Education Department, Syllabus and Instruction – Bible in Schools, 1925-26, Series 2: E2/1926/1a_8/4/32, ANZ.

Film Censor's Files, IA 83, ANZ.

General Assembly Committees, Presbyterian Church of New Zealand, PCANZARC.

J.T. Paul Papers, MS-982, Hocken Library, Dunedin.

John A. Lee Papers, NZMS 828: 9/6, Special Collections, Auckland Public Library.

Knox Presbyterian, Lower Hutt Papers, ATL.

Maurice Gough Gee Papers, MS-Group-0193, ATL.

New Zealand Anglican Bible Class Union, ANG062, Kinder Library, Auckland.

New Zealand Cemetery Records, (microfiche), 1985, Palmerston North City Library.

New Zealand Student Christian Movement, MS-Group-0507, ATL.

Palmerston North Church of England Men's Society Minute Book, 15 March 1910 – 13 December 1922, All Saints' Anglican Church, Palmerston North.

Scripture Union, Historical Documents from the 1930s Box, Scripture Union Archives, Wellington.

Taranaki St Wesleyan Methodist Church, Wellington Papers, ATL.

Terrace Congregational Church, Wellington, MS-Group-1059, ATL.

Wellington Baptist Church, Christian Endeavour Society Papers, ATL.

Wellington Congregational Men's League Minute Book, 1925-30, MS-Group-0159, MSY-4037, ATL.

YMCA (National), Publications and Pamphlets, MS-Group-0362, 95-017-04/1, ATL.

YMCA (Wellington Branch), MS-Group-0662, ATL.

Official publications, papers and proceedings

Appendices to the Journal of the House of Representatives
Census of New Zealand
Gazette Law Reports
Minutes of Annual Conference, Methodist Church of New Zealand
New Zealand Baptist Union Baptist Handbook
New Zealand Parliamentary Debates
Proceedings of the Diocesan Synod of the Diocese of Wellington
Proceedings of the General Assembly of the Presbyterian Church of New Zealand
Proceedings of the General Synod of the Church of the Province of New Zealand
Proceedings of the Synod of the Presbyterian Church of Otago and Southland
Yearbook of the Congregational Union of New Zealand

Newspapers and periodicals

Auckland Star
Auckland Weekly News
Australasian Intercollegian
Biblical Recorder
Break of Day: The Children's Missionary Magazine of the Presbyterian Church of New
    Zealand
Church Chronicle: For the Diocese of Wellington
Church Gazette: For the Diocese of Auckland
Church News: For the Diocese of Christchurch
Citizen: Journal of the Forward Movement
Dunedin Manhood: Official Organ of the YMCA of Dunedin, NZ
Echo: Official Organ of the Wellington District Young Men's Bible Class Union
Evening Post (Wellington)
Four Square: Official Organ of the NZ Presbyterian Young Men's Bible Class Union and
    Institute
Freedom: Official Organ of the New Zealand Youth Movement against Alcoholism
Girl's Chronicle
Grey River Argus
Harvest Field: Magazine of the Presbyterian Women's Missionary Union
Hello Everybody
Knox Collegian
Lyttelton Times
Manawatu Evening Standard
Maoriland Worker
Men: Official Organ of the CEMS in New Zealand
Methodist Bible Class Link: Official Organ of the New Zealand Methodist Young
    Women's and Young Men's Bible Class Movements

Methodist Manhood: Official Organ of the New Zealand Methodist Young Men's Bible Class Movement

Methodist Youth News

New Zealand Baptist

New Zealand Church News

New Zealand Dairy Exporter

New Zealand Herald (Auckland)

New Zealand Journal of Theology

New Zealand Methodist Times

New Zealand Tablet

New Zealand Worker

Open Windows: Monthly Magazine of the New Zealand Student Christian Movement

Otago Daily Times

Otago Liberal

Outlook

Parish Magazine (Parish Magazine of All Saints' Anglican Church, Palmerston North)

Press (Christchurch)

Reaper

School Journal

Socialist

Socialist Church, Monthly Leaflet

Standard

Taranaki Herald

Timaru Herald

Triangle Trail

Wanganui Chronicle

War Cry

Wellington's Manhood: Official Organ of the YMCA of Wellington, NZ

White Ribbon: Official Organ of the New Zealand Women's Christian Temperance Union

Young Man's Magazine

Addresses, pamphlets, tracts and resources

A New Zealand Syllabus of Religious Instruction for Use in the Public Schools of New Zealand Under the Present Voluntary System, Wellington: New Zealand Bible-in-Schools League, 1937.

A Parish Priest in New Zealand, *Conversations on Christian Re-Union*, Dunedin: NZ Tablet, 1924.

A Simple Prayer Book, Wellington: Catholic Enquiry Centre, 1964.

A Syllabus of Religious Instruction for Use in the State Schools of New Zealand Under the Present Voluntary System, Dunedin: Otago Branch of the New Zealand Council of Religious Education, 1933.

'Acceptable Words', 4th ed., Christchurch: Christchurch Bible, Book & Tract Depot, n.d.

Adams, A.S., *Professor Salmond's Blunder. Prohibition: An Effective Social Reform*, Wellington: New Zealand Alliance, 1911.

_____, *The Relation of the Church to the Social Problems of the Age, Wanganui, 1906*, Christchurch: T.E. Fraser, 1906.

Advances in Understanding the Child, 8th ed., London: The Home and School Council of Great Britain, 1948 (1935).

Adventuring! Bible Study Notes, Wellington: Crusader Bookroom, 1935.

Aldridge, George, *Post-Mortem Salvation: A Review of Dr. Salmond's Pamphlet 'The Reign of Grace'*, Dunedin: Mills, Dick & Co., 1888.

_____, *Rhetorical Flourishes: Heresy in Methodism*, Auckland: Printed by Phipps & Hall, 1912.

Allan, John A., *Christianity and Communism*, Wellington: Publications Committee of St John's Young Men's Bible Class, 1936.

_____, *Godlessness, Chaos and the Christ*, Wellington: Publications Committee of St John's Young Men's Bible Class, [1934].

Anderson, William, *How Methodists Meet Heresy: Is Dogma Dead?*, Dunedin: Otago Daily Times Print, 1912.

Bailey, George, *The New Heresy, or, The Scripture Teaching Regarding the Use and Abuse of Intoxicating Liquors*, Invercargill: George Bailey, 1897.

Bates, J.M., *Our Church's Faith: A Study Book on Christian Doctrine*, Christchurch: Presbyterian Bookroom, 1941.

_____, *Ut Omnes Unum Sint*, Lower Hutt: Hartleys Print, 1946.

Black, W. Bower, *Shepherd of Souls*, Christchurch: Presbyterian Bookroom, 1952.

_____, *The House of Quietness*, Christchurch: Presbyterian Bookroom, 1945.

_____, *The Waters of Healing*, Christchurch: Presbyterian Bookroom, 1933.

Blamires, E.O., *A Christian Core for New Zealand Education*, Auckland: Printed by Whitcombe & Tombs, 1960.

Blamires, E.P., *Shall I Join the Church? A Question for Young People*, Christchurch: Literature Committee of the New Zealand Methodist Church, n.d.

Burd, W. Clement, *Methodism in Danger: Heresy in the Methodist Church*, Wellington: Wright & Carman, 1912.

Burley, W.A., *Laymen's Handbook*, Christchurch: Methodist Church of New Zealand, n.d.

Burridge, H.W. (ed.), *When the Boys Come Home: The Problem of the Returned Soldier and the Church*, Dunedin: Presbyterian Church of New Zealand, 1919.

Burton, O.E., *Christian Action*, Levin: Kerslake, Billens & Humphrey Printers, 1970.

_____, *Christian Socialism*, Auckland: Wright & Jaques Printers, 1940 (1928).

_____, *Shall we Fight?*, Auckland: Clark & Matheson Printers, 1923.

_____, *The Master of Men*, Wellington: YMCA, n.d.

_____, *The Stuff of Manhood*, Auckland: Unity Press, 1920.

Campbell, Patrick, *The Mythical Jesus*, with an introduction by James O. Hanlon, Auckland: Waverly Publishing, 1963.

Chapple, A.B. (ed.), *The Church and the Children. Official Report of the First Dominion Conference of Methodist Sunday School Workers*, Christchurch: Lyttelton

Times, 1909.

Clark, F.E., *The Society of Christian Endeavour: What It Is: How It Works*, n.p., The National Christian Endeavour Union of Australia and New Zealand, 1936.

Cohen, Chapman, *Did Jesus Christ Exist?*, London: The Pioneer Press, n.d.

_____, *Freethought and the Child*, London: The Pioneer Press, n.d.

Collins, A.H., *How Far and Why Have the Churches Failed?*, Auckland: Wright & Jaques Printers, 1899.

_____, *The Interest of the Home Churches in Foreign Missions*, Auckland: Wright & Jaques Printers, 1899.

Council of Christian Education (ed.), *Pictures of Jesus for Children: Addresses by Eight Leading Educationists*, London: Religious Tract Society, 1935.

Cunnington, E.W., *The Lectures and Letters of E.W. Cunnington*, edited by her children, Christchurch: Lyttelton Times, 1918.

Dash, George (ed.), *No-License Handbook*, Auckland: Louis P. Christie, for the New Zealand Alliance, 1908.

Desmond, Arthur, *Christ as a Social Reformer*, Auckland: Arthur Cleave, 1890.

Fitchett, W.H., *What Methodism Stands For*, Melbourne: T. Shaw Fitchett Printer, 1915.

Found at Last! The Lost Gospel: The Book That Nobody Knows, Wellington: Evening Post Print, 1931.

Fowlds, George, *Progress Towards Unity: An Address*, Auckland: H. Brett Printer, 1899.

_____, *The Drift Towards Anarchy: Its Causes and Cure*, Auckland: Wright & Jaques Printers, 1914.

_____, *The New Evangel: An Address*, Auckland: NZ Land Values' League, 1911.

Frankland, F.W., *Bible-Religion the Most Important Thing in the World*, Palmerston North: Watson Eyre & Co. Printers, 1909.

Fraser, P.B., *Mental Mutilation of the People's Children by Exclusion of the Bible from Schools*, Oamaru: Andrew Fraser, 1892.

Fuller, J., *Christian Socialism in the Industrial World: How We Can Abolish Industrial Warfare For Ever*, Auckland: Phipps & Hall, 1914.

God and the Little Child, Wellington: Youth Department, Methodist Church of New Zealand, n.d.

Grant, J.G.S., *Critical Examination of 'Ecce Homo'*, Dunedin: Mills, Dick & Co.,1867.

Gray, A. Herbert, *As Tommy Sees Us: A Book For Church Folk*, London: Arnold, 1918.

Greenberg, Len. J., *Personal Adventuring For Christ: A Statement of the Principles of Youth Evangelism*, Wellington: Youth Committee, N.Z. Council of Religious Education, 1934.

_____, *The Great Adventure*, Wellington: Wright and Carman, 1932.

Haddon, A.L., *The Coming of the World Church: A Brief Introduction to the Ecumenical Movement*, Wellington: Youth Committee of the New Zealand Council of Religious Education, 1942.

Hardie, Keir, and Rufus Weeks, *Christianity and Socialism: Two Views: the Miner's and the Millionaire's*, Wellington: New Zealand Times, 1908.

Hartley, Edward R., *A Catholic Pastoral on Socialism. An Open Letter to Archbishop Redwood*, Wellington: Maoriland Worker, 1912.

Hill, H., *Labour, Socialism, and Religion: An Address Delivered Before the Trinity*

Men's Society, May 26th, 1912, Napier: Herald Print, 1912.

Hinman, C.H., *The Deity of Christ. As Seen Before Incarnation. In Incarnation. Among Men. In His Works. In His Death and Resurrection. In His Coming Reign and Glory*, Palmerston North: E. Whitehead Print, 1907.

Howell, Ron, *Christian Pacifism and Social Change*, Auckland: Christian Pacifist Society of New Zealand (Auckland Branch), 1945.

In His Steps: Senior Bible Class Syllabus 1939, Auckland: Youth Committee of the New Zealand Council of Religious Education, 1939.

Intermediate Teachers' Handbook: Teaching Notes on the Intermediate Syllabus of the Graded Lessons of Australia and New Zealand, Melbourne: Joint Board of the Graded Lessons of Australia and New Zealand, 1939.

Jesus Among Men: Junior Bible Class Syllabus, Christchurch: Presbyterian Bookroom, 1933.

Jesus and Life's Problems: Senior Bible Class Syllabus, Christchurch: Presbyterian Bookroom, 1936.

Jesus Christ and Social Need: Addresses Delivered at the Conferences of the Australasian Student Christian Union, 1911-1912, Melbourne: Student Movement Press, 1912.

Jesus the Saviour of Men: Senior Bible Class Syllabus, Christchurch: Presbyterian Bookroom, 1933.

Johnson, John, *'Thou Shalt Love': Study for Summer and Winter Schools of the Methodist Young Men's Bible Class Movement*, Wellington: Wright & Carman, 1935.

Jolly, Isaac, *Why Did God Become Man? A Short Study of the Purpose of the Incarnation of the Son of God*, Christchurch: Presbyterian Bookroom, 1932.

Kane, G. Hope, *Beginners' Department*, Wellington: Youth Board, Methodist Church of New Zealand, n.d.

_____, *The Cradle Roll and Home Department*, Wellington: Youth Board, Methodist Church of New Zealand, n.d.

Kempthorne, S., *The Holy Scriptures, the Only Sound Basis for the Education of Youth*, Auckland: William Atkin Printer, 1870.

Lee, John A., *Expelled From the Labour Party For Telling the Truth*, Auckland: Grey Lynn Democratic Labour Party, 1940.

Luke, Robert, *The Definition of Socialism and Democracy*, Dunedin: The Budget Printers, 1914.

Maclean, Hector, *Jesus' Teaching About the Kingdom of God: A Bible Study Handbook for Conferences and Institutes*, Dunedin: NZ Young Women's Presbyterian Bible Class Union, 1935.

Maples, Frederick G., *Socialism from a Catholic Point of View*, Petone: Hutt and Petone Chronicle, 1908.

McCabe, Jospeh, *The Churches and Social Progress*, Wellington: New Zealand Times, for the editor of Commonweal, 1910.

McKenzie, G.M., *Twelve Splendid Men*, Wellington: N.Z. Student Christian Movement, 1934.

N.Z. National Eucharistic Congress, Wellington, February 1-4 1940: Souvenir

Programme, Christchurch: Printed by Whitcombe & Tombs, 1940.

New Zealand Catholic Schools' Journal: Centenary Number, 1838-1938, Christchurch: Whitcombe & Tombs, 1938.

North, J.J., *Jesus: Son of Man Son of God and Perfectly Both*, Auckland: H.H. Driver, 1939.

_____, *'Me a Christian!!' 'Why Not?'*, Auckland: H.H. Driver, 1939.

_____, *Roman Catholicism: 'Roots and Fruits'*, Napier: Venables Print, 1922.

_____, *Romanism: Five Sermons*, Dunedin: H.H. Driver, 1911.

_____, *The Plain Points of Protestantism*, Auckland: H.H. Driver, 1938.

_____, *The Socialism of Jesus: An Argument*, Christchurch: T.E. Fraser, 1905.

Paul, J.T., *The Duty of the Church to the Labour Movement*, Dunedin: Otago Trades and Labour Council, 1903.

Pettit, W.H., *Experiences in Christian Work Among New Zealand Students*, IVF Papers, no. 2, New Zealand: IVF, n.d.

Prayers for the Home Circle. With a Selection of Bible Readings, Dunedin: Presbyterian Church of New Zealand, 1917.

Prohibition! Opinions of Experts! Papers Read at the Palmerston North Convention on May 24th and 25th, 1898, Palmerston North: Hart & Keeling Printers, 1898.

'Quit You Like Men': NZ Methodist Young Men's Bible Class Movement Study for Easter Camps 1939, n.p., 1939.

Raven, Charles, *The Starting Point of Pacifism*, London: Peace Pledge Union, 1940.

Redwood, Francis, *Jesus Christ Yesterday, To-Day, and For Ever*, Dunedin: NZ Tablet, 1910.

_____, *Lenten Pastoral Letter*, Wellington: Tolan Print, 1933.

_____, *Lenten Pastoral on Socialism*, Wellington: Catholic Times, 1892.

_____, *Pastoral Letter on Socialism*, Dunedin: Tablet Reprints, 1906.

_____, *Pastoral on Socialism*, Dunedin: NZ Tablet Print, 1912.

_____, *The Passion of Our Lord Jesus Christ*, Wellington: Tolan Print, 1926.

Salmond, J.D. (ed.), *Christ and Tomorrow: A Study Book for the Times*, Christchurch: Presbyterian Bookroom, 1936.

_____, *The Church and Her Young People*, Christchurch: Presbyterian Bookroom, 1939.

Salmond, J.D., and Alex Salmond, *The World Crisis and the Gospel*, Dunedin: Otago Daily Times Print, 1931.

Salmond, J.D., and Alex Salmond (eds), *Facing Vital Issues: A Study Book for the Times*, Christchurch: Presbyterian Bookroom, 1932.

Salmond, William, *Prohibition: A Blunder*, 3rd ed., Dunedin: Jolly & Braik Printers, 1911.

_____, *The Reign of Grace: A Discussion of the Question of the Possibility of Salvation for All Men in This Life, or in the Life to Come*, Dunedin: James Horsburgh, 1888.

Sarginson, I., *War, Pacifism and Christianity*, Christchurch: Lyttelton Times, 1927.

Scott, J.A., *The Church and Socialism*, Melbourne: The Australian Catholic Truth Society, 1912.

Scrimgeour, C.G., *Chats: Talks on the 'Friendly Road'*, Auckland: Unity Press, n.d.

Services of Worship (Undenominational) For Use in the Public Schools of New Zealand Under the Present Voluntary System, Wellington: New Zealand Bible-in-Schools

League, 1940.

Shaw, Trevor, *The Jesus Marches*, Auckland: Challenge, 1972.

Smith, J. Gibson, *Eden and After*, Dunedin: Otago Daily Times and Witness Newspapers, 1926.

Sprott, T.H., *Bible in State Schools*, Wellington: Wright & Carman, 1913.

_____, *Redeeming the Time: A Selection of Sermons and Addresses*, Wellington: A.H. & A.W. Reed, 1948.

Stout, Robert, *The Bible in Schools: The Scriptures as Moral Teaching*, Dunedin: Otago Daily Times Print, 1927.

Sullivan, Martin, *Children, Listen: Talks to Boys and Girls*, Christchurch: Whitcombe & Tombs, 1955.

_____, *Listen Again: More Talks to Boys and Girls*, Christchurch: Whitcombe & Tombs, 1956.

Sunday School and Bible Class at Work: Text-Book for Teacher-Training Classes, Study Groups, and General Use, 2nd ed., Melbourne: Joint Board of the Graded Lessons of Australia and New Zealand, 1936.

Sunday School Teachers' Guide, Christchurch: Presbyterian Bookroom, for the Youth Committee of the Presbyterian Church of New Zealand, 1928.

Symons, C.T., *Expression Work for Beginners and Primary Department*, Wellington: Youth Board, Methodist Church of New Zealand, n.d.

_____, *Junior Worship*, Wellington: Youth Board, Methodist Church of New Zealand, n.d.

_____, *Sunday School and Junior Church*, Wellington: Youth Board, Methodist Church of New Zealand, n.d.

_____, *Teaching Temperance: A Guide-Book for Youth Workers*, Wellington: Youth Department, Methodist Church of New Zealand, n.d.

The Bible in Schools: A Criticism of the Proposed Text-book by the Wellington State Schools' Defence League, Wellington: Evening Post, 1905.

The Bible-in-Schools Text Book, As Approved by the Wellington Conference, Wellington: C.M. Banks Printer, 1904.

The Carpenter of Galilee: Studies in Mark's Gospel: Junior Bible Class Syllabus, Christchurch: Presbyterian Bookroom, 1935.

The Life of Jesus in Song and Story, Christchurch: North Canterbury Methodist Sunday School, 1932.

Thomson, William, *Prohibition Fatal to Liberty Temperance and Morality*, Wellington: Whitcombe & Tombs, 1911.

Thornton, Elinor, *Soul Secrets*, Dunedin: Evening Star Printers, 1919.

Toward Unity in Education: Report of the First Conference on National Religious Education, Christchurch: New Zealand Council of Religious Education, 1929.

Williams, William, *Remarks Upon 'Ecce Homo'*, Auckland: Cathedral Press, 1867.

Willis, W.N., *Bible Teaching in State Schools*, Auckland: Wilson and Horton Printers, 1911.

Wilson, A.S., *Concerning Perplexities Paradoxes & Perils in the Spirit-led Path*, Auckland: Scott & Scott, 1932.

_____, *Faith's Fight*, Auckland: Scott & Scott, 1933.

Wood, Rev. A., *A Reply to 'Prohibition a Blunder', by a Presbyterian Minister*, Wellington: New Zealand Alliance, 1911.

Yuille, Tulloch, *There They Crucified Him*, Dunedin: N.Z. Bible and Book Society, 1928.

Books and articles

[Abbott, Edwin Abbott], *Philochristus: Memoirs of a Disciple of the Lord*, Boston: Roberts Brothers, 1878.

Adams, Arthur H., *The Nazarene: A Study of a Man*, London: Philip Welby, 1902.

Averill, A.W., *Fifty Years in New Zealand, 1894-1944: Recollections and Reflections*, Christchurch: Whitcombe & Tombs, 1945.

Bates, J.M., *Presbyterian Theology in New Zealand from 1930-1980: A Personal Retrospect*, Dunedin: Knox Theological Hall, 1995.

Begbie, Harold, *Religion and the Crisis*, London: Cassell & Company, 1913.

Bellamy, Edward, *Looking Backward from 2000 to 1887*, (electronic version), Champaign: Project Gutenberg; NetLibrary, (1888).

Benson, S.V., *The Child's Own Book of Prayers and Hymns*, London: Frederick Warne, 1940.

Bethell, Ursula, *Collected Poems*, Vincent O'Sullivan (ed.), Wellington: Victoria University Press, 1997.

Blaiklock, E.M., *Between the Valley and the Sea: A West Auckland Boyhood*, Palmerston North: Dunmore Press, 1979.

Blamires, E.P., *Youth Movement: The Story of the Rise and Development of the Christian Youth Movement in the Churches of New Zealand – As Seen by a Methodist*, Auckland: Forward Books, 1952.

Blatchford, Robert, *God and My Neighbour*, London: Clarion Press, 1903.

Boyack, Nicholas, and Jane Tolerton, *In the Shadow of War: New Zealand Soldiers Talk About World War One and Their Lives*, Auckland: Penguin, 1990.

Cafferata, H.T., *The Catechism Simply Explained*, rev. ed., London: Burns & Oates, 1954.

Campbell, R.J., *Christianity and the Social Order*, London: Chapman & Hall, 1907.

Carlyle, Thomas, *On Heroes, Hero-Worship and the Heroic in History*, Lincoln: University of Nebraska Press, 1966 (1841).

Catholic Encyclopedia (online edition), 15 vols, New York: Robert Appleton, 1907-1912. URL: http://www.newadvent.org/cathen/index.html.

Chapple, J.H.G., *The Divine Need of the Rebel: Addresses from Texts from the Wider Bible of Literature*, London: C.W. Daniel, 1924.

Cocker, J., *Keep Climbing: Twenty-Five Stories of Great Men and Heroes*, London: H.R. Allenson, 1929.

_____, *The Date Boy of Baghdad: Thirty-Five Story Talks to Young People*, London: H.R. Allenson, 1925.

Cocker, J., and J. Malton Murray (eds), *Temperance and Prohibition in New Zealand*,

London: Epworth Press, 1930.

Collie, J. (ed.), *Rutherford Waddell: Memoir and Addresses*, Dunedin: A.H. Reed, 1932.

Cyclopedia of New Zealand, 6 vols, Wellington: Cyclopedia Company, 1897-1908.

Davidson, Allan K., and Peter J. Lineham (eds), *Transplanted Christianity: Documents Illustrating Aspects of New Zealand Church History*, 2nd ed., Palmerston North: Dunmore Press, 1989.

Dickie, John, *The Organism of Christian Truth: A Modern Positive Dogmatic*, London: James Clarke, 1931.

Don, Alexander, *Light in Dark Isles. A Jubilee Record and Study of the New Hebrides Mission of the Presbyterian Church of New Zealand*, Dunedin: Foreign Missions Committee, Presbyterian Church of New Zealand, 1918.

Donnelly, W. *Heritage of Methodist Youth*, Wellington: New Zealand Methodist Youth Department, 1954.

Dowling, Levi H., *The Aquarian Gospel of Jesus the Christ*, London: L.N. Fowler, 1908.

Driver, H.H., *Our Work for God in India: A Brief History of the N.Z.B.M.S.*, Dunedin: H.H. Driver, 1914.

———, *These Forty Years: A Brief History of the N.Z.B.M.S.*, Dunedin: H.H. Driver, 1927.

Duggan, Eileen, *Selected Poems*, Peter Whiteford (ed.), Wellington: Victoria University Press, 1994.

Ecker, J., *The Catholic School Bible*, Bruges: Charles Beyaert, 1924.

Edmond, Lauris, *An Autobiography*, Wellington: Bridget Williams Books, 1994.

Edmond, Lauris (ed.), *Women in Wartime: New Zealand Women Tell Their Story*, Wellington: Government Printing Office, 1986.

Farrar, F.W., *The Life of Christ*, New York: A.L. Burt, 1907 (1874).

Faulkner, A.N., *The Socialism of John Wesley*, London: Robert Culley, 1908.

Fitzgerald, Gerald Patrick, *Christ in the Culture of Aotearoa-New Zealand*, Dunedin: Faculty of Theology, University of Otago, 1990.

Fletcher, Lionel B., *After Conversion – What?*, London: Marshall, Morgan & Scott, 1936.

———, *The Pathway to the Stars*, London: Marshall, Morgan & Scott, 1933.

Fosdick, Harry Emerson, *The Living of These Days: An Autobiography*, London: SCM Press, 1957.

———, *The Manhood of the Master*, rev. ed., London: Epworth Press, 1958 (1913).

Foston, Herman, *At the Front: A Story of Pluck and Heroism in the Railway Construction Camps in the Dominion of New Zealand*, London: Arthur H. Stockwell, 1921.

———, *In the Bell-Bird's Lair, or 'In Touch with Nature'*, Wellington: Gordon & Gotch, 1911.

Garland, T.T., *Judy Carries On*, Auckland: Whitcombe & Tombs, 1936.

Gee, Maurice, *The Plumb Trilogy*, Auckland: Penguin, 1995.

Glover, T.R., *The Jesus of History*, London: Hodder and Stoughton, 1965 (1917).

Golden Bells: Hymns for Young People, London: CSSM, n.d.

Growing Up in New Zealand Part 28: Sundays and Church Going Before 1925. URL: http://www.nzine.co.nz/features/guinz28.churchgoing.html.

Harcourt, Melville, *A Parson in Prison*, Auckland: Whitcombe & Tombs, 1942.

248

Holland, H.E., *Armageddon or Calvary: The Conscientious Objectors of New Zealand and 'The Process of their Conversion'*, Wellington: H.E. Holland, 1919.

Holland, H.E., and R.S. Ross, *The Tragic Story of the Waihi Strike*, Wellington: Printed by The Worker, 1913.

Hyde, Robin, *The Godwits Fly*, Patrick Sandbrook (ed.), Auckland: Auckland University Press, 2001 (1938).

Jones, E. Stanley, *The Christ of Every Road: A Study in Pentecost*, New York: Abingdon, 1930.

_____, *The Christ of the Indian Road*, London: Hodder and Stoughton, 1926.

Kagawa, Toyohiko, *Brotherhood Economics*, London: SCM Press, 1937.

_____, *The Religion of Jesus*, Helen F. Topping (trans.), London: SCM Press, 1931.

Kemp, Winnie, *Joseph W. Kemp: The Record of a Spirit-Filled Life*, London: Marshall, Morgan & Scott, 1936.

Knight, George A.F., *New Zealand Jesus*, Wellington: Presbyterian Church of New Zealand, 1974.

Lamoreaux, A.A., *The Unfolding Life: A Study of Development with Reference to Religious Training*, Chicago: Religious Publishing Company, 1907.

Lawlor, Pat, *The Demanding God: Some Boyhood Recollections*, Dunedin: NZ Tablet, 1972.

Lee, John A., *Children of the Poor*, London: T. Werner Laurie, 1934.

_____, *Rhetoric at the Red Dawn*, Auckland: Collins, 1965.

_____, *Socialism in New Zealand*, London: T. Werner Laurie, 1938.

_____, *The John A. Lee Diaries, 1936-40*, Christchurch: Whitcoulls, 1981.

Lewis, John, Karl Polanyi and Donald K. Kitchen (eds), *Christianity and the Social Revolution*, London: Victor Gollancz, 1935.

Locke, Elsie, *Student at the Gates*, Christchurch: Whitcoulls, 1981.

Machen, J. Gresham, *Christianity and Liberalism*, London: Victor, 1923.

Major, Henry D.A., *The Gospel of Freedom*, London: T. Fisher Unwin, 1912.

Mander, Jane, *The Story of a New Zealand River*, Christchurch: Whitcombe & Tombs, 1920.

Mason, R.A.K., *Collected Poems*, Allen Curnow (ed.), Christchurch: Pegasus, 1962.

Mathews, Basil, *A Life of Jesus*, New York: R.R. Smith, 1931.

_____, *A Little Life of Jesus*, London: Oxford University Press, 1933.

McCabe, Joseph, *The Sources of the Morality of the Gospels*, London: Watts, 1914.

Mee, Arthur, *The Children's Bible*, London: Hodder and Stoughton, 1924.

Métin, Albert, *Socialism Without Doctrine*, Russel Ward (trans.), Sydney: Alternative Publishing Co-operative, 1977 (1901).

Mirams, Gordon, *Speaking Candidly: Films and People in New Zealand*, Hamilton: Paul's Book Arcade, 1945.

Notovitch, Nicolas, *The Unknown Life of Jesus Christ*, New York: Macmillan, 1894.

Orr, J. Edwin, *All Your Need: 10,000 Miles of Miracle Through Australia and New Zealand*, London: Marshall, Morgan & Scott, 1936.

Papini, Giovanni, *The Story of Christ*, Mary Prichard Agnetti (trans.), London: Hodder and Stoughton, 1923.

Parsons, J. Ernest, *The Lost Santa Claus: Twenty-Five New Addresses*, London: H.R.

Allenson, n.d.

_____, *The Mouse That Stopped the Train: and Other Stories and Parables Told to the Children*, 2nd ed., London, H.R. Allenson, n.d.

_____, *The Splendid Quest: A Story for Children*, Auckland: J.E. Parsons, 1923.

_____, *Three Wonderful Keys: and Other Talks and Stories for Children*, London: H.R. Allenson, 1931.

Phillips, Jock, Nicholas Boyack and E.P. Malone (eds), *The Great Adventure: New Zealand Soldiers Describe the First World War*, Wellington: Allen & Unwin, 1988.

Pope, R. Hudson, *To Teach Others Also*, London: C.S.S.M., 1953.

Reed, A.H. (ed.), *The Isabel Reed Bible Story Book*, Wellington: A.H. & A.W. Reed, 1944.

Renan, Ernest, *The Life of Jesus*, (trans.), London: Trubner, 1863.

Rout, E., *Sexual Health and Birth Control*, London: Pioneer Press, 1925.

Sacred Songs & Solos, and New Hymns & Solos, 888 Pieces, Compiled by Ira D. Sankey, London: Marshall, Morgan & Scott, n.d.

Schweitzer, Albert, *The Quest of the Historical Jesus: A Critical Study of its Progress from Reimarus to Wrede*, W. Montgomery (trans.), 2nd ed., London: A & C Black, 1911.

Seeley, John, *Ecce Homo*, 17th ed., London: Macmillan, 1883 (1865).

Sheldon, Charles M., *In His Steps: What Would Jesus Do?*, London: Frederick Warne, 1928 (1896).

_____, *Jesus is Here! Continuing the Narrative of In His Steps*, New York: George H. Doran, 1914.

Siegfried, André, *Democracy in New Zealand*, E.V. Burns (trans.), Wellington: Victoria University Press, 1981 (1914).

Smith, J. Gibson, *The Christ of the Cross, or, The Death of Jesus Christ in its Relation to Forgiveness and Judgement*, Wellington: Gordon & Gotch, 1908.

Smyth, J. Paterson, *A Peoples' Life of Christ*, London: Hodder and Stoughton, 1921.

Snowden, Rita, *Story-Time Again*, London: Epworth, 1951.

_____, *The Wind Blows*, London: Epworth, 1940.

_____, *Through Open Windows*, London: Epworth, 1939.

Somerset, H.C.D., *Littledene: Patterns of Change*, rev. ed., Wellington: New Zealand Council for Educational Research, 1974.

Soper, Eileen L., *The Green Years*, Dunedin: John McIndoe, 1969.

Stead, F. Herbert, *The Proletarian Gospel of Galilee in Some of its Phases*, London: The Labour Publishing Company, 1922.

_____, *The Story of Social Christianity*, 2 vols, London: James Clarke, 1924.

Stevens, Ewing C., *Jesus*, Dunedin: Logos, 1973.

Strauss, D.F., *A New Life of Jesus*, 2 vols, (trans.), London: Williams and Norgate, 1865.

_____, *The Life of Jesus Critically Examined*, George Eliot (trans.), London: SCM Press, 1975 (1835).

Sullivan, Jim (ed.), *Catholic Boys: New Zealand Men Talk to Jim Sullivan*, Auckland: Penguin, 1996.

Sullivan, Martin, *Watch How You Go*, London: Hodder and Stoughton, 1975.

Sutherland, Martin (ed.), *Baptists in Colonial New Zealand: Documents Illustrating*

Baptist Life and Development, Auckland: N.Z. Baptist Research and Historical Society, 2002.

The Sunday School Hymnary: A Twentieth Century Hymnal for Young People, Carey Bonner (ed.), 17th ed., London: The National Sunday School Union, 1928.

Thomas, Joan Gale, *If Jesus Came to My House*, London: A.R. Mowbray, 1941.

Thomas, W.H. Griffith, *Christianity is Christ*, 2nd ed., London: Longmans, Green and Co., 1909.

Thorn, Margaret, *Stick Out, Keep Left*, Elsie Locke and Jacquie Matthews (eds),` Auckland: Auckland University Press, 1997.

Thornton, Elinor, *Reminiscences*, Auckland: Wright & Jaques, 1943.

Thornton, Guy, *The Wowser: A Tale of the New Zealand Bush*, London: H.R. Allenson, 1916.

Tolerton, Jane (ed.), *Convent Girls: New Zealand Women Talk to Jane Tolerton*, Auckland: Penguin, 1994.

Two Wayfarers, *The Christ of the English Road*, London: Hodder and Stoughton, 1929.

Tyrrell, George, *Christianity at the Crossroads*, London: George Allen & Unwin, 1963 (1909).

Waddell, Rutherford, *The Fiddles of God, and Other Essays*, Wellington: N.Z. Bible and Book Society, 1926.

_____, *Memories and Hopes*, Wellington: N.Z. Book Depot, 1929.

Wills, T.J., *The Church and the Liquor Traffic*, Christchurch: T.E. Fraser, 1894.

_____, *The Liquor Problem, or, The Work of Two Anglican Synods Reviewed*, Christchurch: T.E. Fraser, 1899.

Wilson, A.S., *Definite Experience: Convention Aids and Deterrents*, London: Marshall Morgan & Scott, 1937.

Wilson, Dorothy F., *Child Psychology and Religious Education*, 11th ed., London: SCM Press, 1946.

Secondary sources

Books and pamphlets

Amirthanayagam, Guy, and S.C. Harrex (eds), *Only Connect: Literary Perspectives East and West*, Adelaide: Centre for Research in the New Literatures in English & East-West Centre, 1981.

Archard, David, *Children, Rights and Childhood*, London: Routledge, 1993.

Audoin-Rouzeau, Stéphane, and Annette Becker, *1914-1918: Understanding the Great War*, Catherine Temerson (trans.), London: Profile, 2002.

Australian Dictionary of Biography, 16 vols, Melbourne: Melbourne University Press, 1966-2002.

Barnes, Lewis A., *Oh How I Love Thy Law: Reflections on the Life and Teaching of T.H. Sprott D.D. Vicar of St. Paul's Wellington 1892-1911, Bishop of Wellington 1911-1936*, Hamilton: John Walker, 1985.

Barrowman, Rachel, *Mason: The Life of R.A.K. Mason*, Wellington: Victoria University Press, 2004.

Baugh, Lloyd, *Imaging the Divine: Jesus and Christ-Figures in Film*, Kansas City: Sheed & Ward, 1997.

Beaglehole, Tim, *A Life of J.C. Beaglehole: New Zealand Scholar*, Wellington: Victoria University Press, 2006.

Bebbington, David W., *Evangelicalism in Modern Britain: A History from the 1730s to the 1980s*, Grand Rapids: Baker, 1992.

_____, *The Dominance of Evangelicalism: The Age of Spurgeon and Moody*, Downers Grove: InterVarsity Press, 2005.

_____, *The Nonconformist Conscience: Chapel and Politics, 1870-1914*, London: George Allen & Unwin, 1982.

Beilby, G.T., *A Handful of Grain: The Centenary History of the Baptist Union of N.Z., Volume 3 – 1914-1945*, Wellington: N.Z. Baptist Historical Society, 1984.

Belich, James, *Paradise Reforged: A History of the New Zealanders from the 1880s to the Year 2000*, Auckland: Allen Lane, 2001.

Berry, Christine, *The New Zealand Student Christian Movement, 1896-1996: A Centennial History*, Christchurch: Student Christian Movement of Aotearoa, 1998.

Birchard, Robert S., *Cecil B. DeMille's Hollywood*, Lexington: University of Kentucky Press, 2004.

Bosch, David, *Transforming Mission: Paradigm Shifts in Theology of Mission*, New York: Orbis, 1991.

Bottigheimer, Ruth B., *The Bible for Children: From the Age of Gutenberg to the Present*, New Haven: Yale University Press, 1996.

Bourke, Joanna, *Dismembering the Male: Men's Bodies, Britain and the Great War*, Chicago: University of Chicago Press, 1996.

Bradstock, Andrew, Sean Gill, Anne Hogan and Sue Morgan (eds), *Masculinity and Spirituality in Victorian Culture*, Basingstoke: Macmillan, 2000.

Bradwell, Cyril, *Fight the Good Fight: The Story of the Salvation Army in New Zealand 1883-1983*, Wellington: Reed, 1982.

Breward, Ian, *A History of the Churches in Australasia*, New York: Oxford University Press, 2001.

_____, *Godless Schools? A Study of Protestant Reactions to Secular Education in New Zealand*, Christchurch: Presbyterian Bookroom, 1967.

Brookes, Barbara, Annabel Cooper and Robin Law (eds), *Sites of Gender: Women, Men and Modernity in Southern Dunedin, 1890-1939*, Auckland: Auckland University Press, 2003.

Brown, Bruce, *The Rise of New Zealand Labour: A History of the New Zealand Labour Party from 1916 to 1940*, Wellington: Price Milburn, 1962.

Brown, Callum G., *The Death of Christian Britain: Understanding Secularisation, 1800-2000*, London: Routledge, 2001.

_____, *The Social History of Religion in Scotland Since 1730*, London: Methuen, 1987.

Brown, Colin, *Jesus in European Protestant Thought, 1778-1880*, Grand Rapids: Baker, 1988.

Bunge, Marcia J. (ed.), *The Child in Christian Thought*, Grand Rapids: Eerdmans, 2001.

Burrow, J.W., *The Crisis of Reason: European Thought, 1848-1914*, New Haven: Yale University Press, 2000.

Byrne, James M., *Religion and the Enlightenment: From Descartes to Kant*, Louisville: Westminster John Knox Press, 1996.

Byrnes, Giselle (ed.), *The New Oxford History of New Zealand*, Melbourne: Oxford University Press, 2009.

Burton, O.E., *Percy Paris*, Wellington: The Friends of Percy Paris, 1963.

Campion, Edmund, *Australian Catholics*, Ringwood: Penguin, 1988.

Carnes, Mark C., and Clyde Griffen (eds), *Meanings for Manhood: Constructions of Masculinity in Victorian America*, Chicago: University of Chicago Press, 1990.

Castle, Frank W., *Annals of the Auckland Unitarian Church*, Auckland: Auckland Unitarian Church, 1981.

Chambers, J.B., *'A Peculiar People': Congregationalism in New Zealand, 1840-1984*, Wellington: Congregational Union, 1984.

Christoffel, Paul, *Censored: A Short History of Censorship in New Zealand*, Wellington: Department of Internal Affairs, 1989.

Ciaran, Fiona, *Stained Glass Windows of Canterbury, New Zealand: A Catalogue Raisonné*, Dunedin: University of Otago Press, 1998.

Clifford, J. Ayson, *A Handful of Grain: The Centenary History of the Baptist Union of N.Z., Volume 2 – 1882-1914*, Wellington: N.Z. Baptist Historical Society, 1982.

Cooke, Bill, *A Rebel to His Last Breath: Joseph McCabe and Rationalism*, New York: Prometheus, 2001.

_____, *Heathen in Godzone: Seventy Years of Rationalism in New Zealand*, Auckland: NZ Association of Rationalists and Humanists, 1998.

Cooper, Kate, and Jeremy Gregory (eds), *Signs, Wonders, Miracles: Representations of Divine Power in the Life of the Church*, Woodbridge: Ecclesiastical History Society, 2005.

Couvares, Francis G. (ed.), *Movie Censorship and American Culture*, Washington: Smithsonian Institution Press, 1996.

Crawford, John, and Ian McGibbon (eds), *New Zealand's Great War: New Zealand, the Allies and the First World War*, Auckland: Exisle, 2007.

Crotty, Martin, *Making the Australian Male: Middle-Class Masculinity 1870-1920*, Melbourne: Melbourne University Press, 2001.

Cunningham, Hugh, *Children and Childhood in Western Society since 1500*, London: Longman, 1995.

Curran, Charles E., *Catholic Social Teaching, 1891-Present: A Historical, Theological and Ethical Analysis*, Washington: Georgetown University Press, 2002.

Daley, Caroline, *Girls & Women, Men & Boys: Gender in Taradale, 1886-1930*, Auckland: Auckland University Press, 1999.

_____, *Leisure & Pleasure: Reshaping & Revealing the New Zealand Body, 1900-1960*, Auckland: Auckland University Press, 2003.

Dalley, Bronwyn, *Family Matters: Child Welfare in Twentieth-Century New Zealand*,

Auckland: Auckland University Press, 1998.

Davidson, Allan K., *Christianity in Aotearoa: A History of Church and Society in New Zealand*, Wellington: Education for Ministry, 1991.

Davis, R.W., and R.J. Helmstadter (eds), *Religion and Irreligion in Victorian Society: Essays in Honor of R.K. Webb*, London: Routledge, 1992.

Davis, Richard P., *Irish Issues in New Zealand Politics 1868-1922*, Dunedin: University of Otago Press, 1974.

Dictionary of New Zealand Biography (online edition). URL: http://www.teara.govt.nz/en/biographies.

Elder, John Rawson, *The History of the Presbyterian Church of New Zealand, 1840-1940*, Christchurch: Presbyterian Bookroom, 1940.

Elworthy, Gertrude, and Anthony Elworthy, *A Power in the Land: Churchill Julius, 1847-1938*, Christchurch: Whitcombe & Tombs, 1971.

Emilsen, Susan, and William W. Emilsen (eds), *Mapping the Landscape: Essays in Australian and New Zealand Christianity. Festschrift in Honour of Professor Ian Breward*, New York: Peter Lang, 2000.

Fairburn, Miles, *The Ideal Society and its Enemies: The Foundations of New Zealand Society, 1850-1900*, Auckland: Auckland University Press, 1989.

Faulkner, Ian F., *The Decisive Decade: Some Aspects of the Development and Character of the Methodist Central Mission, Auckland, 1927-1937*, Christchurch: Wesley Historical Society, 1982.

Fishburn, Janet Forsythe, *The Fatherhood of God and The Victorian Family: The Social Gospel in America*, Philadelphia: Fortress Press, 1981.

Ford, David F., and Mike Higton (eds), *Jesus*, Oxford: Oxford University Press, 2002.

Fox, Richard Wightman, *Jesus in America: Personal Savior, Cultural Hero, National Obsession*, San Francisco: HarperSanFrancisco, 2004.

Frantzen, Allen J., *Bloody Good: Chivalry, Sacrifice, and the Great War*, Chicago: University of Chicago Press, 2004.

Girouard, Mark, *The Return to Camelot: Chivalry and the English Gentleman*, New Haven: Yale University Press, 1981.

Grant, David, *A Question of Faith: A History of the New Zealand Christian Pacifist Society*, Wellington: Philip Garside, 2004.

Greene, Colin J.D., *Christology in Cultural Perspective: Marking Out the Horizons*, Grand Rapids: Eerdmans, 2003.

Grenz, Stanley J., and Roger E. Olson, *20th-Century Theology: God & the World in a Transitional Age*, Downers Grove: InterVarsity Press, 1992.

Gustafson, Barry, *From the Cradle to the Grave: A Biography of Michael Joseph Savage*, Auckland: Penguin, 1988.

_____, *Labour's Path to Political Independence: The Origins and Establishment of the New Zealand Labour Party 1900-19*, Auckland: Auckland University Press, 1980.

Hall, Donald E. (ed.), *Muscular Christianity: Embodying the Victorian Age*, Cambridge: Cambridge University Press, 1994.

Hames, E.W., *Coming of Age: The United Church 1913-72*, Auckland: Institute Press, 1974.

_____, *Out of the Common Way: The European Church in the Colonial Era 1840-1913*,

254

Auckland: Institute Press, 1972.

Harper, Glyn (ed.), *Letters from the Battlefield: New Zealand Soldiers Write Home, 1914-18*, Auckland: HarperCollins, 2001.

Hendrick, Harry, *Images of Youth: Age, Class, and the Male Youth Problem 1880-1920*, Oxford: Clarendon Press, 1990.

Heywood, Colin, *A History of Childhood: Children and Childhood in the West from Medieval to Modern Times*, Malden: Polity, 2001.

Hinchliff, Peter, *God and History: Aspects of British Theology, 1875-1914*, Oxford: Oxford University Press, 1992.

Hitchcock, Tim, and Michèle Cohen (eds), *English Masculinities, 1660-1800*, London: Longman, 1999.

Holcroft, M.H., *Mary Ursula Bethell*, Wellington: Oxford University Press, 1975.

Holmes, Arthur F., *Fact, Value, and God*, Grand Rapids: Eerdmans, 1997.

Houlden, Leslie (ed.), *Jesus in History, Culture and Thought: An Encyclopedia*, 2 vols, Santa Barbara: ABC-CLIO, 2003.

Howe, K.R., *Singer in a Songless Land: A Life of Edward Tregear, 1846-1931*, Auckland: Auckland University Press, 1991.

Hughes, Richard T. (ed.), *The American Quest for the Primitive Church*, Urbana: University of Illinois Press, 1988.

Hughes, Richard T., and C. Leonard Allen, *Illusions of Innocence: Protestant Primitivism in America, 1630-1875*, Chicago: University of Chicago Press, 1988.

Hutchinson, Mark, and Stuart Piggin (eds), *Reviving Australia: Essays on the History and Experience of Revival and Revivalism in Australian Christianity*, Sydney: Centre for the Study of Australian Christianity, 1994.

Jackson, H.R., *Churches & People in Australia and New Zealand, 1860-1930*, Wellington: Allen & Unwin, 1987.

Johnston, Robert K., *Reel Spirituality: Theology and Film in Dialogue*, Grand Rapids: Baker Academic, 2000.

Jonas, Raymond, *France and the Cult of the Sacred Heart: An Epic Tale for Modern Times*, Berkeley: University of California Press, 2000.

Jupp, Peter C., and Glennys Howarth (eds), *The Changing Face of Death: Historical Accounts of Death and Disposal*, New York: St Martin's Press, 1997.

King, Michael, *God's Farthest Outpost: A History of Catholics in New Zealand*, Auckland: Penguin, 1997.

Kirkman, Allison, and Pat Moloney (eds), *Sexuality Down Under: Social and Historical Perspectives*, Dunedin: University of Otago Press, 2005.

Koopman-Boyden, Peggy G. (ed.), *Families in New Zealand Society*, Wellington: Methuen, 1978.

Koops, Willem, and Michael Zuckerman (eds), *Beyond the Century of the Child: Cultural History and Developmental Psychology*, Philadelphia: University of Pennsylvannia Press, 2003.

Kuschel, Karl-Josef, *The Poet as Mirror: Human Nature, God and Jesus in Twentieth-Century Literature*, London: SCM Press, 1999.

Larsen, Timothy, *Contested Christianity: The Political and Social Context of Victorian Theology*, Waco: Baylor University Press, 2004.

Law, Robin, Hugh Campbell and John Dolan (eds), *Masculinities in Aotearoa/New Zealand*, Palmerston North: Dunmore Press, 1999.

Lightman, Bernard, *The Origins of Agnosticism: Victorian Unbelief and the Limits of Knowledge*, Baltimore: Johns Hopkins University Press, 1987.

Lineham, Peter J., *New Zealanders and the Methodist Evangel: An Interpretation of the Policies and Performance of the Methodist Church of New Zealand*, Auckland: Wesley Historical Society, 1983.

Maas, Jeremy, *Holman Hunt & The Light of the World*, London: Scolar Press, 1984.

Maclean, Chris, and Jock Phillips, *The Sorrow and the Pride: New Zealand War Memorials*, Wellington: GP Books, 1990.

Macquarrie, John, *Jesus Christ in Modern Thought*, London: SCM Press, 1990.

Maindonald, John, *A Radical Religious Heritage: Auckland Unitarian Church and its Wider Connections*, Auckland: Auckland Unitarian Church, 1993.

Martin, John E., and Kerry Taylor (eds), *Culture and the Labour Movement: Essays in New Zealand Labour History*, Palmerston North: Dunmore Press, 1991.

Marty, Martin E. (ed.), *Protestantism and Social Christianity*, Munich: K.G. Saur, 1992.

Massam, Katherine, *Sacred Threads: Catholic Spirituality in Australia, 1922-1962*, Sydney: New South Wales University Press, 1996.

McClure, Margaret, *A Civilised Community: A History of Social Security in New Zealand, 1898-1998*, Auckland: Auckland University Press, 1998.

McDannell, Colleen, *Material Christianity: Religion and Popular Culture in America*, New Haven: Yale University Press, 1995.

McEldowney, Dennis (ed.), *Presbyterians in Aotearoa, 1840-1990*, Wellington: The Presbyterian Church of New Zealand, 1990.

McGeorge, Colin, and Ivan Snook, *Church, State and New Zealand Education*, Wellington: Price Milburn, 1981.

McGrath, Alister, *The Making of Modern German Christology, 1750-1990*, 2nd ed., Grand Rapids: Zondervan, 1994.

McKay, F.M., *Eileen Duggan*, Wellington: Oxford University Press, 1977.

McLeod, Hugh, *Religion and the People of Western Europe, 1789-1970*, Oxford: Oxford University Press, 1981.

_____, *Secularisation in Western Europe, 1848-1914*, Basingstoke: Macmillan, 2000.

McLintock, A.H. (ed.), *Encyclopaedia of New Zealand*, 3 vols, Wellington: Government Printer, 1966.

Moloney, Pat, and Kerry Taylor (eds), *On the Left: Essays on Socialism in New Zealand*, Dunedin: University of Otago Press, 2002.

Morgan, David, *Visual Piety: A History and Theory of Popular Religious Images*, Berkeley: University of California Press, 1998.

Mullin, Robert Bruce, *The Puritan as Yankee: A Life of Horace Bushnell*, Grand Rapids: Eerdmans, 2002.

Murray, Stuart, *Never a Soul at Home: New Zealand Literary Nationalism and the 1930s*, Wellington: Victoria University Press, 1998.

Nichols, Stephen J., *Jesus Made in America: A Cultural History from the Puritans to the Passion of the Christ*, Downers Grove: IVP Academic, 2008.

Nolan, Melanie, *Kin: A Collective Biography of a Working-Class Family*, Christchurch:

Canterbury University Press, 2005.

O'Farrell, Patrick J., *Harry Holland: Militant Socialist*, Canberra: Australian National University, 1964.

_____, *The Catholic Church and Community: An Australian History*, rev. ed., Kensington: New South Wales University Press, 1985.

_____, *Vanished Kingdoms: Irish in Australia and New Zealand*, Kensington: New South Wales University Press, 1990.

Olssen, Erik, *Building the New World: Work, Politics and Society in Caversham 1880s-1920s*, Auckland: Auckland University Press, 1995.

_____, *The Red Feds: Revolutionary Industrial Unionism and the New Zealand Federation of Labour 1908-1913*, Auckland: Oxford University Press, 1988.

Openshaw, Roger, and David McKenzie (eds), *Reinterpreting the Educational Past: Essays in the History of New Zealand Education*, Wellington: New Zealand Council for Educational Research, 1987.

Pals, Daniel L., *The Victorian 'Lives' of Jesus*, San Antonio: Trinity University Press, 1982.

Patrick, Bruce (ed.), *New Vision New Zealand, Volume II*, Auckland: Vision New Zealand, 1997.

Pearson, Clive, Allan Davidson and Peter Lineham, *Scholarship and Fierce Sincerity: Henry D.A. Major, The Face of Anglican Modernism*, Auckland: Polygraphia, 2005.

Pelikan, Jaroslav, *Jesus through the Centuries: His Place in the History of Culture*, New Haven: Yale University Press, 1985.

Pelling, Henry, *The Origins of the Labour Party, 1880-1900*, London: Macmillan, 1954.

Phillips, Jock, *A Man's Country? The Image of the Pakeha Male – A History*, rev. ed., Auckland: Penguin, 1996.

Phillips, Jock, and Chris Maclean, *In the Light of the Past: Stained Glass Windows in New Zealand Houses*, Auckland: Oxford University Press, 1983.

Phillips, Paul T., *A Kingdom on Earth: Anglo-American Social Christianity, 1880-1940*, Pennsylvania: Pennsylvania State University, 1996.

Pope, Robert, *Seeking God's Kingdom: The Nonconformist Social Gospel in Wales, 1906-1939*, Cardiff: University of Wales Press, 1999.

Pope, Robert (ed.), *Religion and National Identity: Wales and Scotland c.1700-2000*, Cardiff: University of Wales Press, 2001.

Prothero, Stephen, *American Jesus: How the Son of God Became a National Icon*, New York: Farrar, Straus and Giroux, 2003.

Putney, Clifford, *Muscular Christianity: Manhood and Sports in Protestant America, 1880-1920*, Cambridge: Harvard University Press, 2001.

Rice, Geoffrey W. (ed.), *The Oxford History of New Zealand*, 2nd ed., Auckland: Oxford University Press, 1992.

Roper, Michael, and John Tosh (eds), *Manful Assertions: Masculinities in Britain Since 1800*, London: Routledge, 1991.

Royle, Edward, *Radicals, Secularists and Republicans: Popular Freethought in Britain, 1866-1915*, Manchester: Manchester University Press, 1980.

Scott, Jamie S. (ed.), *'And the Birds Began to Sing': Religion and Literature in Post-*

Colonial Cultures, Amsterdam: Rodopi, 1996.

Segel, Harold B., *Body Ascendant: Modernism and the Physical Imperative*, Baltimore: Johns Hopkins University Press, 1998.

Shiels, W.J. (ed.), *The Church and Healing*, Oxford: Basil Blackwell, 1982.

Simpson, Tony, *The Sugarbag Years*, 2nd ed., Auckland: Penguin, 1984.

Sinclair, Keith, *A Destiny Apart: New Zealand's Search for National Identity*, Wellington: Allen & Unwin, 1986.

_____, *Walter Nash*, Auckland: Auckland University Press, 1976.

Sizer, Sandra S., *Gospel Hymns and Social Religion: The Rhetoric of Nineteenth-Century Revivalism*, Philadelphia: Temple University Press, 1978.

Smith, Gary Scott, *The Search for Social Salvation: Social Christianity and America 1880-1925*, Lanham: Lexington, 2000.

Stenhouse, John, and Brett Knowles (eds), with Antony Wood, *The Future of Christianity*, Adelaide: ATF Press, 2004.

Stenhouse, John, and Jane Thomson (eds), *Building God's Own Country: Historical Essays on Religions in New Zealand*, Dunedin: University of Otago Press, 2004.

Sturm, Terry (ed.), *The Oxford History of New Zealand Literature*, Auckland: Oxford University Press, 1991.

Susman, Warren I., *Culture as History: The Transformation of American Society in the Twentieth Century*, New York: Pantheon Books, 1984.

Tatum, W. Barnes, *Jesus at the Movies: A Guide to the First Hundred Years*, Santa Rosa: Poleridge Press, 1997.

Taylor, Gary, *Socialism and Christianity: The Politics of the Church Socialist League*, Sheffield: IHS Press, 2000.

Thomson, David, *A World Without Welfare: New Zealand's Colonial Experiment*, Auckland: Auckland University Press, 1998.

Thomson, Mathew, *Psychological Subjects: Identity, Culture, and Health in Twentieth-Century Britain*, Oxford: Oxford University Press, 2006.

Thorn, James, *Peter Fraser: New Zealand's Wartime Prime Minister*, London: Odhams Press, 1952.

Tolerton, Jane, *Ettie: A Life of Ettie Rout*, Auckland: Penguin, 1992.

Tosh, John, *A Man's Place: Masculinity and the Middle-Class Home in Victorian England*, New Haven: Yale University Press, 1999.

Vance, Norman, *The Sinews of the Spirit: The Ideal of Christian Manliness in Victorian Literature and Religious Thought*, Cambridge: Cambridge University Press, 1985.

Watson, Chris, and Roy Shuker, *In the Public Good? Censorship in New Zealand*, Palmerston North: Dunmore Press, 1998.

Welch, Claude, *Protestant Thought in the Nineteenth Century: Volume I, 1799-1870*, New Haven: Yale University Press, 1972.

White, Ronald C., and C. Howard Hopkins, *The Social Gospel: Religion and Reform in Changing America*, Philadelphia: Temple University Press, 1976.

Wilkinson, Alan, *Christian Socialism: Scott Holland to Tony Blair*, London: SCM Press, 1998.

Winter, Jay, *Sites of Memory, Sites of Mourning: The Great War in European Cultural History*, Cambridge: Cambridge University Press, 1995.

Winters, Donald E., *The Soul of the Wobblies: The I.W.W., Religion, and American Culture in the Progressive Era, 1905-1917*, Westport: Greenwood, 1985.

Worrall, B.G., *The Making of the Modern Church: Christianity in England Since 1800*, 3rd ed., London: SPCK, 2004.

Worsfold, James E., *A History of the Charismatic Movements in New Zealand*, Bradford: Julian Literature Trust, 1974.

_____, *The Reverend and Gilbert and Mrs Alice White*, Wellington: Julian Literature Trust, 1995.

Wright, Anthony, *Socialisms: Theories and Practices*, Oxford: Oxford University Press, 1986.

Yerkes, James, *The Christology of Hegel*, Missoula: Scholars Press, for the American Academy of Religion, 1978.

Ziolkowski, Theodore, *Fictional Transfigurations of Jesus*, Princeton: Princeton University Press, 1972.

Articles

Albert, John, 'The Christ of Oscar Wilde', *American Benedictine Review*, 39:4, 1988, pp.372-403.

Barber, Laurie H., 'James Gibb's Heresy Trial, 1890', *NZJH*, 12:2, 1978, pp.146-57.

Bassett, Michael, 'How Ideal was the Savage Ideal', M.J. Savage Memorial Lecture, La Trobe University, 4 September 1998. URL: http://www.michaelbassett.co.nz/article_savage.htm.

Bergman, Jay, 'The Image of Jesus in the Russian Revolution: The Case of Russian Marxism', *International Review of Social History*, 35:2, 1990, pp.220-48.

Bevir, Mark, 'The Labour Church Movement, 1891-1900', *Journal of British Studies*, 38:2, 1999, pp.217-45.

_____, 'Welfarism, Socialism and Religion: On T.H. Green and Others', *The Review of Politics*, 55, 1993, pp.639-61.

Carlyon, Jennifer, 'Friendly Societies 1842-1938: The Benefits of Membership', *NZJH*, 32:2, 1998, pp.121-42.

Davidson, Allan K., 'A Protesting Presbyterian: The Reverend P.B. Fraser, and New Zealand Presbyterianism 1892-1940', *JRH*, 14:2, 1986, pp.193-217.

De Jong, Mary G., '"I Want to Be Like Jesus": The Self-Defining Power of Evangelical Hymnody', *Journal of the American Academy of Religion*, 54:3, 1986, pp.461-93.

Gilling, Bryan D., '"Almost Persuaded Now to Believe": Gospel Songs in New Zealand Evangelical Theology and Practice', *JRH*, 19:1, 1995, pp.92-110.

Graham, Jeanine, 'Child Employment in New Zealand', *NZJH*, 21:1, 1987, pp.62-78.

Guy, Laurie, 'One of a Kind? The Auckland Ministry of A.H. Dallimore', *Australasian Pentecostal Studies*, 8, 2004, pp.125-45.

Inglis, K.S., 'English Nonconformity and Social Reform, 1880-1900', *Past & Present*, 13, 1958, pp.73-88.

Jackson, Hugh, 'Churchgoing in Nineteenth-Century New Zealand', *NZJH*, 17:1, 1983, pp.43-59.

Lineham, Peter J., 'Christian Reaction to Freethought and Rationalism in New Zealand', *JRH*, 15:2, 1988, pp.236-50.

_____, 'Freethinkers in Nineteenth-Century New Zealand', *NZJH*, 19:1, 1985, pp.61-81.

_____, 'How Institutionalised was Protestant Piety in Nineteenth-Century New Zealand?', *JRH*, 13:4, 1985, pp.370-82.

_____, 'The Nature and Meaning of Protestantism in New Zealand Culture', *Turnbull Library Record*, 26:1-2, 1993, pp.59-75.

Milburn, Josephine F., 'Socialism and Social Reform in Nineteenth-Century New Zealand', *Political Science*, 12:1, 1960, pp.62-70.

Moffat, Kirstine, 'The Puritan Paradox: An Annotated Bibliography of Puritan and Anti-Puritan New Zealand Fiction, 1860-1940. Part 1: The Puritan Legacy', *Kotare*, 3:1, 2000, pp.36-86.

_____, 'The Puritan Paradox: An Annotated Bibliography of Puritan and Anti-Puritan New Zealand Fiction, 1860-1940. Part 2: Reactions Against Puritanism', *Kotare*, 3:2, 2000, pp.3-49.

Olssen, Erik, 'The "Working Class" in New Zealand', *NZJH*, 8:1, 1974, pp.44-60.

Picard, Andrew, 'Church Responses to Social Issues in Depression New Zealand, 1933', *New Zealand Journal of Baptist Research*, 9, 2004, pp.24-48.

Quartly, Marian, 'Making Working-Class Heroes: Labor Cartoonists and the Australian Worker, 1903-16', *Labour History*, 89, 2005, pp.159-78.

Roth, Herbert, 'The Labour Churches and New Zealand', *International Review of Social History*, 4, 1959, pp.361-66.

Ryan, Greg, 'An Undertaking Worthy Only of Fanatics: Catholic Opinion on Temperance and Prohibition in New Zealand, c.1870-1910', *Australasian Journal of Irish Studies*, 10, 2010, pp.16-36.

Sharpe, Maureen, 'ANZAC Day in New Zealand: 1916 to 1939', *NZJH*, 15:2, 1981, pp.97-114.

Smith, Brian, '"Wherefore Then This Thusness": The Social Composition of Baptist Congregations in New Zealand', *New Zealand Journal of Baptist Research*, 3, 1998, pp.71-83.

Stenhouse, John, 'Christianity, Gender, and the Working Class in Southern Dunedin, 1880-1940', *JRH*, 30:1, 2006, pp.18-44.

_____, 'God's Own Silence: Secular Nationalism, Christianity and the Writing of New Zealand History', *NZJH*, 38:1, 2004, pp.52-71.

Stuart, Robert, '"Jesus the *Sans-Culotte*": Marxism and Religion during the French *Fin de Siècle*', *The Historical Journal*, 42:3, 1999, pp.705-27.

Sutherland, M.P., 'Pulpit or Podium? J.K. Archer and the Dilemma of Christian Politics in New Zealand', *The New Zealand Journal of Baptist Research*, 1, 1996, pp.26-46.

Troughton, Geoffrey, 'Jesus and the Ideal of the Manly Man in New Zealand After World War One', *JRH*, 30:1, 2006, pp.45-60.

_____, 'Moody and Sankey Down Under: A Case Study in "Trans-Atlantic" Revivalism in Nineteenth-Century New Zealand', *JRH*, 29:2, 2005, pp.145-60.

_____, 'Religion, Churches and Childhood in New Zealand, c.1900-1940', *NZJH*, 40:1, 2006, pp.39-56.

_____, 'Religious Education and the Rise of Psychological Childhood in New Zealand', *History of Education Review*, 33:2, 2004, pp.30-44.

_____, '*The Light of the World* at the End of the World, 1906', *Journal of New Zealand Art History*, 28, 2007, pp.1-15.

_____, 'The *Maoriland Worker* and Blasphemy in New Zealand', *Labour History*, 91, 2006, pp.113-29.

van der Krogt, Christopher, 'A Catholic-Labour Alliance? The Catholic Press and the New Zealand Labour Party 1916-1939', *Australian Catholic Record*, 78:1, 2001, pp.16-29.

_____, 'Imitating the Holy Family: Catholic Ideals and the Cult of Domesticity in Interwar New Zealand', *History Now/Te Pae Tawhito o te Wa*, 4:1, 1998, pp.13-19.

Veldman, Meredith, 'Dutiful Daughter Versus All-Boy: Jesus, Gender, and the Secularization of Victorian Society', *Nineteenth Century Studies*, 11:6, 1997, pp.1-24.

Walsh, Cheryl, 'The Incarnation and the Christian Socialist Conscience in the Victorian Church of England', *Journal of British Studies*, 34:3, 1995, pp.351-74.

Weitzel, R.L., 'Pacifists and Anti-militarists in New Zealand, 1909-1914', *NZJH*, 7:2, 1973, pp.128-47.

Theses, dissertations and unpublished manuscripts

Barber, L.H., 'The Social Crusader: James Gibb at the Australasian Pastoral Frontier 1882-1935', PhD thesis, Massey University, 1975.

Buckley, Barry, 'The Holy Name Society: A Short History of the Society in Auckland', BA Hons research exercise, Massey University, 2001.

Cadogan, Bernard F., 'Lace Curtain Catholics: The Catholic Bourgeoisie of the Diocese of Dunedin', 1900-1920, BA Hons dissertation, University of Otago, 1984.

Clements, Kevin P., 'The Churches and Social Policy: A Study in the Relationship of Ideology to Action', PhD thesis, Victoria University of Wellington, 1970.

Coles, David J., 'The Remodelling of the New Zealand Sunday School', MA thesis, University of Auckland, 1966.

Cooke, Bill, '"The Best of Causes": A Critical History of the New Zealand Association of Rationalists and Humanists', PhD thesis, Victoria University of Wellington, 1998.

Cutfield, Lisa, 'Silent Film and Censorship in New Zealand, 1908-1928', BA Hons long essay, University of Otago, 1994.

Dalton, Sarah, 'The Pure in Heart: The New Zealand Women's Christian Temperance Union and Social Purity, 1885-1930', MA thesis, Victoria University of Wellington, 1993.

Elliott, Nerida J., 'Anzac, Hollywood and Home: Cinemas and Film-going in Auckland 1909-1939', MA thesis, University of Auckland, 1989.

Hanson, E.F.I., 'The Relationship between Sunday School and Church in the History of New Zealand Methodism', DTheol thesis, Melbourne College of Divinity, 2002.

Hickey, Carina, '"Man in His Time Plays Many Parts": Life Stories of William Jordan', MA thesis, Massey University, 2003.

Keen, David S., 'Feeding the Lambs: The Influence of Sunday Schools on the Socialization of Children in Otago and Southland, 1848-1901', PhD thesis, University of Otago, 1999.

King, Geoffrey S., '"Organising Christian Truth": An Investigation of the Life and Work of John Dickie', PhD thesis, University of Otago, 1998.

MacDonald, D.V., 'The New Zealand Bible in Schools League', MA thesis, Victoria University of Wellington, 1964.

MacPherson, S.C., 'A "Ready Made Nucleus of Degradation and Disorder"? A Religious and Social History of the Catholic Church and Community in Auckland 1870-1910', MA thesis, University of Auckland, 1987.

McArthur, Margaret J., 'Collectivist Tracts and Altruistic Sermons: A Study of "Socialism" in Late Nineteenth Century New Zealand', MA thesis, University of Canterbury, 1981.

Morrison, Hugh D., '"It is our Bounden Duty": The Emergence of the New Zealand Protestant Missionary Movement, 1868-1926', PhD thesis, Massey University, 2004.

Pearson, Clive R., 'H.D.A. Major and English Modernism, 1911-1948', PhD thesis, University of Cambridge, 1989.

Plumridge, E.W., 'Labour in Christchurch: Community and Consciousness, 1914-1919', MA thesis, University of Canterbury, 1979.

Rathgen, D.G.S., 'The Church in New Zealand 1890-1920, With Special Reference to W.A. Orange', LTh Hons thesis, New Zealand Board of Theological Studies, 1969.

Reid, A.J.S., 'Church and State in New Zealand, 1930-35: A Study of the Social Thought and Influence of the Christian Church in a Period of Economic Crisis', MA thesis, Victoria University, 1961.

Smith, Justine, '"Dunedin Manhood: Official Organ of the Dunedin YMCA". The "Manufacturing" of Christian Men in Dunedin, 1933-1938', BA Hons thesis, University of Otago, 1999.

Thompson, Susan J., 'Knowledge and Vital Piety: Methodist Ministry Education in New Zealand from the 1840s to 1988', PhD thesis, University of Auckland, 2002.

van der Krogt, Christopher J., 'More a Part than Apart: The Catholic Community in New Zealand Society 1918-1940', PhD thesis, Massey University, 1994.

Wood, Simon, 'Liberalism and Heresy: An Examination of the Controversy Surrounding William Salmond's *The Reign of Grace*', BA Hons research essay, University of Otago, 1991.

Index